WORKING TOGETHER

A PERSONALITY-CENTERED
APPROACH TO MANAGEMENT

WORKING TOGETHER

A PERSONALITY-CENTERED
APPROACH TO MANAGEMENT

OLAF ISACHSEN, Ph.D.
LINDA V. BERENS, Ph.D.

Published by: **Institute for Management Development**

P.O. Box 82010
Phoenix, AZ 85071-2010
(602) 942-1256

Second Edition 1991
Third Edition 1995

ISBN 978-1-877808-01-2 (Deluxe Bind)
ISBN 978-1-877808-02-9 (Spiral Bind)

ACKNOWLEDGEMENTS

In this second edition, it would be impossible to acknowledge all of the contributors to this book since it represents the thoughts and works of many people both known and unknown to us. However, the basis for this text is in many ways a sculpting of the works of Carl Gustav Jung, Ernst Kretschmer, Isabel Myers and David Keirsey. In addition to these major thinkers, we thank all of our clients and friends for the many examples of typology they have revealed to us. It is truly through them that this book may provide some practical value to managers.

In our more immediate circle, we owe a great deal of gratitude to John Greer who has had a major hand in making this second edition a more comprehensive and improved version of the original text, as we have learned so much from our respective work environments during the past years - and John has assisted us greatly in focusing more on the pragmatic and real life issues than otherwise would have been the case.

A special thanks goes to Sylvia Neville who has tirelessly worked on the editing and assisted us in making more meaningful use of the English language. Without her enthusiasm and energy this edition would have been a lesser text.

Finally, we are indebted to:

John Berens	Mary Ellen Reynolds
Dan Gudeman	Mary Ricci
Lance Merker	Velda Williams

who all made this new edition possible.

TABLE OF CONTENTS

INTRODUCTION

A NEW PERSONALITY-CENTERED
APPROACH TO MANAGEMENT

The book you are about to read we think you will find somewhat unusual. *Working Together* is perhaps more of a map of
territories where people work than it is a literary contribution.
The text has been designed to be a "hands on" practical guide
causing people at any level in an organization to understand
themselves and those they work with better. Indeed, our intent
is to shed more light on situations which traditionally may
have generated unproductive heat. Since the initial publication of this book both of us have increasingly become aware of
the immense power in comprehending and understanding
human typology and temperament. Indeed, we have experienced how mediocre work environments have changed per-
manently, and sometimes dramatically, to become highly efficient and productive, which is ultimately reflected in the
bottom line. For example, a nationwide manufacturer and
distributor of graphic paper has increased market share, improved the bottom line and increased productivity in excess of
15% during a period when the industry is experiencing a
reduction in demand.

Our mission for *Working Together* is simple. Through this text
we want you to become more aware of why people you work
and deal with on a daily basis seem to react, function and
behave the way they do. As that happens you will be more
readily able to accept realities as they are rather than wishing
they would be different.

Unlike so many present day "quick fix" fads and shallow
theories about how managers can become more effective, the

philosophical base of *Working Together* is based on and has its roots in the life long work of highly recognized researchers and practitioners alike. Individuals such as Ernst Kretschmer, Carl Gustav Jung, Isabel Myers and David Keirsey have made individual, unique contributions allowing scholars of the next generation to build on earlier findings, concepts and ideas.

Throughout our professional lives both of us have had so many rich opportunities to work with individuals as well as within corporate structures. We assisted in discovering how profoundly human typology and temperament impact others, as well as the overall work environment and we hope the new unusually highly successful individuals and organizations of today will become the norm in the next century. The bottom line of what we have learned is simple: a manager cannot motivate people. Motivation comes from within, hence the challenge for anyone guiding others at work is one of creating an environment where people are allowed and encouraged to be all they can. The theme of *Working Together* therefore is one of empowering individuals to become star performers where they shine as opposed to wasting time and negative energy on "corrective action." Indeed, we have witnessed exceptional performance by ordinary people because their leaders and managers have learned to work with people from the "inside out" instead of the "outside in."

When work is satisfying, meaningful and enjoyable, people will strive to perform. When it is conflict-ridden, unreasonable and threatening, people will be preoccupied with surviving or searching for better opportunities elsewhere, and productivity must pay the price and suffer accordingly. Consequently, we wish to assist you in arranging your work environment so that the former, not the latter, condition will persist.

People we have worked with during the past few years seem uniformly to have gained four insights, allowing them to function much more efficiently in a day-to-day work situation. As a result of their knowledge and application of the concepts and ideas about typology and temperament they have come to accept that:

> All the conditions are present for things to be the way they are and no conditions are present for them to be different. Hence, they have come to accept people for who they are rather than being upset with the fact they are not molded into some other kind of personality.

> Judging people from their own objective point of view is less productive than assisting them in their subjective realities. In other words, they have begun to manage people from the "inside out" as opposed to the "outside in."

> Modern day platitudes, cliches and jargon cannot substitute for the truth. They have become far more conscious of how people work and have thus abandoned attempts to manipulate situations in their favor.

> As a result of the above, they no longer impose their personal values, beliefs and norms on others. They have learned to suspend their own needs for expressing their point of view and opinion for the benefit of the people they work with.

Working Together, then, is a tool allowing you first of all to better understand how you tend to function in everyday working situations. As you begin to comprehend your own inner driving force, so to speak, it will become increasingly obvious and clear to you that others legitimately may be quite different.

It is our ambition and hope that *Working Together* will become part of your approach in working with others; that it will assist you in both accepting and understanding others from their frame of reference; and enable you to build on their strengths rather than agonize over their weaknesses.

Olaf Isachsen
Linda V. Berens

April 30, 1991

USERS GUIDE

This book is designed so that you can start wherever you want. There is no need to read Chapter One to understand Chapter Five. We recommend you start with what interests you first.

- If you are one to begin from a historical perspective and you want to know that the concepts in this book are not out of thin air, start with Chapter Two.

- If your attitude is one of "So What!" - by all means read Chapter One first so you can see some potential outcomes.

- If you want to start from a personal perspective, i.e., "What's my type?" - start with the self-assessment section and move on to Chapters Three and Four.

- If you want the descriptions of the temperaments and types, Chapter Three should entice you.

- If you want a brief overview of how to manage each type, skip right to Chapter Five for a one-page sketch of each of the 16 types.

Wherever you start, we hope this becomes a ready reference and that eventually you find each and every page packed with interesting and useful insights.

1

**KEYS TO INDIVIDUAL
AND ORGANIZATIONAL
SUCCESS**

KEYS TO INDIVIDUAL
AND ORGANIZATIONAL SUCCESS

"Each of us really understands
in others only the feelings he is
capable of producing himself."
— Andre Gide, 1921

A few weeks ago, we sat in on a staff meeting in a major real estate firm located on the West Coast. The president summarized the session by pointing out that the firm, in his opinion, was moving smartly ahead, and that he certainly appreciated the contribution made by each person present.

The following three days we met with each one of the key managers in the group in order to better understand their views and perceptions of where the firm seemed to be heading. To provide you with a glimpse of the picture, we asked for feedback about the president, and these are some of the verbatim remarks we registered:

> "There is no way his plan is going to work. We didn't make it last year, so what's different now?"

> "You know, we used to be a team...now look at this mess."

> "I really like John (the president) and I have supported him for a long time; I just wish he could listen to us."

"Get a load of this: he wants us to increase production by 50% and we don't even have the land inventoried."

"He sure is a great dealmaker...but he is a marginal manager."

"There are too many people in the executive office who have their own agendas, and eventually it will hurt all of us."

If the above sounds familiar, welcome to the typical, everyday work life in America. It is normal and not necessarily unhealthy for people working together to have a myriad of opinions and attitudes. The challenge facing the manager in any organization is one of attempting to get all these butterflies to fly in some kind of formation toward a common goal. Some people would label that need and phenomenon "synergy"--we call it "organizational climate."

Ultimately, we believe that all managers want to establish a climate where people, of their own free will and desire, want to work well together and optimize their own performance. The implications are clear: no one in a formal power situation can motivate people to work. That motivation comes from within, and the only thing an intelligent manager can do is to set the stage, so to speak, and create conditions where superior performance will take place.

A basic premise in all human behavior is very simple: people tend to do what they perceive as most rewarding to them. Hence, the first step in beginning to understand the energy direction in any work situation is to become aware of how people subjectively view their work environment. In other words, if a person does not perceive a problem, it does not exist, at least in his or her reality. Therefore, we are less inclined to trust the concept of MBO (Management By Objectives) and more inclined to suggest that MBS (Management By Subjectives) in the long haul will determine how much energy anyone is willing to measure out in any situation. The wise manager will know that for people to work well together, they need to like each other, or better, people who tend to perform to the best of their capacity are provided with an opportunity to like and enjoy themselves in the presence of their superiors, peers and subordinates. They gain a very real feeling of being significant by the dignity they are given. Another way of expressing the above is to suggest that people who enjoy self-respect at work perform.

Year after year managers, supervisors and individual contributors march off by the thousands to seminars and workshops to improve their interpersonal skills, be it in managing people, sales, negotiations, and on and on. Typically, they return all excited and enthused about the new concepts and ideas on how to become a more effective person, only to sink back to "business as usual" - often sooner than later. The reasons are simple. Not much can change by learning new behavioral patterns unless these are supported by the internal environment. Hence, for any organization to begin to optimize its performance calls for, in a sense, "back to basics." Unless everyone is afforded an opportunity to come to grips with the role they play and personally assess its usefulness, nothing really changes in the long haul. Anyone responsible to owners and superiors for the performance of others cannot succeed without abandoning contradiction, lack of logic and meaningless cliches. Every successful manager we have come across is authentic, consistent, predictable and, above all, a person of high integrity who people can and want to trust.

Indeed, we have come to realize that superior performance is created from within any organization. Unless people at work can begin to understand and accept each other for what they are as opposed to what they might wish others would be, performance cannot become a soaring experience.

Superior performance emerges from superior strategies, i.e. the ability of a firm to bring to its side the best possible conditions given its resource limitations. For any firm, a critical issue will always remain one of determining what range of strategies is available given its financial, physical and human resources.

Within the scope of our work, we have found that the strategic position of a firm is significantly strengthened when people working together become astutely aware of how the overall organizational climate seems to impact performance. Indeed, we have learned that when top management has an opportunity to really hear and understand how people at multiple levels of an organization react to their work environment, productive, strategic and profound change takes place. The approach for top management to learn about how employees view their work environments is accomplished through what we have come to label an "Organizational Climate Study" (OCS). An OCS, put very simply, is a vehicle designed to listen to employees at all levels comment on how they experience the effectiveness and efficiency of their organization. By "effectiveness" we ask people to assess the degree to which their organization seems to be doing the "right things" and by "efficiency" we ask employees to gauge the degree to which "things are done right." It is astounding to experience the constructive, long range change taking place in organizations having the courage to take a long hard look at themselves.

Every year we conduct several OCS's and the payoff, as shall be explained, has impacted the performance of each organization so profoundly that as the CEO of a leading realtor organization expressed, "I believe the OCS assisted us in becoming much more honest about our performance. We abandoned the gimmicks, the confusing jargon and quick fix theories. I can honestly say that I personally learned three lessons from the OCS which have remained with our firm to this day:

- My knowledge of the firm is incomplete, biased and distorted. An unbiased outside review is far more valuable in comprehending our overall situation than the most thoughtful self-assessment.

- Attempting to be brilliant is not enlightened; as a matter of fact, it results in poor management.

- It is more important to know the simple, candid truth than say things that sound good."

The way an OCS is conducted is simple. There is no magic, no platitudes, no cliches, no slogans, no shortcuts, no search for anything. As the study is conducted by an outside skilled interviewer, the risk of internal bias is eliminated; and while initially individuals and groups may experience some suspicion, people contributing quickly come to appreciate the opportunity to share some of their most important beliefs and insights about their work environment.

Typically, top management will, with the help of the interviewer, explain the purpose of an OCS and then participate in determining a schedule for interviews. Each interview, typically, is conducted on a one-to-one basis, especially with members of the top team. Other sessions can be conducted with focus groups where up to seven people at one time have an opportunity to share in their perceptions of the work environment.

Upon completing the OCS, the interviewer typically will spend time, often on a one-to-one basis, with top management so as to be able to report the findings in great detail. It is important to emphasize, however, that each interview is conducted confidentially so as to assure that no one contributor is exposed in a negative fashion.

While an OCS is an open-ended communication vehicle, allowing and encouraging participants to discuss issues of importance to them as opposed to the perceptions of executive management, filtered into the conversations are usually three subject matters:

- What would you like to change in this organization if you had the opportunity?

- Where do we have strengths - and where, in your opinion, can we improve performance?

- Who are our critical competitors and what seem to be their strategies?

Always, the participants receive a written report reflecting the findings and often containing specific, action-oriented recommendations. The reason the OCS report is important is that it provides feedback validating the contribution made by the participants.

In essence, beginning to understand the organizational climate of any work environment is based upon a fundamental four-step process:

First, understand the motives, beliefs, values and norms of people in important formal positions.

Second, understand the motives, beliefs, values and norms of people in important informal positions.

Third, and as a result of the above, provide feedback for all participants.

Fourth, and in our minds the most significant long-term issue with the highest payoff, determine the human style and temperament of everyone, allowing the organization to more strongly position itself in its competitive environment.

To provide you with living examples, we will share from our experience with five different organizations we have worked with for several years. Each of them conducted an OCS, and all employees at some point participated in and learned about human styles through the Myers-Briggs Type Indicator (MBTI)®. As will be evidenced in the following chapters, the MBTI constitutes the central theme of this text. It is a relatively simple instrument comprised of 126 questions and it provides a comprehensive understanding of how a person tends to function in everyday life.

While the purpose and mission of each firm was very different, they all had four things in common:

1. They went from describing themselves as a somewhat mediocre to a high-performance organization.

2. The MBTI legitimized the opportunity for every member in both top and middle management to influence the thinking of his or her peer group, as well as subordinates and superiors.

3. Each firm became more focused and more strategic. In other words, a great deal of energy was freed up for management to bring about the conditions most favorable to their firm in the overall competitive environment.

4.   As a result of the above, each firm was able to better
      define the overall purpose of its respective organi-
      zation, and a superordinate goal emerged for each
      firm.

Preceding the application of the MBTI, each firm conducted an
OCS. In addition to staking out the future for each organiza-
tion, there are three additional and important outcomes of the
OCS:

First, top management implicitly acknowledges and
requests individuals to express their insights and views
on the overall organization in a safe, non-judgmental
atmosphere where an outside consultant, in confidence,
makes every effort to understand and reflect on the
values, beliefs and attitudes of the interviewees.

Second, the process is therapeutic. We have yet to
discover anyone experiencing the exercise negatively.
Sometimes, participants are skeptical, but in time the
disbelief wears thin or, in most cases, disappears as the
result of significant organizational change.

Third, when the written report has been drafted, it is
returned to each contributor for further comments and
eventual approval. Each person who participates in an
OCS tends to take more and more ownership in the
exercise. The organization makes tangible efforts to
upgrade and change the work climate to better accommodate and support individuals and groups, who in
turn contribute a higher sense of personal significance
and value to the firm and ultimately improve the overall organizational effectiveness.

Typically, an OCS is a forerunner for the MBTI exercise. As can
be expected, participants may initially joke and feel somewhat

insecure about the Indicator and believe there are "right" and "wrong" answers. As the tremendous contribution provided by Jung, Myers and Keirsey starts to unfold, however, we are amazed by how each individual comes to accept the realities of their organizations along with their own, as well as the style of those they work with. The energies freed up are dramatic and usually reflected in improved earnings within six to twelve months.

The performance of the firms we are about to describe improved practically overnight, not because employees were reprogrammed or manipulated, but because they gained an enduring life-long awareness. Indeed, each individual is afforded an opportunity to understand how she or he can make the highest and best personal contribution to their respective employer, not based on criticism or antiquated performance evaluation procedures, but from an authentic joy of wanting to contribute . . . usually to the very height of their capacity.

We have selected five very different firms in our example so as to provide a spectrum of non-related organizations.

- A law firm in Northern California.
- An architectural firm in Southern California.
- A real estate firm in Chicago.
- A nationwide producer of office forms and vouchers for large industrial customers.
- A construction firm in the Pacific.

These organizations have been able to improve their performance beyond tradition-bound expectations as a result of utilizing the OCS and the MBTI. They are existing client companies, but at their request, their names have been changed.

THE LAW FIRM OF "KING, BREWSTER, & HOWE" (KB&H) SAN FRANCISCO, CALIFORNIA

KB&H was established in the late 1940s, and only Mr. Howe remained with the firm as an active, practicing lawyer. The other partners had retired and a new, younger generation of lawyers were in effect working their way into the organization.

On a Friday afternoon, a board meeting was scheduled to take place, and the three major agenda items dealt with succession planning, business development and compensation issues. The board consisted of twelve partner-attorneys, all of whom considered themselves reasonably successful, and several of whom did not fully identify with the organization for a variety of reasons. Mr. Dugal, for example, felt that he brought more business to the firm than anyone else but was not adequately compensated for his contribution. Mr. Rittmeyer, on the other hand, felt that his colleagues were too greedy and really did not care that much about the overall growth of the firm. Finally, Mr. Verdun, the young, 43-year old managing partner, was not all that enthused about having to manage the firm, as practicing law seemed more rewarding than, as he said, "trying to get all these butterflies to fly in formation toward a common goal."

As expected, the board meeting turned out to be somewhat less than successful. Several name-calling and yelling matches occurred, one attorney left, and after a three-hour session, the board agreed to establish yet another committee to deal with business development issues. In a later interview, some of the key players admitted that their frustration levels were substantial.

During the next few months, there were similar kinds of meetings and, if anything, the partners experienced less light and more heat in each session. At some point, two of the partners learned about the OCS and the MBTI, and a decision was reached by the board to engage our services. In short order, the OCS provided the partners with a fairly realistic picture of how energies in the firm were directed toward counterproductive activities, and upon completion of the MBTI exercise, the partners agreed to spend one day in a strategic planning session in order to determine how the firm would define itself in the marketplace.

In the beginning of 1988, three years after the introduction of the OCS and the MBTI, revenues of KB&H had increased by roughly 60% annually. A compensation package had been developed and accepted unanimously by all partners. In addition, the firm was able to attract the brightest students from western law schools and the partners frequently talked about KB&H as one of the leading firms in its field. That year, the firm was recognized by a highly respected law publication as one of the top ten in the San Francisco Bay area.

Strategic planning has now become a way of life for KB&H. Growth is expected to continue at 25% annually, and each employee continues to benefit from the OCS and the MBTI. An introductory program has been developed for new hires, and it is commonly recognized that they probably are employed by the leading law firm in the region.

THE "FOREMOST ARCHITECTURAL GROUP"
NEWPORT BEACH, CALIFORNIA

Back in 1978, George Oppenheimer, a nationally recognized force in the design of single-family homes, became acquainted with the MBTI. At the time, the overall economy was weak and, as a result, business was quite slow for Foremost. George understood the value of human typology, however, and each member of his twenty-person staff was afforded an opportunity to benefit from the MBTI Seminar.

The overall atmosphere in the firm could probably have been described as highly individualistic. Each architect was into "doing his or her own thing" and the overall efficiency of the organization was not all that impressive. In addition, as seems to be the case in most architectural firms, designers were viewed as far superior to those individuals involved in production and less creative kinds of work. A sense of "them against us" prevailed, and the firm clearly was not benefitting from the optimum contribution available from the group as a team.

In 1981, an OCS was conducted and soon thereafter the firm literally made such a turnaround that it is now recognized as a clear leader in a highly competitive field. Indeed, it has won more awards for its superior performance than any other competitor in its field in Southern California. In summary, these are the major achievements attained by the Foremost organization:

- There is practically no turnover in the firm, and George is of the opinion that their overall labor force is superior.

- The style of Henry, the managing partner, is more one of enabling the architects to perform and less one of demonstrating personal brilliance as a design architect.

- A carefully selected advisory board has supported George over the years to enhance the overall strategic position of the firm.

- And, most importantly, every employee in the firm knows instinctively that he works for the best firm in the business.

"THE CHICAGO COMMERCIAL LAND
DEVELOPMENT CORPORATION" (CC)
CHICAGO, ILLINOIS

"Well, you see, it's like this. I got fed up working for the ABC Corporation toward the end of 1985 and decided the time had come for me to go out on my own. Sure, I was scared, concerned and worried, but I knew I had to give it a shot. I always wanted to go out on my own, and I kind of knew that if I used whatever little bit of knowledge I have about typology, I would be ahead when it came to building the organization from scratch."

Jim Hauge was reflecting over the success he had experienced in the very short time he had been in business for himself. In less than three years he had gone from no revenue at all to earning well over $2 million a year in management and leasing fees from commercial real estate transactions in the greater Chicago area.

For some time, Jim had been aware of the MBTI, and in starting up his new organization he continuously placed individuals who would complement his own style in key positions. Jim knew that his forte was in thinking up, examining, and evolving new concepts and ideas, so he attracted a number of employees who complemented his intuitive style with a more "hands-on" orientation.

CC quickly became a leader in its field. Much of the credit belongs to the ideas that Jim developed and manifested at a rate that enabled the firm to grow and earn a significant share of specific markets. Moreover, very early in the game Jim developed a strategic plan which he kept changing all the time; but, as he explains, "It is better to plan and fail than not to plan at all."

Jim's plan was quite simple, but he went to great lengths to attract the right kind of people to support his ambitious goals and aspirations. Jim spared no energy in explaining to each one of his key employees their styles as well as the styles of their peer group, and the acceptance people came to have for one another was really nothing short of amazing. It became obvious to everyone that their realities, preferences and personal driving forces were different and very complementary. Perhaps the marketing manager explained the overall organizational climate best when he suggested that, "I have never worked in a place like this; everyone seems to like each other. Perhaps it can be explained by the fact that we have a common comfort level, and no one places undue expectations upon anyone around here."

Jim is planning to double his business this year and we will be surprised if he doesn't exceed that goal, as usual.

"THE EDGEWOOD GRAPHICS CORPORATION"
SAN DIEGO, CALIFORNIA

Mr. Clarence Edgewood, Jr., an enthusiastic member of the Young Presidents' Organization, from time to time went to National University, where he had an opportunity to participate and learn about new developments in managing a business. One of the lectures focused on the Myers-Briggs Type Indicator, and Clarrie, as he was called by his staff, returned to his company bubbling with excitement for what he felt could be accomplished with the OCS and the MBTI in the ninety-year old organization.

Prior to arranging for the OCS, Mr. Edgewood explained to our researcher that the "management team had worked together for a long time and has kind of run out of steam." His observation was strongly confirmed through the interview sessions with both top and middle management. The senior executives over the years had become territorial and developed the attitude that if something was not invented by them, it wouldn't work. Middle management, on the other hand, turned out to be quite open for change and testing new ideas. Moreover, they took great pride in the performance of their respective plants and went to great lengths to meet and exceed their performance goals.

As a result of participation in the OCS and MBTI, the firm did not change overnight, but it did change over time. The senior managers became less possessive of their territories and started to cooperate in managing the everyday operations of Edgewood. More importantly, a succession plan was developed and the younger managers in the firm were able to assume more responsibility in preparing for future promotions.

The industry is very competitive and success is often measured by a company's share of a specific market segment. Over the past two years, Edgewood has gained considerably by focusing on bringing about conditions most favorable to its side. One of the reasons for this development is that one of the senior managers has a highly inventive bent that was somehow hidden in administrative minutiae. Once the senior group understood the valuable contribution this manager could make, someone said, "Before, we tended to be empire builders; now we have become results orientated."

Edgewood does not enjoy the same rapid growth as the younger organizations we have described, but for a ninety-year old lady in a maturing industry, increasing annual revenues by some 17% is nothing to be ashamed of. Management, through knowing each others' styles and temperaments, has come to enjoy their working environment, or as Clarrie declared, "We all seem to be on our second wind and I think we shall be riding this wave of success for a long time."

"THE HAWAIIAN
PACIFIC CONSTRUCTION
CORPORATION" (HPCC)
AGANA, GUAM

It was a hot, humid afternoon in Agana, on the island of Guam, and Bob Brown, the President of HPCC, reluctantly had agreed to be interviewed by one of our researchers working for a major bank in the Western Pacific. The purpose of the interview was to provide feedback for the bank as to how important customers viewed the service and performance of the financial institution.

Initially, the interview was not all that pleasant, since Mr. Brown could only be described as a dictator, sometimes benevolent and other times not. It turned out that Mr. Brown knew the president of the bank, and the opportunity to unload hostility and frustration was a welcome event for him. Toward the end of the interview, Mr. Brown was clearly pleased with himself, and he invited our researcher to take a walk in the yard where all the construction equipment was stored, maintained and repaired. During the walk, some employees seemed scared and others were overly respectful to Mr. Brown, and they were described by him as relatively incompetent and irresponsible.

A few weeks after the interview, Mr. Brown called our researcher and referred to a personal conversation with the bank president, who had said to him in effect, "Robert, you owe it to yourself to benefit from the MBTI." To make a long story short, by the end of 1987, HPCC increased sales by well over 50% from the previous year, and perhaps most gratifying of all, the "incompetent and irresponsible" employees managed the operation so well that Mr. Brown no longer goes on fire fighting trips to Guam; he is now able to enjoy life a great deal more in his beautiful Hawaiian home. As a matter of fact, in a conversation with him a few weeks ago, Bob admitted that he had now learned to "take the good with the good." End of story.

The above examples are not exceptional; they are typical and harvested from the everyday life of ordinary people. What is extraordinary is that they all had the initial guts to depart from "business as usual" and, indeed, business in these cases never did return to past normalcy; they reached into a new realm where no one hopes that "the old days" will return again.

We would now like to turn your attention to the individuals who in their life have probably done more than anyone else to develop managers and individual contributors in organizational settings, without really having intended to do so.

The lesson to be learned is simple: profound, permanent and meaningful change does not take place within a person or within an organization by reaching for recipes of the moment. It occurs as a result of time-tested, applicable, meaningful and constructive knowledge. All too often, companies go through programs, seminars and workshops seeking long-term change. Usually the results are short-lived gusts of excitement and enthusiasm, and the companies eventually fall back into the same old trenches of interpersonal relationships that don't result in long-term performance improvements and fundamental and permanent acceptance of individual human styles and temperaments.

Those individuals who learn about personality types and apply their knowledge to their relationships and who encourage this knowledge to be widespread throughout their company will find:

- interpersonal relationships will improve
- stress will decrease
- team work will increase
- productivity will increase

The choice is yours.

A BRIEF HISTORY OF
THE STUDY OF
PERSONALITY TYPES

A BRIEF HISTORY OF
THE STUDY OF PERSONALITY TYPES

*"It is easier to go to Mars
or to the Moon than it is to
penetrate one's own being."*
— Carl Gustav Jung, 1956

The fundamental purpose of this text is to provide you with superior tools to become more efficient and effective in working with people. This chapter will help you to understand how and why the whole notion of human typology has come about. Personality has been studied and described in many ways down through the ages. In the first quarter of the twentieth century, several great minds, independent of one another, were at work in this area. Their contributions were nearly lost to us with the advent of behaviorism. We are fortunate that their work has been revived, reconfigured and reborn into practical working tools by two individuals, Isabel Myers and David Keirsey, working separately, yet coming to describe human behavior in similar ways. Let us examine first the contributions of their primary predecessors from the 1920s.

The Contribution Made by Carl Gustav Jung

On July 26, 1875, Carl Gustav Jung was born in Kesswill, a small town on Lake Constance in Switzerland. His father and uncles were ministers, and he was expected to maintain the family tradition by entering the ministry. In the year 1900, however, Jung graduated from the University of Basel with a degree in medicine. He decided to pursue psychiatry, and while working as a private practitioner, he continued his post-doctoral work at Burghölzli, the psychiatric clinic at the University of Zurich.

His contribution to understanding the human psyche can be described as gigantic. Unlike many of his contemporaries, he did not approach the understanding of people from a purely Freudian point of view. As a matter of fact, all of those who worked with him found Jung to be enormously inquisitive, with an ability to view events around him in a non-judgmental and non-dogmatic fashion.

During Jung's lifetime, Sigmund Freud, the famous Viennese psychologist who was 19 years his senior, seemed to command a great deal more attention than he, yet now it seems that the contributions made by Jung have found more practical and useful inroads than Freudian psychoanalysis. This is partly evidenced by the fact that The Jungian Institute in Kustnach by the Lake of Zurich is becoming increasingly influential as an organization focused on the application of psychological theory in the healing professions, in family life, and in any type of organizational setting. There are C. G. Jung Institutes located in many metropolitan areas of the United States.

In 1921, Jung published the text *Psychologische Typen*, or *Psychological Types*, which provides a fundamental understanding of human typology.

Jung determined that the population was made up of two basic human "types," the extraverted and the introverted. He considered the introverted to be an abstract type and the extraverted an object-oriented type. He then proceeded to take into account the processes of thinking and feeling, and of intuition and sensation. He made a significant and lasting contribution by suggesting that human typology could be reduced to the following:

Extraverted-Thinking
Extraverted-Feeling
Extraverted-Sensing
Extraverted-Intuiting
Introverted-Thinking
Introverted-Feeling
Introverted-Sensing
Introverted-Intuiting

During this early stage of theory development, Jung did not seem to differentiate these kinds of human characteristics in categories other than psychological functions. As shall be seen later in this text, since the early 1920s, new insights and contributions have caused us to become far more sophisticated in understanding why certain categories of our fellow human beings seem to react predictably different to the events both within and outside themselves.

Jung's contribution opened up ways of thinking about people and the way they handle themselves in all kinds of situations, providing some behavioral predictability and making it possible to render more reasonable judgments of those who do not seem to fit into our own mold and comfort zone. Perhaps one of the most telling insights provided by Jung is best described in his own words:

"Merely to establish the fact that certain people have this or that physical appearance is of no significance, if it does not allow us to infer a psychic correlative."[1]

The Contribution Made by Ernst Kretschmer

Ernst Kretschmer, a contemporary of Carl Gustav Jung, was considered the leading German medical psychologist during his lifetime. His descriptions of a constitutional psychology that encompasses physical build, behavior under normal circumstances, and behavior under abnormal circumstances have made an enormous contribution to our ability to understand and observe patterns of human behavior.

Kretschmer was born October 8, 1888 in Wüstenrot, Germany. He studied medicine at Tübingen and Munich and achieved recognition and status as a psychiatrist and neurologist. He served as director of the psychiatric clinic of the University of Marburg and was later Chair of Psychiatry and Neurology at Tübingen. He was president of the German Society of Psychotherapy, a position he resigned when Hitler came to power and attempted to exert control over the Society.

Kretschmer is best known for his book, *Körperbau und Charakter (Physique and Character)*, which was published in 1921 when he was 33. He had protested and reacted to the Kraepelinian typology of abnormal behavior in an earlier work and had worked toward a more multi-dimensional diagnosis. He also wrote *Men of Genius* (1929), which applied his typological theories to understanding genius, and he wanted the general public to have access to his theories as well.

Kretschmer died February 2, 1964, and in an obituary notice for the British Journal of Psychology, Hans Eysenck praised him for his tolerance and openness to the contributions of any and all theories and for his ability to clearly and succinctly describe character. Kretschmer continued to refine his theories and his *Physique and Character* was published in German in over twenty editions. His contribution was tremendous, yet somewhat lost. Eysenck lamented,". . . if only psychologists could be called away from their worship of the Rorschach to an investigation of the brilliant ideas pioneered by Kretschmer, how much more quickly would psychology advance!"

As a psychiatrist and neurologist, Kretschmer saw a connection between an individual's physical expression (body type or physique) and the psychological expression (the normal, well-functioning personality characteristics, as well as the malfunctioning personality characteristics). In essence, he viewed the individual as an integrated whole and as unique. However, he was able to discern and describe groupings of characteristics which led to his typology. What is important for us to understand is that he did not see individuals in an either/or framework, but along a continuum of having a grouping of characteristics, i.e., of being more like a certain type than another. For our purposes, it is useful to examine this typology for the insights it can give us into the dimensions of human behavior.

Kretschmer outlined two basic types, (1) the cyclothymic, whose functioning varied according to mood, cheerfulness or sadness, and (2) the schizothymic, who were capable of splitting their awareness and having an abstract attitude. Cyclothymes were described as practical, observing first and then looking at the principles. Schizothymes were described as somewhat removed from direct experience, focusing first on the abstraction and sequence of thought, then on the experience.

Each of these types have sub-types. The hypomanic cyclothymes are characterized as having enormous energy and quickness of response to the right moment. Their thinking seems to be conditioned by whatever is going on at the time, rather than systematic. The melancholic cyclothymes, on the other hand, are described as dependable, conscientious and persevering. If they are faced with sudden and violent changes, they tend to become depressed. The hyperaesthetic schizothymes show an oversensitivity, in other words, a lot of feeling and emotion. This sensitivity reveals itself in a tendency for dramatic responses and enthusiasm in written and spoken language. The anesthetic schizothymes, on the other hand, exhibit very little sensitivity and seem emotionally detached. They can be characterized by their highly systematic thinking and tendency to build logical, abstract systems.

Kretschmer believed this basic typology to be the most decisive factor in determining differences among individuals and, as we will see, there is a nearly revolutionary impact possible from the roots of his work.

The Contribution Made by Isabel Myers

In 1886, two highly gifted individuals, Katharine Cook and Lyman Briggs, were married. Katharine, an independent thinker, very early in life became fascinated by the ideas and theories of Carl Gustav Jung. Lyman, on the other hand, devoted his energies to science, and his contribution in stratospheric studies in Antarctica has been memorialized by the establishment of the Lyman Briggs College at Michigan State University.

Katharine and Lyman had one child, Isabel, who was born in 1899. After being educated at home except for a year or two in public school, Isabel was accepted at Swarthmore College at the age of 16, and eventually graduated first in her class. During her junior year, she married Clarence Myers, and while the two of them pursued different life careers, Clarence provided Isabel with a great deal of support in her life-long work of understanding people.

Briggs had observed some basic human differences among people and had formulated her own theory of individual differences. When she and her daughter came upon Jung's descriptions of types, they were amazed at the similarities between his theories and theirs. They began to work to develop new ways of thinking about people and their actions, anchored in the theories of Jung.

In the early 1940s, Briggs and Myers developed a simple indicator to measure psychic functions and attitudes, allowing anyone to better understand himself or herself as well as those individuals he interacts with on a regular basis, in family or work situations. The Myers-Briggs Type Indicator (MBTI) emerged as a new and different methodology of comprehending, understanding, and eventually accepting differences in human behavior. Not surprisingly, the academic community turned out to be quite skeptical of the instrument, and to this day that skepticism has continued in spite of the thorough research behind it. Nonetheless, the practical insights provided by these two women far outpaced the complex theories and deep philosophical pontifications put forth by more esoteric theoreticians.

The Myers-Briggs Type Indicator is probably the most insightful and useful instrument available to very quickly understand how and why people tend to behave and contribute in work situations the way they do. No amount of coaching, well intended resolutions, and pronouncements can really alter what individuals like, dislike, enjoy, detest, want, and do not want . . . at least in the long haul.

As free-thinking, self-determined individuals, Briggs and Myers found that they disagreed in part with some of Jung's thoughts and ideas, and as a result, they evolved further refinements and more applicable theories in understanding human behavior. While Jung focused primarily on psychic functions, Briggs and Myers further refined the concept of attitudes. To further differentiate the types, they clarified an attitude of "judging" vs "perceiving."

The MBTI provides each participant with insights into their functions and attitudes. Every person relies upon one rational function, either thinking or feeling, and one irrational function, either sensing or intuition. In other words, thoughts and feelings can be turned on or off and can be directed at will. Sensing and intuition are just there and seem to have a life of their own.

Attitudes toward the outer world are either wanting or not wanting to structure most events. A structured individual enjoys a sense of direction and goal setting, while a perceptive type is usually quite content to flow with events as they happen.

Attitudes toward the interaction with the external world are reflected in the notion of extraversion or introversion. A person who has an extraverted attitude toward living is energized in the presence of others and seems to derive a great deal of satisfaction from active involvement with other people. The introverted individual, on the other hand, tends to be energized when alone and seems to derive satisfaction from less interaction with others, and therefore enjoys a rich inner life and sense of personal being.

The following illustration should help you to quickly understand:

People attend to and take in data through:
SENSING (S)   or   INTUITION (N)
———————————— | ————————————

People process data and make decisions through:
THINKING (T)   or   FEELING (F)
———————————— | ————————————

People have modes of meeting the world around them through:
JUDGMENT (J)   or   PERCEPTION (P)
———————————— | ————————————

People have attitudes toward others and are energized by:
EXTRAVERSION (E)   or   INTROVERSION (I)
———————————— | ————————————

Neither Jung nor Myers suggested that a person is purely one way or the other. By preference, Jung meant that a person prefers and therefore chooses, fairly consistently, one way of doing or being over another way. Individuals can be extraverted to some degree, as well as introverted to some degree, thinking as well as feeling, etc.

Rather, our preferences are similar to the way in which we "prefer" to use either the right hand or the left hand for writing our name. Some of us are more flexible in shifting back and forth than others. Most of us, however, have a distinct preference for using one hand over the other, just as we have a preference for either extraversion or introversion.

The mother/daughter team felt that it was important to reliably know what types people are in order to resolve conflicts between people of different types. If a person is to be freed from the prison of his or her own typo-centric view of the world, it is critical to know one's own type. It follows that if one wants to develop a genuine tolerance for an individual of another type, one must know one's own type and that of the other person.

There are different schools of thought about whether a person's preferences may strengthen or weaken as time passes and situations change. The question of whether these preferences are inborn or developed later is still being debated. Jung apparently believed that they are inborn.

The contribution made by Myers and Briggs clearly opened a door of awareness that had been shut for many years, and the opportunity to apply their insights and methodology is available for anyone at any time. It is interesting to note that as they worked on theories and concepts, students and teachers tended to be the natural forum for experimentation. Only in the 1980s does the full ramification of their work seem to enter into business and industry, and its impact appears to be much more profound than recent popularized texts providing shortcuts to performance (only to eventually evaporate into relatively useless reams of business publications).

While the contribution provided through the MBTI is formidable in everyday work life, differentiating the 16 human types becomes difficult, cumbersome, and sometimes frustrating for individuals who need to perform on a day-to-day basis according to predictable standards. Read on to discover how yet another researcher, from a practical and user-friendly point of view, has contributed to assisting leaders, managers, and supervisors to swiftly and effectively utilize these valuable concepts.

The Contribution Made by David W. Keirsey

Perhaps the most applicable and pragmatic contribution made to the concept of human typology was by Dr. David Keirsey in the development of what he has labeled "temperament theory." Keirsey was born in Ada, Oklahoma in 1921. He spent his childhood in Tustin, California, where his mother was a teacher and his father grew oranges and ran a nursery. After high school, he graduated from Santa Ana Junior College and went on to serve three and one-half years in the Marine Corps as a fighter pilot on a carrier in the Pacific during World War II. After the war, he completed his degree in psychology at Pomona College and attended Claremont Graduate School. After working as a counselor in a reform school and then as a school psychologist, he returned to Claremont to complete his doctoral studies.

It was just before this, in 1956, that Keirsey started formulating the temperament theory of behavior based primarily on his studies of Ernst Kretschmer's work. He had read the collected works of Jung and Kretschmer and, in 1958, he became aware of the Myers-Briggs Type Indicator. It was then that he rebased the Jungian ideas on the Kretschmer base of temperaments. As a pathologist and personologist of the Gestalt, field-systems school, Keirsey rejected the notion of functions as autonomous "parts" of the psyche; yet he found that some of Isabel Myers' descriptions fit some of the four temperaments quite well.

In 1970, Keirsey joined the faculty of the counseling program at California State University, Fullerton. Always an independent thinker, he was the architect of one of the most innovative and successful counselor training programs in the country. Using a total team approach, he and the late Marilyn Bates implemented a program that taught would-be counselors what successful therapists do, rather than just the theories they espouse. They also taught them about the four temperaments and their behaviors, needs, values and pathologies, all in a systems context. The tremendous value of this knowledge was that the counselors, or change agents, could then meet clients at their view of the world and have instant empathy and increased likelihood of change. He and Bates co-authored the book *Please Understand Me*, which he published in 1974 after her death. This self-published book has sold over one million copies and has been translated into Spanish and German. The tremendous potential of this concept of how people are different and the patterns behind their behavior is only just now beginning to be realized.

One of the contributions of Keirsey was to unify the many descriptions of the same four basic patterns of behavior that had been observed over the ages. In so doing, he identified some underlying themes of these descriptions. While he used Kretschmer's basic contribution of a comprehensive constitutional psychology as the basis for his descriptions of the temperaments, he also incorporated heavily the work of another contemporary of Jung and Kretschmer - Eduard Spränger.

A brief look at Spränger's work helps to deepen our understanding of Keirsey's four temperaments and what motivates them.

Spränger distinguished four primary value types: aesthetic, economic, religious and theoretic. Overall, Spränger was interested in the structure or configuration of the whole personality around a theme. This theme could be found in observing those acts, objects, achievements, experiences, etc. an individual found most valuable. He isolated four basic value tendencies which can be illustrated by considering an object such as a book from each perspective. A book could be viewed as having aesthetic value, being attractive or not; having economic value, being saleable; having religious value, being of some worth toward understanding the higher purpose in life; or having theoretic value, being an intellectual achievement.

His four types would prefer one of these perspectives over another and, by their daily choices, would consistently show a value preference for one of the four basic types. The aesthetic type focuses on experiencing the concrete world, with an aversion to the conceptual. There is a quality of self-enjoyment and response to impulse. Those of the economic type mainly choose actions that are useful in the preservation of life or in making life pleasant. They would focus on products and production. The religious types seek the total value of life in the highest way. They are concerned with unity, identity and meaning that goes beyond the senses. The theoretic types have a passion for objective knowledge and tend to be observers rather than doers. According to Spränger, understanding these "idealized" types would help us comprehend the behaviors of individuals even though they might not exactly match the "idealized" types.

Now let us look at the basics in understanding the four Keirseyan temperaments. Keirsey defined temperament as a "... thematization of the whole, a uniformity of the diverse. One's temperament is that which places a signature or thumb print on each of one's actions, making it recognizably one's own."[2] The emphasis is on the theme or core value of the type and on the configuration of the whole. The four temperaments are described in terms of the pattern of their behavior, which is taken as given and inborn, and in terms of the theme of that configuration. The Idealists value ethics and want to be authentic and whole. The Rationals value knowledge and competence and want mastery over nature. The Guardians value enculturation and civilization and want to have membership. The Artisans value art and play in their infinite variations and want to be free to choose the next act.

As noted before, Keirsey came across Myers' descriptions of the 16 types and noted some major similarities. He was then able to adapt the MBTI to his temperament theory. Jung and Myers' "Intuitives" seemed to be like Kretschmer's schizothymes and their "Sensing" seemed to be like Kretschmer's cyclothymes. Myers' iNtuitive Feeler (ENFJ, INFJ, ENFP and INFP) descriptions seemed to fit both Kretschmer's hyperaesthetic schizothymes and Spränger's religious type. The iNtuitive Thinker (ENTJ, INTJ, ENTP and INTP) descriptions seemed to fit both the anaesthetic schizothymes and the theoretic type. On the Sensing side, Myers' descriptions of the types with Introverted Sensing[3] (ESTJ, ISTJ, ESFJ and ISFJ) fit the melancholic cyclothymes and the economic types and those with Extraverted Sensing[4] (ESTP, ESFP, ISTP and ISFP) fit the hypomanic cyclothymes and the artistic type. The Keirseyan adaptations of the MBTI are as follows: Idealist, the four types with N and F (iNtuition and Feeling); Rationals, the four types with N and T (iNtuition and Thinking); Guardians, the four types with S and J (Sensing and Judging); and Artisans, the four types with S and P (Sensing and Perceiving).

Of course, other theories and descriptions were adapted, and the contributions of Kretschmer, Spränger and their predecessors are outlined in the following matrix[5] as they relate to Jung and the MBTI:

	Schizoid (Kretschmer) Intuition (Jung/Myers)	Cycloid (Kretschmer) Sensation (Jung/Myers)
Hippocrates Paracelsus Kretschmer Spränger Myers Keirsey	Choleric Nymph/Water Hyperaesthetic Religious Intuition, Feeling (NF) Idealist (NF)	Melancolic Gnome/Earth Depressive Economic Sensing, Judging (SJ) Guardian (SJ)
Hippocrates Paracelsus Kretschmer Spränger Myers Keirsey	Phlegmatic Sylph/Air Anaesthetic Theoretic Intuition, Thinking (NT) Rational (NT)	Sanguine Salamanders/Fire Hypomanic Aesthetic Sensing, Perceiving (SP) Artisan (SP)

In the next chapter let's rearrange the contributions of Jung, Kretschmer, Spränger, Briggs and Myers, Keirsey and others into a logical set of descriptions which can greatly increase your understanding of human motivation and behavior.

REFERENCES

[1]*Jung, A Biography*, by Gerhard Wehr: Shambhala, 1988.

[2]*Please Understand Me*, by David Keirsey and Marilyn Bates, page 25: Prometheus Nemesis, Del Mar, CA, 1984.

[3]While Myers' Introverted Sensing descriptions were written about the ISTJ and ISFJ, Keirsey found that the descriptions of the melancholic cyclothymes and the economic types fit all four of the types with both S and J.

[4]While Myers' Extraverted Sensing descriptions were written about the ESTP and ESFP, Keirsey found that the descriptions of the hypomanic cyclothymes and the artistic types fit all four of the types with both S and P.

[5]Adapted with permission from Keirsey's history matrix in *Portraits of Temperament*, 1986.

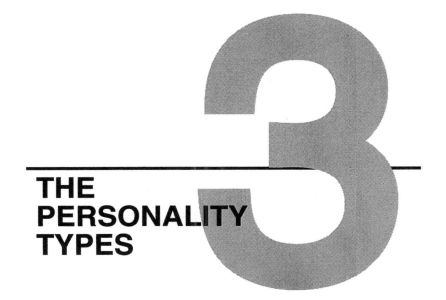

3

THE PERSONALITY TYPES

THE PERSONALITY TYPES

"If a man does not keep
pace with his companions, perhaps
it is because he hears a different drummer."
— Henry David Thoreau, 1854

For many of you this may be the ideal starting place in this book. These brief descriptions are offered here to present managers and those they manage with some basis for their use of these tools.

FOUR KINDS OF PEOPLE

Let us start with descriptions of the four temperaments to give us a brief picture of each one as a basis for our attempt to understand human behavior.[1]

The IDEALISTS
(NFs in Myers-Briggs Type Indicator language -
  includes ENFJ, INFJ, ENFP and INFP)

The Idealists want to be authentic, benevolent and empathic. They search for identity, meaning and significance. In fact, life is one constant search for identity. They are relationship oriented and they must have meaningful relationships for their life to be worth living. They devote a lot of time to nurturing those relationships. They tend to be romantic, idealistic and want to make the world a better place. They are future oriented. NFs trust their intuition, their imagination and their fantasy. These are as real and significant to them as an actual tree or a chair. Their focus tends to be on developing potential, fostering and facilitating growth through coaching, teaching, counseling and communicating. They will add these dimensions to whatever job they hold. If a job description does not call for these inclinations, they will do these things on their own, often providing a greater value to the organization by virtue of greasing the wheels and diffusing tension than the contribution they make doing their prescribed job. Generally, they are enthusiastic, especially about the ideas or causes that interest them. Their natural thinking style is one of integrating and seeing similarities. They look for universal principles and usually hold a global view. NFs are usually gifted in the use of language, oral and written. Metaphors abound in their language and they use this gift to bridge different perspectives and create harmony. Idealists are usually diplomatic; they put their many people and communication talents to work in the service of their ideals and morale.

The RATIONALS
(NTs in Myers-Briggs Type Indicator language -
 includes ENTJ, INTJ, ENTP and INTP)

The Rationals seek knowledge, competence, and achievement. They strive to understand what makes the world run and people tick. Rationals are fascinated by and drawn to theories. Everything is conditional and relative to the context in which it is found or expressed. Like the Idealists, they are future oriented. They trust logic and reason. Everything must be logical and proceed from carefully defined premises. Rationals want to have a rationale for everything and are natural skeptics. They think in terms of differences, delineating categories, definitions, structures and functions. If their job is too routine, they formulate hypotheses and theories to make it interesting. They hunger for precision, especially in thought and language. Long-range planning, inventing, designing and defining are their areas of strength and they bring these gifts to any job even if these are not called for. Their mood is generally calm and they prefer a peaceful environment. They foster individualism rather than conformity. Frequently they gravitate toward technology and the sciences and are well suited for engineering and devising strategy.

The GUARDIANS
(SJs in Myers-Briggs Type Indicator language - includes ESTJ, ISTJ, ESFJ and ISFJ)

The Guardians want to belong, to have membership in whatever group is theirs. They hunger for responsibility and accountability. Frequently, they take on too much responsibility and become overworked. They expect others to work hard and be accountable. They favor generosity, service and duty. They establish and maintain institutions and standard operating procedures. SJs want to preserve the world and protect their charges, so they stand guard, so to speak. They can be found to give warnings when someone or something is going off course or varying too much from the prescribed norm. They look to the past and tradition for security and standards. Frequently, they foster enculturation with ceremonies, rules and rituals. Guardians trust contracts and authority and distrust chance. They want security and stability. SJs think in terms of convention, association and discrete elements, and thus emphasize memory and drill as paths to mastery. Generally they are serious and concerned, with a fatalistic stance. Guardians are skilled at ensuring that things and people are in the right place, in the right amounts, the right quality and at the right time. Frequently, they gravitate towards business and commerce, especially in the areas where safekeeping and logistics are required.

The ARTISANS
(SPs in Myers-Briggs Type Indicator language -
includes ESTP, ISTP, ESFP and ISFP)

Artisans want the freedom to choose the next act. They must experience and act on impulses. They want to be graceful, bold and impressive and to have an impact on their "audience." They are generally excited and optimistic, expecting lady luck to be on their side. SPs may become so absorbed in the action of the moment that they lose sight of distant goals. The flip side: they see opportunities that others miss (which they seize if at all possible). Artisans are oriented toward the present and they seek adventure and experiences. They hunger for spontaneity. SPs trust their impulses, luck and their ability to solve any problem they run into. Thus, they frequently rush in when others hold back with fear and hesitation. Artisans are natural negotiators and enjoy getting others to concede even some small part. They think in terms of variation, thus the name Artisan. The capacity for producing variations on a theme shows up in all that they do, not just in the limited sense of "arts and crafts." No matter what their job, they will find some way to vary it. They have a keen ability to notice and describe detail. They like the freedom to move, festivities and games. Gifted tacticians, figuring out the best move to make at the instant, Artisans do the expedient thing, not the acceptable, friendly or logical thing. Frequently they are drawn to the manual, visual and performing arts as well as entrepreneurial aspects of business.

Keirsey aligned the four temperaments in a matrix which displays the dimensions and similarities of these four basic types in such a way as to give us a scaffolding to use to build our human interaction skills. An adaptation of his matrix follows:[2]

	NFs and NTs have in common	SJs and SPs have in common
	Abstract/Symbolic Consciousness	Concrete/Real Consciousness
NFs and SJs focus on affiliation, consensus and the social values of care and cooperation.	**NF** IDEALISTS	**SJ** GUARDIANS
NTs and SPs focus on pragmatism, autonomy and the use of power for the sake of expediency.	**NT** RATIONALS	**SP** ARTISANS

Idealists (NFs) and Rationals (NTs) have in common that they prefer thinking and talking in symbols and abstractions. They are more interested in connections between ideas and in representations than in a more concrete reality. On the other hand, Guardians (SJs) and Artisans (SPs) prefer the real, sensory based world. In other words, things as they are.

Another set of similarities lies along a dimension of affiliation and pragmatism. Idealists (NFs) and Guardians (SJs) prefer cooperative and affiliative means to achieving goals. Focusing more on social values and consensus, they want people to work together. Rationals (NTs) and Artisans (SPs) seek a pragmatic solution. That is, their focus is first on doing whatever it takes to get the job done. This does not mean that they will not cooperate. It means that affiliation is not their first and foremost priority. Their first inclination is to do whatever it takes. If it takes a cooperative effort, then so be it. If not, well the important thing is that the job got done!

Perhaps this brief matrix[3] will capture for you the essentials of the four temperaments before we go on to Jung and Myers' four dimensions that allow us to more easily grasp variations on these four basic patterns.

THE FOUR TEMPERAMENTS

	Abstract Symbolic	Concrete Real

Affiliators	**Idealists**
	Intuitive Feeling - NF
	
	• Wants to Grow
	• Meaning and Significance
	• Guide Others
	• Make a Better World
	• Self-Realization
	• "Catalyst"
	• "Becoming" Is
	  Most Important
		Guardians
		Sensing Judging - SJ
		
		• Wants A Place
		• Membership
		• Responsibility
		• Accountability
		• Duty
		• "Traditionalist"
		• "Serving" Is
		  Most Important

Pragmatists	**Rationals**
	Intuitive Thinking - NT
	
	• Wants To Know
	• Competence
	• Knowledge
	• Power Over Nature
	• Intellect
	• "Visionary"
	• "Knowing" Is
	  Most Important
		Artisans
		Sensing Perceiving - SP
		
		• Wants Spontaneity
		• Freedom To Choose
		  the Next Act
		• Excitation
		• Action
		• Grace
		• "Negotiator"
		• "Doing" Is
		  Most Important

FOUR DIMENSIONS OF BEHAVIOR

Now for the descriptions of the dimensions outlined by Jung and added to by Myers as functions and attitudes.

EXTRAVERSION vs. INTROVERSION

The person who is energized by having interaction with other people is said to be Extraverted (E), while a person who prefers introspection and solitude is said to be Introverted (I). Estimates are that about 75% of the population is Extraverted, while only 25% are Introverted. When dealing with an Extravert, you are meeting with the General and the Aide is in the tent; when you meet an Introvert, you meet with the Aide and the General is in the tent. If you will remember this, it will give you some insight into the difference and effects of these two preferences.

EXTRAVERSION vs.	INTROVERSION
Sociability	Solitary
Interaction	Private
External	Internal
Breadth	Depth
Extensive	Intensive
Relationships	Deep friendship
Expand	Conserve
Actions	Reactions
External events	Internal reactions

SENSING vs. INTUITION

Those who have a natural preference for Sensing (S) probably describe themselves as practical, while those who have a natural preference for iNtuition (N) may describe themselves as innovative. It is estimated that 75% of the general population in America would report a preference for Sensing while only 25% would indicate a preference for iNtuition.

To help you quickly assess the difference between Sensing and iNtuitive people, the following might be useful:

SENSING	vs.	INTUITION
Experience		Hunches
Past		Future
Realistic		Speculative
Perspiration		Inspiration
Actual		Possible
Down to earth		Head in clouds
Utility		Fantasy
Practicality		Ingenuity
Sensible		Imaginative

THINKING vs. FEELING

Persons who choose the impersonal basis of choice are called Thinking (T) types by Jung. Persons who choose the personal basis are called Feeling (F) types. Both of these ways of selecting what to do or not to do are necessary and useful. It is a matter of preference. Some people are more comfortable with impersonal, objective judgments and are less comfortable with personal value judgments. Others are more comfortable with value judgments and less comfortable with logic and objectivity. The more extreme "F" types are a bit put off by rule-governed choice, regarding the act of being impersonal as being inhumane. The more extreme "T" types, on the other hand, sometimes look upon the emotion-laden decisions of Feelers as unintelligent. Each person is quite capable of both types of decision. It is, again, a matter of preference. The distribution of Thinking and Feeling types is approximately equal.

THINKING	vs.	FEELING
Objective		Subjective
Principles		Values
Policy		Society
Laws		Circumstances
Firmness		Persuasion
Impersonal		Personal
Standards		Good or bad
Critique		Appreciate
Analyze		Sympathize
Practicality		Beauty

JUDGING vs. PERCEIVING

Persons who choose closure over open options are likely to be the Judging (J) types. Persons preferring to keep things open and fluid are the Perceiving (P) types. "Js" are apt to report a sense of urgency until they make a pending decision and then be at rest once the decision has been made. The "P" person, in contrast, is more apt to consider new possibilities and, after a decision has been made, to keep options open and available. Current estimates indicate that of the total population, 60% tend to prefer Judging while 40% tend to prefer Perceiving.

JUDGING	vs.	PERCEIVING
Settled		Pending
Decided		Open
Fixed		Flexible
Plan ahead		Adapt as you go
Closure		Options
Decisions		Opportunities
Planned		Spontaneous
Completed		Emergent
Urgency		Excitement
Structured		Unstructured

Let us summarize functions and attitudes in a more orderly and chronological fashion so that at this initial stage you can understand what we have suggested to this point:

- We absorb impressions and data from the outside world through the function of either Sensing or iNtuition.

- We formulate decisions and opinions through the function of Thinking or Feeling.

- We tend to go about living everyday life either in a Structured or Perceptive manner.

- Finally, the mode of our personal energy and the attitude we have toward others is expressed in Extraversion or Introversion.

Taking the concepts one step further, according to the MBTI there are two opposite attitudes and two opposite functions:

- The function of Sensing versus the function of iNtuiting. Both of these functions are irrational, not usually under conscious direction.

- The function of Thinking versus the function of Feeling. Both of these functions are rational, more likely to be under our direction.

- The attitude of Judging versus Perceiving - an attitude you have toward your actions in the world.

- The attitude of Extraversion versus the attitude of Introversion - an attitude you have toward interactions with others.

If what you have read so far makes sense to you, then let us take these concepts further and put them into the more holistic realm of the types that Jung described.

- The four Sensing types: ISTJ, ISFJ, ESTP, and ESFP. All of these personalities rely primarily upon their sensing and secondarily upon their thinking or feeling in their day-to-day living. Approximately 38% of the population are Sensors.

- The four Thinking types: ISTP, INTP, ESTJ, and ENTJ. All of these personalities rely primarily upon their thinking and secondarily upon their sensing and intuition in their day-to-day living. Approximately 26% of the population are Thinkers.

- The four Feeling types: ISFP, INFP, ESFJ, and ENFJ. All of these personalities rely primarily upon their feelings and secondarily upon their sensing or intuition in their day-to-day living. Approximately 24% of the population are Feelers.

- Finally, the four iNtuitive types: INTJ, INFJ, ENTP, and ENFP. All of these personalities rely primarily upon their intuition and secondarily upon their thinking or feeling in their day-to-day living. Approximately 12% of the population are iNtuitors.

In the context of what we have written about both functions and attitudes, it is important to understand that the intensity or the relative importance of each one of these functions and attitudes can vary significantly. While the individual MBTI score is not an absolute indicator, it is possible that the higher the score in any one of these categories, the stronger the preference or conviction.

VARIATIONS ON 4 THEMES - 16 TYPES

Now to put Jung's types into the context of the four temperaments. Each temperament has four variations. The unique
configuration of each temperament's variations is based on
observation, but fits nicely with our understanding of the
functions and attitudes. Let's take a look at the variations. The
branching diagrams which follow illustrate how we start with
the core values and needs of the temperament and arrive at the
varieties in their behaviors using Jung and Myers' dimensions.

IDEALISTS
Idealists (NFs) are at their core concerned with identity and
self-realization of some higher good.

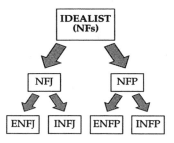

NFJs
Two varieties of Idealists (NFs) rely primarily on their judging
preference in dealing with the outer world (NFJ). They tend to
be very comfortable giving directives and structure to others.
They are **role directive**.

NFPs
The two varieties of Idealists who rely primarily on their
perceptive preference in dealing with the outer world (NFP)
are less comfortable with telling people what to do and structuring others. Instead, they tend to give information, leaving
the decision to act to the other person. They are **role informative**.

The Extraversion-Introversion dimension tells us even more about the varieties of Idealists (NFs). Those Idealists (NFs) who prefer Extraversion are more gregarious and tend to initiate in relationships more comfortably than those who prefer Introversion. The Introverted Idealists tend to wait for someone to make the first move and then to respond to that move. However, given a desire for structure, an Introverted, Role Directive Idealist (INFJ) will be likely to make the first move before an Introverted, Role Informative Idealist (INFP).

RATIONALS
Rationals (NTs) are at their core concerned with knowledge and competence.

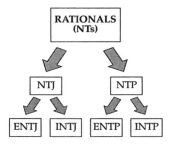

.NTJs
Two varieties of Rationals (NTs) rely primarily on their judging preference in dealing with the outer world (NTJ). They tend to be very comfortable giving directives and structure to others. They are **role directive**.

NTPs
The two varieties of Rationals who rely primarily on their perceptive preference in dealing with the outer world (NTP) are less comfortable with telling people what to do and structuring others. Instead, they tend to give information, leaving the decision to act to the other person. They are **role informative**.

The Extraversion-Introversion dimension tells us even more about the varieties of Rationals (NTs). Those Rationals (NTs) who prefer Extraversion are more gregarious and tend to initiate in relationships more comfortably than those who prefer Introversion. The Introverted Rationals tend to wait for someone to make the first move and then to respond to that move. However, given a desire for structure, an Introverted, Role Directive Rational (INTJ) will be likely to make the first move before an Introverted, Role Informative Rational (INTP).

GUARDIANS

Guardians (SJs) are at their core concerned with belonging and the preservation of resources.

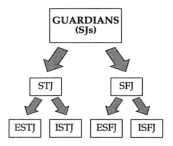

STJs

Two varieties of Guardians (SJs) prefer to rely on objective criteria when making decisions (STJ). They tend to be very comfortable giving directives and structure to others. They are **role directive**.

SFJs

The two varieties of Guardians who rely primarily on personal criteria for decisions (SFJ) are less comfortable with telling people what to do and structuring others. Instead, they tend to give information, leaving the decision to act to the other person. They are **role informative**.

The Extraversion-Introversion dimension tells us even more about the varieties of Guardians (SJs). Those Guardians (SJs) who prefer Extraversion are more gregarious and tend to initiate in relationships more comfortably than those who prefer Introversion. The Introverted Guardians tend to wait for someone to make the first move and then to respond to that move. However, given a desire for structure, an Introverted, Role Directive Guardian (ISTJ), will be likely to make the first move before an Introverted, Role Informative Guardian (ISFJ).

ARTISANS
Artisans (SPs) are at their core concerend with variation and spontaneity.

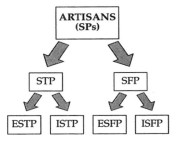

STPs
Two varieties of Artisans (SPs) prefer to rely on objective criteria when making decisions (STP). They tend to be very comfortable giving directives and structure to others. They are **role directive**.

SFPs
The two varieties of Artisans who rely primarily on personal criteria for decisions (SFP) are less comfortable with telling people what to do and structuring others. Instead, they tend to give information, leaving the decision to act to the other person. They are **role informative**.

The Extraversion-Introversion dimension tells us even more about the varieties of Artisans (SPs). Those Artisans (SPs) who prefer Extraversion are more gregarious and tend to initiate in relationships more comfortably than those who prefer Introversion. The Introverted Artisans tend to wait for someone to make the first move and then to respond to that move. However, given a desire for structure, an Introverted, Role Directive Artisan (ISTP) will be likely to make the first move before an Introverted, Role Informative Artisan (ISFP).

Another way to look at these variations is through the expanded temperament matrix[4] on the following page:

THE FOUR KEIRSEYAN TEMPERAMENTS
AND THEIR VARIANTS

	Directive *	Informative **	Directive	Informative
Introversion (Responsive)	INFJ FORESEER DEVELOPER	INFP PROPONENT ADVOCATE	ISTJ OVERSEER INSPECTOR	ISFJ PROVIDER NOURISHER
	IDEALIST iNtuitive Feeling NF		**GUARDIAN** Sensing Judging SJ	
Extraversion (Assertive)	ENFJ FORESEER MOBILIZER	ENFP PROPONENT MESSENGER	ESTJ OVERSEER SUPERVISOR	ESFJ PROVIDER CARETAKER
Introversion (Responsive)	INTJ DIRECTOR STRATEGIST	INTP INVENTOR DESIGNER	ISTP MANEUVERER OPERATOR	ISFP PERFORMER COMPOSER
	RATIONAL iNtuitive Thinking NT		**ARTISAN** Sensing Perceiving SP	
Extraversion (Assertive)	ENTJ DIRECTOR COMMANDANT	ENTP INVENTOR IMPROVISOR	ESTP MANEUVERER PROMOTER	ESFP PERFORMER ENTERTAINER

* describes a preference for giving directives among people who score NJ & ST
** describes a preference for giving information among people who score NP & SF

In the chapters that follow, we hope you find these basic descriptions and matrices helpful in organizing your understanding so that you can put these valuable theories to work in your own environment.

REFERENCES

[1]The summary descriptions were adapted, with permission, from the works of David Keirsey including *Please Understand Me* and *Portraits of Temperament*.

[2]Adapted with permission from *Temperament Report Form* by Linda V. Berens, Telos Publications, Huntington Beach, CA, 1988.

[3]From *Introduction to Temperament*, Telos Publications, Huntington Beach, CA. © Copyright 1987 Giovannoni, Berens & Cooper.

[4]From *Introduction to Temperament*, Telos Publications, Huntington Beach, CA. © Copyright 1989 Giovannoni, Berens & Cooper.

4

HOW TO
IDENTIFY TYPES -
A LAYMAN'S GUIDE

HOW TO IDENTIFY TYPES — A LAYMAN'S GUIDE

" A moment's insight is
sometimes worth a life's experience."
— Oliver Wendell Holmes, 1860

Before you continue to read it would seem useful and appropriate for you to gain some insight into what your own style and temperament might be. Not surprisingly, we recommend that you use the MBTI.[1] When it is adequately and professionally interpreted, it is the best and most accurate indicator for your style and temperament. In order to gain some preliminary insight into how you tend to function and your personality style, however, you may want to use the descriptions and lists in this chapter to "discover" or "uncover" your own type. If so, first complete the checklist and then read the description matching your type in the Appendix and see how well it fits you.

If you already know your type, or you are seeking to identify the type of someone you know, skip the checklist and read on. Use the vignettes of the sixteen styles for contrast and comparison.

This checklist is not meant to replace a professionally administered and interpreted personality assessment.

THE TEMPERAMENT
SELF-ASSESSMENT CHECKLIST

PART ONE - BEHAVIORS:

INSTRUCTIONS: Read the following paragraphs and decide which one fits you best. Rank that paragraph #1. Then decide which one fits you least. Rank that paragraph #4. After that assign the ranks of #2 and #3 to the remaining paragraphs.

_____**A.** You spend a lot of time relating to others, either one-on-one or in a group. You may spend hours talking and listening empathically, as people frequently come to you with their problems. You also like to fantasize, envisioning what might happen. Philosophizing about how to make things better and lamenting lost potential of others also occupies a great deal of your time. For you, life without meaning is not worth much, so you may devote your energy to helping others find meaning and feel lost yourself when you do not have a sense of purpose. Frequently, you find that you can predict what someone feels or thinks and even what may happen. Teaching in some way or revealing the truth behind an issue appeals to you. You want to bring out the best in others and are often a catalyst for others to be creative. You are happiest with some kind of cause to foster or even fight for.

_____**B.** Theorizing and philosophizing are favorite pastimes for you. You may be frequently found deep in thought about a design or a plan. In fact, you prefer to spend your time planning, inventing, engineering and designing. You may even spend a lot of time telling people what you know. When you are dealing with ideas, facts, events and people, you cannot help but analyze. You want the categories set forth and a strategic, long-range plan developed. It is important to you to be competent and knowledgeable as well as efficient. You abhor redundancy and routine. There should be a rationale for everything. You are likely to have very high standards and will raise those standards on yourself as you achieve each goal. You are most content when life is calm and you are clear-headed and when all of the factors have been considered.

_____C. As a rule, you are very industrious. You tend to be busy doing what should be done and will work steadily to complete whatever it is. You are usually extremely loyal to those who are in charge by position and title. Risk is something to be avoided and change approached cautiously, for what is most important is preservation of what already works. Philosophizing can be a waste of time. You are likely to follow the rules and to be upset when others do not. You may be concerned with making sure that others are comfortable and they get their physical needs met. You also want to make sure that there is no waste or misuse of material. You are most happy when people are getting along and working together for the good of the organization.

_____D. You want excitement and variation in all you do. You have the ability to become totally absorbed in the activities of the moment, whether they involve people, tools or some other medium. Risk is no stranger to you as you frequently test the limits. The risks you take may not feel like risks to you and may not necessarily be highly visible and physical. You might enjoy doing "zany" things like getting people to laugh; financial wheeling and dealing; ignoring protocol, procedures and customs or anything requiring operating on the edge. You may especially like to get a response from others. You are at your best in a crisis and can take instant action to save the day. You likely have an uncanny sense of the "what's in it for me" of those you come in contact with. You are happiest when there is an opportunity to seize, an action to take and when you are left alone to do it your way.

PART TWO - LANGUAGE:

INSTRUCTIONS: Read the following paragraphs and decide which one fits you best. Rank that paragraph #1. Then decide which one fits you least. Rank that paragraph #4. After that assign the ranks of #2 and #3 to the remaining paragraphs.

_____**A.** When asked about your work, you will frequently talk about **relationships** at work. When just conversing, you are prone to philosophizing about making the world a better place, your ideals, finding your true self, the meaning of life and the significance of events. Your language is rich with metaphors. Flowing and rapturous, it is often full of redundancies and exaggerations for dramatic effect. You may not like to be pushed to fill in the concrete details and are more likely masterful at stating things in a global, general way.

_____**B.** When asked about your work, you are likely to talk about your goals and **strategies** and the problems you are involved in solving. You talk about future plans, possibilities, how things work, problems or puzzles to solve, design flaws and efficiency. You do not favor small talk. Often you will ask for the rationale behind an assertion, a comment, a law or a procedure and then proceed to challenge it. Your language is frequently filled with conditionals, such as the "if ..., then" statement, "tends to," "might be," "possible," etc. Your language is syllogistic or self-consistent. It is usually terse and highly qualified, since you hate to be redundant and inaccurate.

_____**C.** When asked about your work, you tend to tell how you do the prescribed tasks, your **duties**. Given free choice, you talk about real events, operating procedures, what you have done. Frequently, over the course of a conversation you will mention something you worry about or give a caution or warning about avoiding trouble or correcting a performance. Your language is filled with shoulds and should nots, oughts and ought nots. It is factual, detailed, quantitative, rarely metaphoric or sonorous. There are frequent comparisons and references to the past and to convention or tradition.

_____**D.** When asked about your work, you frequently talk about the **activities** involved and the tools you use. When conversing, you tend to mirror the conversation of others, that is, you tend to feed back to others what they want to hear. You have quite a knack for noticing when other's eyes light up and their minimal non-verbal cues. Whenever you are free to talk about whatever you want and are not invested in persuading someone, you may have lots of stories about your adventures and experiences. You like to talk about chances you have taken, deals you have made, risks you have survived and interesting characters you have known. Anything to make an impact on the listener. Your language is rich with these anecdotes and usually quite colloquial.

PART THREE - PERSONALITY PREFERENCE:

INSTRUCTIONS: On the following page, read the pairs of words or phrases. Select the one in each pair that is most like you or that would most often describe you. Total each column. The column with the most choices indicates your likely preference.

EXTRAVERSION   ## INTROVERSION

EXTRAVERSION			INTROVERSION
Externally focused	☐	☐	Internally focused
Outward thrust	☐	☐	Inward pull
Uses many words	☐	☐	Economical with words
Wants to talk	☐	☐	Wants to be quiet
More sociable	☐	☐	Less sociable
Go go	☐	☐	Hesitate
Silence is embarrassing	☐	☐	Silence is a blessing
Talk . . . think	☐	☐	Think . . . talk
Talk . . . feel	☐	☐	Feel . . . talk
Scattered energy	☐	☐	Concentrated energy
TOTAL - E	☐	☐	TOTAL - I

(If equal, give one more point to E.)

SENSING   ## INTUITION

SENSING			INTUITION
What is real	☐	☐	What can become
Concrete	☐	☐	Abstract
To do	☐	☐	To envision
Specific/actual	☐	☐	Theoretical
Action	☐	☐	Insight
Realistic	☐	☐	Futuristic
Tangible	☐	☐	Conceptual
Today	☐	☐	Tomorrow
Practical	☐	☐	Vision
TOTAL - S	☐	☐	TOTAL - N

(If equal, give one more point to S.)[2]

THINKING   FEELING

THINKING			FEELING
Head	☐	☐	Heart
Criteria	☐	☐	Values
Impersonal	☐	☐	Personal
Explain	☐	☐	Understand
Tough	☐	☐	Compassion
Aloof	☐	☐	Personable
Principles	☐	☐	Circumstances
Justification	☐	☐	Humane
Objective	☐	☐	Subjective
TOTAL - T	☐	☐	TOTAL - F

(If equal, give one more point to F.)

JUDGING   PERCEIVING

JUDGING			PERCEIVING
Priorities	☐	☐	Projects
Anticipate and schedule	☐	☐	See what happens and respond
Get on with it	☐	☐	Keep going
Finished	☐	☐	Another angle
On time	☐	☐	On a roll
Urgency	☐	☐	Lots of time
Agenda	☐	☐	Loose leaf
Order	☐	☐	Options
Task	☐	☐	Process
TOTAL - J	☐	☐	TOTAL - P

(If equal, give one more point to P.)

Summary Sheet

Paragraph Rankings   Rank #1   Rank #2

Behaviors   _____   _____
Language   _____   _____

Preferences   E or I   S or N   T or F   J or P

                     _____   _____   _____   _____

Preferred Roles

Do you:
a. _____tend to be comfortable telling others what to do?
b. _____tend to be uncomfortable telling others what to do?

Are you:
a._____less often inclined to offer information, preferring
instead the time-saving method of giving a directive?
b._____more often inclined to offer information and leave the
decision to act up to the individual?

If you chose the behavior and language patterns of paragraph
A and you have preferences of N and F, you are most likely an
NF Idealist. If you selected choice (a) on the two preceding
questions and have a preference for J, you are most likely a
directive Idealist (ENFJ or INFJ). If you selected choice (b) on
those questions and have a preference for P, you are most likely
an informative Idealist (ENFP or INFP).

If you chose the behavior and language patterns of paragraph
B and have preferences of N and T, you are most likely an NT
Rational. If you selected choice (a) on the two preceding

questions and have a preference for J, you are most likely a directive Rational (ENTJ or INTJ). If you selected choice (b) on those questions and have a preference for P, you are most likely an informative Rational (ENTP or INTP).

If you chose the behavior and language patterns of paragraph C and you have preferences of S and J, you are most likely an SJ Guardian. If you selected choice (a) on the two preceding questions and have a preference for T, you are most likely a directive Guardian (ESTJ or ISTJ). If you selected choice (b) on those questions and have a preference for F, you are most likely an informative Guardian (ESFJ or ISFJ).

If you chose the behavior and language patterns of paragraph D and you have preferences of S and P, you are most likely an SP Artisan. If you selected choice (a) on the two preceding questions and have a preference for T, you are most likely a directive Artisan (ESTP or ISTP). If you selected choice (b) on those questions and have a preference for F, you are most likely an informative Artisan (ESFP or ISFP).

If your preferences do not match your first ranked paragraph selections, look to see if they match your second ranking. If they still do not match, you might want to ask someone who knows you well to tell you their selections on the paragraphs, the pairs of words and the preferred roles. If your preference and paragraph selections were close, read the corresponding descriptions in the appendix and decide which one fits you best. Remember, you may share some of the characteristics of several of the types, but it is the overall theme and pattern that we are looking for.

This checklist is not meant to replace a professionally administered and interpreted personality assessment.

OBSERVABLE BEHAVIORS

Type identification of others is something most "type-enthusiasts" do for fun. It has its hazards, as well as its benefits. Since you can't go around giving the MBTI to everyone you meet, it is useful to try to identify another person's type through application of knowledge of "pure" types. To use your knowledge of these "pure" types to improve your human relationships, you may want to begin to form hypotheses about individuals' temperaments when you first meet them. Then check out those hypotheses by varying your communications with them and by observing them further.

One key to developing an ability to identify temperaments is to look for patterns of behavior that indicate a person's core values. Put another way, look for what they are interested in. Behavior often offers clues to an individual's temperament. Alfred Adler, a contemporary of Jung, Freud and Kretschmer, said something to the effect that if you want to know what people are up to, watch their feet. That is to say, what behaviors do they engage in, what actions do they take, what do they do? Herein lies the real key to identifying and verifying temperament, for we do not always report ourselves accurately, for whatever reason. In fact, the MBTI is estimated to be accurate only 75% of the time. So it behooves us to take the MBTI results as a starting point for a hypothesis and check it out against behaviors, or in "typing" yourself and others to look and listen closely to what people do and say.

Sometimes the core values are evident in language. Given the opportunity to talk about whatever they choose, people will talk about what is important to them, their values.

SP ARTISAN LANGUAGE

When asked about their work, SP Artisans frequently talk about the **activities** involved and the tools they use. When conversing, their temperament is a little harder to pinpoint since they are masters at mirroring the conversation of others. In other words, they tend to feed back to you what you want to hear, given their knack for noticing when your eyes light up and other minimal non-verbal cues. However, if you listen carefully, especially when SPs are free to talk about anything and are not invested in persuading you, you may hear evidence of their hunger for risk and excitement and trust in chance, their desire for freedom and variation, and their love of making a deal. Their language is rich with anecdotes, colorful, sometimes terse, colloquial and sonorous.

SJ GUARDIAN LANGUAGE

When asked about their work, the SJ Guardians tend to tell you how they do the prescribed tasks, their **duties**. Given free choice, they talk about real events, operating procedures, what they have done. Frequently, over the course of a conversation they will mention something they worry about or give a caution or warning about avoiding trouble or correcting a performance. Their language is filled with shoulds and should nots, oughts and ought nots. It is factual, detailed, quantitative, rarely metaphoric, rarely sonorous. There are frequent comparisons and references to the past and to convention or tradition.

NF IDEALIST LANGUAGE

When asked about their work, NF Idealists will frequently talk about **relationships** at work. When just conversing, they are prone to philosophize about making the world a better place, their ideals, finding their true selves, the meaning of life and the significance of events. Their language is rich with metaphors; something is always something else. It is often exaggerated, redundant, flowing and rapturous.

NT RATIONAL LANGUAGE

When asked about their work, NT Rationals are likely to talk about their goals and **strategies** and the problems they are involved in solving. They talk also about future plans, possibilities, how things work, problems or puzzles to solve, design flaws and efficiency. They do not favor small talk. Often they will ask for the rationale behind an assertion, a comment, a law or a procedure. Their language is frequently filled with conditionals, such as the "if..., then" statement, "tend to," "might be," "possibly," etc. NT language is syllogistic or self-consistent. It is terse and highly qualified, since Rationals hate to be redundant and inaccurate.

SP ARTISAN BEHAVIORS

In observing SPs, one will notice a lot of risk taking, but not always the highly visible and physically risky behaviors. Look for more subtle risk taking as well. Doing "zany" things, financial wheeling and dealing, ignoring protocol, procedures and customs. Look also for evidence of their desire for variation. Total absorption in whatever their impulses dictate at the moment is also characteristic of the Artisans.

SJ GUARDIAN BEHAVIORS

In observing SJs, one will notice how industrious they are. They tend to be busy doing what should be done. They may exhibit extreme loyalty to the powers that be. There will be very little risk taking and very little philosophizing. They frequently follow the rules to the letter and insist that everyone else do so as well. Very often the activities they engage in will involve inspecting, storing material, assuring there is no waste, and making sure that the right people get the right things and the wrong people do not. You may find them concerned with making others comfortable and making sure their physical needs are met.

NF IDEALIST BEHAVIORS

One of the first things to notice about NFs is that they spend a lot of time relating to others. They may spend hours talking and listening empathically. They also may engage in fantasizing. Philosophizing about how to make things better, teaching and developing the potential in others also occupies a lot of their time. They frequently are involved in predicting what someone feels or thinks or even what may happen, as well as revealing the truth behind an issue.

NT RATIONAL BEHAVIORS

Like the NFs, the NTs may spend a lot of time talking and cogitating. Theorizing and philosophizing are favorite pastimes for them. They are frequently found deep in thought about a design or a plan. Indeed, they prefer to spend their time planning, inventing, engineering and designing. They like to categorize. They may also get involved in marshalling the forces to carry out a plan.

FROM THE FOUR TEMPERAMENTS
TO THE SIXTEEN TYPES

We have found it useful to start with the temperament and then to look at the scales of the MBTI (Extraversion/Introversion; Sensing/Intuition; Thinking/Feeling; and Judging/Perceiving) to help us determine the variation of the temperament. So let's examine how the concepts emerged and how you might approach that challenge.

While by no means a comprehensive explanation, the concepts emerging from the work of Jung and Myers certainly provide insights of significant value in better understanding how people tend to react to the external events and how these clearly influence the state they seem to be in at various points in time. Initially, Jung labeled these notions "attitudes." They were, as you know by now, labeled:

> Sensing....................Intuition
> Thinking..................Feeling
> Extraversion............Introversion

In the 1940s, Myers added the dimension of:

> Structure.......Perceiving

It is probably more useful to consider these categories from a somewhat different point of view, that of (a) functions and (b) attitudes. Accordingly, each person has two attitudes and two functions. The attitudes are:

> Structure vs. Perceiving
> Extraversion vs. Introversion

and the functions are:

Sensing vs. Intuition
Thinking vs. Feeling

It is useful to understand that Sensing/Intuition are irrational functions. In other words, we are really not in command or in charge of how our Sensing and/or Intuitive capabilities are put to work for us. They just happen to be there so we can draw from them in living everyday life. Also note, if you will, that people predominantly influenced by the Sensing function tend to be concrete and therefore do not enjoy abstractions, at least not in great quantity. On the other hand, individuals drawing on their Intuition tend to function from the opposite side of the continuum, so to speak; concrete issues for them may be mundane and uninteresting, while abstractions can be a source of energy and enthusiasm.

Thinking/Feeling, however, are rational functions. Although Thinkers at times may accuse Feelers of being irrational, both functions are rational. In other words, individuals preferring to approach events and issues from an objective point of view can direct their thinking in ways they choose in order to understand and explore. Similarly, individuals relying on their Feelings can direct their value orientation in the directions they desire.

Let us address both the attitudes and functions, then, in a way that hopefully will be useful for you in identifying types.

- Do you absorb data and feed your awareness of what seems to be happening either by sensation, i.e., concreteness, or by intuition, i.e., abstraction?

- In reaching decisions, do you rely predominantly on your thinking process, i.e., logic (objectivity or impersonal basis), or do you rely on your value orientation, i.e., feelings (personal basis)?

- Facing everyday life, are you more comfortable structuring and prioritizing, or perceiving and constantly being open to unanticipated changes?

- Energies are derived through Extraversion/Introversion. Do you tend to be energized and motivated by being with and dealing with people? Or do you tend to experience time alone or with small groups as far more energizing?

Here are some words to help you identify yourself and the people around you as extraverted or introverted.

EXTRAVERSION	INTROVERSION
Externally focused	Internally focused
Outward thrust	Inward pull
Uses many words	Economical with words
Wants to talk	Wants to be quiet
Silence is embarrassing	Silence is a blessing
More sociable	Less sociable
Likes to make the first move	Let others make the first move, then respond
Expansive gestures[3]	Close to the body gestures
Go go	Hesitation
Talk . . . think	Think . . . talk
Talk . . . feel	Feel . . . talk
Scattered energy	Concentrated energy

The list could probably go on, yet we believe you are now able to observe behaviors of people around you and determine whether or not individuals are extraverted or introverted. It is useful to also understand that the degree to which a person appears to be extraverted or introverted can vary significantly.

Early on in life, introverts usually learn to behave in an extraverted fashion so you may want to take a cautious approach in your categorization.

Now, let us turn to two other attitudes - those of Judging and Perceiving. There are several "give aways" in terms of determining whether you are dealing with one or the other. We have found that asking people to drop everything at the spur of the moment provides a quick insight into their need for structure. As you would expect, perceiving people are usually delighted to switch mid-stream and do something else, while structured individuals tend to be bothered sometimes to the point of irritation (as they usually have a need to finish whatever they are working on). A structured person, then, has a need for completion, while a non-structured person enjoys keeping several things going at the same time.

Here are some outward manifestations of whether or not you are interacting with a structured, judicious person or a perceptive, spontaneous person.

STRUCTURED (JUDGING)	NON-STRUCTURED (PERCEIVING)
There is a time and place for everything	There are many times and places for all kinds of things
See you at 1:00 p.m. sharp	See you sometime tomorrow
Priorities	Projects
Anticipate and schedule	See what happens, respond
Finished	Another angle
On time	On a roll
Urgency	Lots of time
Agenda	Loose leaf
Order	Options
Task	Process

Again, the list could be expanded, yet we hope the above will provide you with beginning insights into whether you are communicating with a structured or a non-structured person.

In terms of the functions, let us first address the two irrational ones by providing you with some words which hopefully will enable you to better observe the differences between a person who prefers to use his or her Sensing capabilities in absorbing data, as opposed to the person who prefers Intuition.

SENSING	INTUITION
What is real	What can become
Concrete	Abstract
To do	To envision
Specific/Actual	Theoretical
Action	Insight
Realistic	Futuristic
Tangible	Conceptual
Today	Tomorrow
Practical	Vision

If we were to distill all of the above into a more comprehensive concept, it could probably be expressed by suggesting that the Sensing preference causes individuals to assess most events in terms of their past or present value, whereas the Intuitives tend to make a similar assessment in terms of their future value. For the Sensor, there needs to be a tangible payoff soon, while for the Intuitor, a promise in the future can go a long way.

Finally, we need to consider the Thinking/Feeling functions. These are both rational; in other words, they are more easily controlled and directed at will. Thinking evolves around the objective and impersonal, while Feeling focuses on values and sentiments. Clearly they are complementary in everyday life, and to suggest that one is more important or valuable than the other is absurd. The synergy of the two is likely to produce a better outcome than reliance upon only one of the preferences. Here are some words describing the two preferences.

THINKING	FEELING
Head	Heart
Criteria	Values
Impersonal	Personal
Explain	Understand
Tough	Compassion
Aloof	Personable
Principles	Circumstances
Justification	Humane
Objective	Subjective

As you continue to work with these concepts, over time you will find that more often than not you will be able to determine how other people tend to function, as well as gaining insights into their attitudes. Over the years, we have found that it is quite useful to determine individual styles by following this guideline:

Once the temperament is identified, then we look at the scales in this fashion:

In the case of the NF Idealists:
a) Are they Structured - NFJ or b) Perceiving - NFP?

Then do they live most of their lives in the:
a) Introverted INFJ/INFP attitude or
b) Extraverted attitude ENFJ/ENFP?

In the case of the NT Rationals:
a) Are they Structured - NTJ or b) Perceiving - NTP?

Then we ask are they:
a) Gregarious ENTJ/ENTP or b) Solitary INTJ/INTP?

In the case of the SJ Guardians (first we look to the Thinking-Feeling scale):
a) Are they tougher and more impersonal - STJ or
b) More personal and subjective - SFJ?

Then we ask are they:
a) Gregarious ESTJ/ESFJ or b) Solitary ISTJ/ISFJ?

In the case of the SP Artisans:
a) Are they STP or b) SFP?

Then we ask are they:
a) ESTP/ESFP or b) ISTP/ISFP?

Understanding people and their realities is no easy task. Hence, do not expect to become an instant expert. We have found that practice seems to go hand in hand with success. Keep forming your hypotheses and testing them against what you observe people doing and saying. When these differences become real for you, your ability to make the fine distinctions among the sixteen varieties will become second nature.

Knowing the above, hopefully it will be easier for you to understand and accept that all the conditions are present for people to be the way they are, and any energy spent wishing they were different is not an investment which is likely to pay off. In fact, it will produce more heat and less light and become a source of frustration and irritation over time. Your personal power will be greatly enhanced and facilitated when you understand and accept that the state of each person you meet during the remainder of your life makes a great deal of sense to him or her. Your ability to facilitate her or his state of being is the difference between using your human intelligence or living in the bliss of ignorance.

REFERENCES

[1]For assistance in locating a professional qualified to administer and interpret the MBTI, contact either the Temperament Research Institute or the Institute for Management Development.

[2]The selection of Sensing preferences over Intuition preferences is the opposite of the scoring convention of the MBTI. We have chosen this difference based on our observations that in business settings many of those who score "N" have a true preference for "S." Our hypothesis about this is that the focus in higher education and management training is on strategy and theories, so the "N" preference is seen as preferred. Research is needed to check out this hypothesis, so for now we re-emphasize the need to confirm the person's reported preference.

[3]With gestures as with many characteristics, be careful of cultural variations.

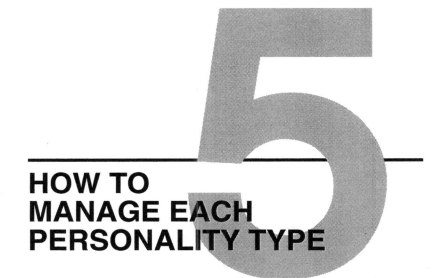

HOW TO
MANAGE EACH
PERSONALITY TYPE

HOW TO MANAGE EACH PERSONALITY TYPE

*"Do not judge, and you will
never be mistaken."*
— Rousseau, 1762

The pages in this chapter provide a quick review for understanding how each of the sixteen types functions in the work environment. The reader may benefit by gleaning in a nutshell specific characteristics for each of the sixteen types. Not only is it of great value to understand our preferences, it is equally important to grasp the strengths, areas which need improvement, desires, frustrations and values for each of the other fifteen types.

We suggest that this "quick reference" section be viewed and used as just that - quick and incomplete. As you continue to work through the text, we would like for you to know that the heart and soul of our efforts are reflected in the appendix, "How To Get Along With Each Personality Type."

Also, we would like to caution you that no one person is pure. In other words, our attitudes and functions can have degrees of strength in preference. Since we deal with four distinct variables, it follows then that they seldom, if ever, would tend to have equal weight or significance.

Have fun - we hope you find these "quickies" useful and fun to work with.

MANAGING THE
EXTRAVERTED SENSING THINKING PERCEPTIVE
(ESTP)

WORK LABEL - PROMOTER

- Rides with the tide
- An adaptable realist
- Makes the most of every situation
- Highly observant
- Fun loving

STRENGTHS	OPPORTUNITIES FOR GROWTH
- Procuring	- Set goals and work toward them
- Operating	- Set priorities and follow-through
- Situational	- Be open to the "big picture"
- Flexible	- See opportunities in input from others
- Realistic	- Become sensitive to others' needs

TO FUNCTION BEST ESTPs NEED: Challenge and excitement. They love to put out fires and to rally the troops. Lots of action and adventure. Don't tell them, they love to be asked.

THEY ARE FRUSTRATED BY: Restrictions. Being told how to do their work. Complex theory. Long explanations. Orders and demands. Too much structure.

THEY IRRITATE OTHERS BY: Not adhering to set priorities and structure. Preparing in haste and eliminating important details. Shooting from the hip (and getting away with it).

THEY VALUE: Flexibility, action and excitement.

ON A TEAM: They fight fires or start them.

MANAGING THE
INTROVERTED SENSING THINKING PERCEPTIVE
(ISTP)

WORK LABEL - OPERATOR

- Quiet and reserved
- Cool observer of life
- Usually interested in impersonal principles
- Interested in the how and why of things
- Does not waste personal energy

STRENGTHS	OPPORTUNITIES FOR GROWTH
- Spontaneous	- Develop a sensitivity to others
- Objective	- Push to have ideas understood
- Independent	- Be open to the "big picture"
- Concretely analytical	- Set long-term personal goals
- Skillful	- Communicate more

TO FUNCTION BEST ISTPs NEED: Variety, skills and techniques to master. Challenge of problems to solve and something to fix. Freedom to work independently. A sense of bringing about something new and important.

THEY ARE FRUSTRATED BY: Restrictions, emotional situations. Being told how to work. Anything slow. Social requirements.

THEY IRRITATE OTHERS BY: Not communicating. Shooting from the hip. Lack of follow-through. Appearing anti-social and cold.

THEY VALUE: Flexibility, challenge and adventure.

ON A TEAM: They do their own thing.

MANAGING THE
EXTRAVERTED SENSING FEELING PERCEPTIVE
(ESFP)

WORK LABEL - PERFORMER

- A hands-on operator
- Able to "smell the roses"
- A natural negotiator
- Life of the party, a lot of fun
- Exciting company

STRENGTHS	OPPORTUNITIES FOR GROWTH
- Easy going	- Study and develop the mind
- Accepting	- Set priorities and follow through
- Situational	- Be open to the "big picture"
- Flexible	- Take time to listen to own values
- Realistic	- Deal with conflict and anxiety

TO FUNCTION BEST ESFPs NEED: Challenge, excitement, and the opportunity to be a hero. Respect for their skills, talents, and approach to problems and needs of the organization. Positive feedback and recognition.

THEY ARE FRUSTRATED BY: Restrictions. Being told how to work. Anything slow. Not being allowed to operate and contribute. Injustice and cruelty.

THEY IRRITATE OTHERS BY: Not keeping to priorities and structure. Preparing in haste and eliminating important details. Shooting from the hip (and getting away with it).

THEY VALUE: Action, excitement and emotion.

ON A TEAM: They keep 'em laughing.

MANAGING THE
INTROVERTED SENSING FEELING PERCEPTIVE
(ISFP)

WORK LABEL - COMPOSER

- Quietly friendly and warm
- Modest about his/her abilities
- A loyal follower
- Guided by values
- A free spirit

STRENGTHS	OPPORTUNITIES FOR GROWTH
- Sensitivity	- Set goals and keep them in mind
- Adaptability	- Try to be objective
- Perfectionist	- Be open to the "big picture"
- Flexible	- Stick to principles
- Harmonious	- Take some action toward goals

TO FUNCTION BEST ISFPs NEED: Challenge and variation. Opportunity to act on their values. Freedom to incorporate and internalize music, rhythm, color and texture into their life.

THEY ARE FRUSTRATED BY: Restrictions. Being told how to do work. Limitations and time constraints. Social functions and being forced to conform.

THEY IRRITATE OTHERS BY: Not adhering to priorities and lack of follow-through. Insufficient and hasty preparation. Not asserting themselves. Avoiding conflict.

THEY VALUE: Variety, sensual experiences and challenge.

ON A TEAM: They are loyal and value driven.

MANAGING THE
EXTRAVERTED SENSING THINKING JUDGING
(ESTJ)

WORK LABEL - SUPERVISOR

- Practical and realistic
- A natural in business and applied mechanics
- Likes to run things
- Gets things done
- Has no time to waste

STRENGTHS	OPPORTUNITIES FOR GROWTH
- Responsible	- Slow down, be patient
- Matter-of-fact	- Recognize other workable solutions
- Industrious	- Be open to the "big picture"
- Can organize	- Be sensitive to others' needs
- Decisive	- Listen more

TO FUNCTION BEST ESTJs NEED: Predictability and order. Standards and measurements for success. Tell them what needs to be done, they'll make it happen.

THEY ARE FRUSTRATED BY: A lack of realism. Missed deadlines. Broken rules and wasted time. Emotional responses.

THEY IRRITATE OTHERS BY: Being impatient. Making decisions too fast. Not taking the time to listen. Insensitivity to the needs of others.

THEY VALUE: The system, authority and control.

ON A TEAM: They take responsibility and get things done.

MANAGING THE
INTROVERTED SENSING THINKING JUDGING
(ISTJ)

WORK LABEL - INSPECTOR

- Serious and quiet
- Responsible and trustworthy
- Will see the job through to the end
- A "no-nonsense" person
- Task oriented

STRENGTHS	OPPORTUNITIES FOR GROWTH
- Practical	- Consider other possible solutions
- Careful	- Be open to the "big picture"
- Determined	- Listen more to those around you
- Dependable	- Be sensitive to others' needs
- Organized	- Make time for fun

TO FUNCTION BEST ISTJs NEED: Organization and structure in which to work. Projects to complete and tasks to accomplish. Opportunities to organize and preserve data or materials. An understanding of their role.

THEY ARE FRUSTRATED BY: Unrealistic and emotional situations. Wasted time and broken rules. Permissiveness and a lack of respect for the system.

THEY IRRITATE OTHERS BY: Being too task oriented. Making decisions on an impersonal basis. Ignoring peoples' wishes. Going like a steamroller. Looking only for the bottom line.

THEY VALUE: Responsibility, tradition and accuracy.

ON A TEAM: They follow the rules and guard the process.

MANAGING THE
EXTRAVERTED SENSING FEELING JUDGING
(ESFJ)

WORK LABEL - PROVIDER

- Warm-hearted
- Active committee member
- Sociable
- Strong value systems
- Always doing something nice for someone

STRENGTHS	OPPORTUNITIES FOR GROWTH
- Warm	- Give people a second chance
- Cooperative	- Take care of own needs
- Involved	- Be open to the "big picture"
- Caring	- Keep an open mind, listen
- Harmonious	- See values as less absolute

TO FUNCTION BEST ESFJs NEED: Harmony, encouragement, praise and emotional support. A structured work environment with many opportunities to work with people.

THEY ARE FRUSTRATED BY: Criticism and a lack of appreciation for peoples' needs. Complex theory and abstract thought. Impersonal decisions. The challenging and breaking of established rules.

THEY IRRITATE OTHERS BY: Becoming impatient and refusing to listen or see new and better ways. Subjectivity and lack of logic in interpersonal situations. Being too focused on social acceptability.

THEY VALUE: Tradition, human beings and stable relationships.

ON A TEAM: They bring human comforts to light.

MANAGING THE
INTROVERTED SENSING FEELING JUDGING
(ISFJ)

WORK LABEL - PROTECTOR

- Quiet and conscientious
- A loyal and devoted worker
- A sympathetic listener
- A very dependable person
- A real team player

STRENGTHS	OPPORTUNITIES FOR GROWTH
- Considerate	- Take the initiative more often
- Responsible	- Take care of personal needs
- Patient	- Be open to the "big picture"
- Dedicated	- Seek out objective viewpoint
- Realistic	- Recognize the value of conflict

TO FUNCTION BEST ISFJs NEED: An orderly work environment with human interaction. Opportunities to respond to the needs of others. Harmonious relationships. Praise and appreciation.

THEY ARE FRUSTRATED BY: Criticism and injustice. Having to stop in the middle of a project. Too much complexity and cold, impersonal logic.

THEY IRRITATE OTHERS BY: Being subjective and overly sensitive to criticism. Not speaking up about unpleasant things that need to be aired.

THEY VALUE: Relationships, responsibility and harmony.

ON A TEAM: They care and do the work.

MANAGING THE
EXTRAVERTED INTUITIVE THINKING JUDGING
(ENTJ)

WORK LABEL - FIELD MARSHALL

- Frank and decisive
- A natural leader
- He/she thinks on his/her feet
- Exudes confidence
- Is well-informed

STRENGTHS	OPPORTUNITIES FOR GROWTH
- Energetic	- Slow down, experience today
- Futuristic	- Spend time reflecting on values
- Conceptual	- Make effort to praise others
- Logical	- Be sensitive to others' needs
- Dynamic	- Take care of routine and details

TO FUNCTION BEST ENTJs NEED: Mental challenges and interesting problems to solve. Recognition. Positive feedback and an absence of routine. Respect for ideas.

THEY ARE FRUSTRATED BY: Emotional responses to rational situations. Routine and petty details. The inabilities and weaknesses of their co-workers. Wasted time.

THEY IRRITATE OTHERS BY: Appearing arrogant. Inflated confidence and self-image. Being cold and impersonal. A lack of execution and attention to detail.

THEY VALUE: Intelligence, concepts and expertise.

ON A TEAM: They are the leaders. They cannot not lead.

MANAGING THE
INTROVERTED INTUITIVE THINKING JUDGING
(INTJ)

WORK LABEL - STRATEGIST

- An original thinker
- Interested and innovative
- Single-minded concentration
- Unimpressed with authority
- A naturally high achiever

STRENGTHS	OPPORTUNITIES FOR GROWTH
- Pragmatic	- Be sensitive to others' needs
- Conceptual	- Take care of routine details
- Autonomous	- Learn to yield to others' points
- Tenacious	- Take time to smell the roses
- Analytical	- Try to be more empathic in relationships

TO FUNCTION BEST INTJs NEED: Support for ideas and projects. Freedom from routine and mundane details. Problems to solve. To see ideas worked out and applied.

THEY ARE FRUSTRATED BY: Routine, redundancy, being sidetracked by others' needs and opinions. Being told what to do or how to do things.

THEY IRRITATE OTHERS BY: Refusing to yield. Being overly demanding or insistent on having their own way. Arrogance, skepticism and hair-splitting. Moving too fast. Lack of execution.

THEY VALUE: Logic, ideas and ingenuity.

ON A TEAM: They analyze the alternatives.

MANAGING THE
EXTRAVERTED INTUITIVE THINKING PERCEPTIVE
(ENTP)

WORK LABEL - INVENTOR

- A creative thinker
- Stimulating company
- Alert and outspoken
- Argues on both sides of an issue
- Confident of abilities

STRENGTHS	OPPORTUNITIES FOR GROWTH
- Ingenious	- Self-discipline and follow-through
- Conceptual	- Pay attention to details
- Resourceful	- Recognize the value in other styles
- Enthusiastic	- Complete old projects before new
- Analytical	- Don't take on too much at once

TO FUNCTION BEST ENTPs NEED: A working environment where they can go from one project to another, solving major problems and leaving details to others. Recognition and support for ideas.

THEY ARE FRUSTRATED BY: Dull routine, boring details, emotional responses to rational issues. Redundancy and restrictions. Being told how to do things.

THEY IRRITATE OTHERS BY: Appearing arrogant and knowing it all. Moving fast, becoming impatient. Lack of execution. Hurting others' feelings. Questioning authority.

THEY VALUE: Ideas, energy and ingenuity.

ON A TEAM: They offer solutions and identify opportunities.

MANAGING THE
INTROVERTED INTUITIVE THINKING PERCEPTIVE
(INTP)

WORK LABEL - DEFINER

- Reserved and impersonal
- Lives in a world of ideas
- Skilled with hair-splitting logic
- Strongly defined interests
- Enjoys theoretical and/or scientific subjects

STRENGTHS	OPPORTUNITIES FOR GROWTH
- Independent	- Improve follow-through
- Creative	- Nurture relationships
- Conceptual	- Remember to communicate
- Analytical	- Be sensitive to others' needs
- Imaginative	- Take care of details

TO FUNCTION BEST INTPs NEED: Freedom to work independently. Opportunities to design, problems to solve. Variety and support for ideas. Positive feedback, recognition and a reason for what they are doing.

THEY ARE FRUSTRATED BY: Being told what to do and how to do it. Unintelligent demands. Routine and redundancy. Overly emotional responses.

THEY IRRITATE OTHERS BY: Appearing arrogant and not communicating. Hurting feelings. Skepticism. Refusing to deal with details and lack of execution.

THEY VALUE: Concepts, intelligence and ingenuity.

ON A TEAM: They work alone for the group.

MANAGING THE
EXTRAVERTED INTUITIVE FEELING JUDGING
(ENFJ)

WORK LABEL - MENTOR

- Responsive and responsible
- Popular and sociable
- Charismatic charm
- A natural communicator
- Warmly enthusiastic

STRENGTHS	OPPORTUNITIES FOR GROWTH
- Dependable	- Take time for yourself
- Persuasive	- Take care of routine details
- Cooperative	- Seek out an objective viewpoint
- Conceptual	- Set priorities and stick to them
- Considerate	- Be open-minded and listen

TO FUNCTION BEST ENFJs NEED: Opportunities to lead people, especially through face-to-face interaction. Harmony, support for ideas. Recognition, appreciation, and a cause or leader to work for.

THEY ARE FRUSTRATED BY: Cold, impersonal logic. Overly task-oriented jobs. Being left out. A lack of feedback. Criticism and a lack of appreciation.

THEY IRRITATE OTHERS BY: Becoming overly emotional, moralistic and unrealistic. Being too anxious to please. Wanting to know everything and everyone.

THEY VALUE: Cooperation, harmony and self-determination.

ON A TEAM: They are enthusiastic communicators.

MANAGING THE
INTROVERTED INTUITIVE FEELING JUDGING
(INFJ)

WORK LABEL - FORESEER

- Quietly forceful
- Concerned for others
- Serves the common good
- Puts his/her best effort into work
- Single-minded concentration

STRENGTHS	OPPORTUNITIES FOR GROWTH
- Conceptual	- Be objective and flexible
- Conscientious	- Try to see beyond own values
- Compassionate	- Put insights in language of others
- Determined	- Set priorities and stick to them
- Harmonious	- Be open-minded and listen

TO FUNCTION BEST INFJs NEED: Support for ideas and opportunity to put them into practice. Variety and freedom from dull routine. Recognition and appreciation for their unique contribution. A cause to work for.

THEY ARE FRUSTRATED BY: Being told how to do things. Not being listened to. Lack of feedback and impersonal attitudes. Criticism and confrontations.

THEY IRRITATE OTHERS BY: Taking an emotional stand and being moralistic. Being too anxious to please.

THEY VALUE: Participation, cooperation and determination.

ON A TEAM: They are the ones to put it in writing.

MANAGING THE
EXTRAVERTED INTUITIVE FEELING PERCEPTIVE
(ENFP)

WORK LABEL - CATALYST

- Warm and enthusiastic
- Charming and interesting
- People oriented
- Knows everyone and everything going on
- Able to do almost anything he/she wants

STRENGTHS	OPPORTUNITIES FOR GROWTH
- Creative	- Develop self-discipline to be true to self
- Imaginative	- Look on the objective side
- Communicator	- Recognize value of others' motives
- Energetic	- Take time alone to set goals
- Spontaneous	- Structure time to take care of details

TO FUNCTION BEST ENFPs NEED: Acceptance and appreciation for their unique contribution and creativity. Recognition for achievements and a lot of encouragement. They need harmony and care.

THEY ARE FRUSTRATED BY: Criticism and cold logic. Impersonal attitudes and doing things by the book. Lack of positive feedback and dull routine.

THEY IRRITATE OTHERS BY: Getting too excited. Taking an emotional stand. Being too anxious to please. Being moralistic and illogical.

THEY VALUE: Recognition, approval and relationships on their terms.

ON A TEAM: They can be great integrators.

MANAGING THE
INTROVERTED INTUITIVE FEELING PERCEPTIVE
(INFP)

WORK LABEL - ADVOCATE

- A peacekeeper
- Undertakes a great deal
- Absorbed in projects
- Deeply caring
- Idea oriented

STRENGTHS	OPPORTUNITIES FOR GROWTH
- Dedicated	- Communicate more to others
- Conceptual	- Take care of important details, routine
- Ingenious	- Try to see beyond own values
- Idealistic	- Be more objective and realistic
- Perfectionist	- Develop and use a social network

TO FUNCTION BEST INFPs NEED: To handle significant projects from start to finish. Support for ideas. Encouragement and respect for their unique contribution. Freedom from structure and rules.

THEY ARE FRUSTRATED BY: Their own inner standards of perfection. Routine and inconsequential details. Conflict and unpleasantness. A lack of purpose.

THEY IRRITATE OTHERS BY: Appearing reserved and detached. Refusing to deal with unpleasantness. Undertaking too much and being moralistic.

THEY VALUE: Harmony, self-determination and meaning.

ON A TEAM: They act as peacekeepers.

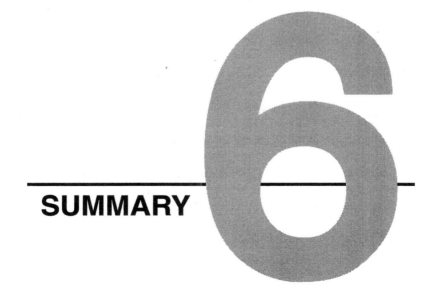

SUMMARY

SUMMARY

*"It is better to light a candle
than to curse in the darkness."*
— Chinese Proverb

We hope this book will help you live a richer, more insightful and complete life. We are indebted to Carl Gustav Jung, Isabel Briggs Myers, Ernst Kretschmer, Eduard Spränger and David Keirsey and know that their work will outshine our lives and remain important. As you contemplate the rest of your life, understand that the tools you have acquired in understanding type and temperament can be applied in any situation when working and being together with people.

As we at TRI train other professionals in the use of these ideas to help managers, we have found the blending of all of these contributors to be invaluable. It seems that the synergistic use of all of them goes way beyond what one can do with just one of them. As we have added the personality centered focus to other teamwork tools such as listening, giving feedback and resolving conflicts, we have vastly increased their power.

In the training programs we conduct at the Institute for Management Development we ask at some point, "What is the worst thing that could happen to you?" - and invariably the answer is, "I could die." We suggest that perhaps an even more detrimental event would be one of not having had the opportunity to live and become aware of and take part in the riches of living life to the hilt as an SJ, SP, NT or NF.

Your sense of personal power needs to emerge from knowing that all the conditions are present for the environments you move in and out of to be exactly the way they are simply because they are not something else.

Similarly, whatever temperament and style of people you encounter, no conditions prevail for them to be much different. Accepting people for who they are as opposed to wishing they would be different is another strength you can develop.

The above is not merely to suggest that personal strength is gained from accepting and expecting things to remain the same and never change. On the contrary, it will allow you, by evaluation, to maneuver a work situation toward optimizing performance. We know of no organization that benefited in the long run from knee-jerk management.

Wise leaders and managers alike understand that they can maneuver circumstances so that people are allowed to contribute from their strengths as opposed to miserably failing from preoccupation with their weakness. To be upset with what is not happening takes away energy from creating conditions so as to eventually be content with what is achieved.

Strength in working together comes from accepting people for who they are and not what they do. Enlightened managers do not impose their priorities on people, rather they follow others and provide leadership as the opportunities emerge. From now on, no one you meet and work with shall again be labeled as "good" or "bad," "right" or "wrong,""appropriate" or "inappropriate." Rather, your acceptance and ability to understand their realities will allow you to be received by them as someone for whom they would like to deliver superior performance. Judgement produces defensiveness or offensiveness, ultimately usurping positive energy, producing more heat and less light.

Please use *Working Together* as a management tool. We sincerely hope that this text will be next to you until you become unconsciously competent and skillful enough to understand the temperament and typology of just about everyone.

We would like to support you in whatever endeavors you undertake to understand people better. Please write us with your questions, comments and inquiries at either of the following addresses:

Olaf Isachsen:

**INSTITUTE FOR
MANAGEMENT
DEVELOPMENT**

31831 Camino Capistrano
Suite 201
San Juan Capistrano, CA
92675
(714) 489-8010
FAX (714) 489-7875

Linda Berens:

**TEMPERAMENT
RESEARCH
INSTITUTE**

16125 Beach Boulevard
Suite 179
Huntington Beach, CA
92647
(714) 841-0041
(800) 700-4TRI (4874)

APPENDIX -
HOW TO GET
ALONG WITH EACH
PERSONALITY TYPE

HOW TO GET ALONG WITH EACH
PERSONALITY TYPE

*"People only see what
they are prepared to see."*
— Ralph Waldo Emerson, 1863

We have now arrived at what we think of as the very essence of this text. It is based upon prior research and years of practical experience in listening to and working with hundreds of people, all of whom know their MBTI typology. The following pages are probably more a labor of love than anything else. We are both NTs, and therefore we know that what we have written is not perfect. It is, however, the best we are capable of at this particular point in time. We know and want to continue to improve upon this appendix so that over time it will become the most accurate reference we can offer to you.

It has been written from a pragmatic management point of view and it is intended to be immediately useful and applicable for you. Because some of the types have a great deal in common, you may find some redundancy in the descriptions. Each of the 16 descriptions was built from the temperament base. This is so we describe the essential aspects and do not leave out important characteristics of each type.

Uniformly, each one of the sixteen styles has been addressed according to the following topics:

• **Management Style**: Managing and being managed. For our purpose, we shall define "management style" as the way in which an individual determines what needs to be done and then create the necessary conditions to achieve the desired results. You will quickly discover that each one of the sixteen types substantially differ in how they manage and how they like to be supervised. It is important to understand that we focus on process, not substance. Put another way, attitudes are shaped by process; hence, the wise manager eventually learns to direct his or her energies towards creating conditions enabling people to optimize and maximize their performance.

• **Values**: We like to define values as what the individual style seems to favor—the situations and circumstances occurring that will most likely be conducive to an individual liking himself or herself in any given work situation.

• **Attitude**: Attitude may be defined as a set of expectations about how the world works. Attitude can be inferred from what an individual says or does.

• **Skills**: Let us define the concept for our purposes as the natural ability and proficiency of the distinct type. Again, you will very quickly discover that the favorite skills of each type are very different, and the more individuals are allowed to utilize their God-given skills, the more they will be able to optimize their natural contribution in an organizational setting.

• **Driving Force**: Driving force can be thought of as a cause for conditions which are a real "turn on," given the individual style and temperament of the people you are working with or for.

• **Energy Direction**: Consider energy direction to be the natural allocation and conservation of the resourcefulness of a particular style. In other words, the direction of energy contributed by each type is different, important and, more often than not, complementary to other types.

• **Authority Orientation**: What we are attempting to focus on here may best be described as the way each type views authority and asserts authority. They differ widely and not knowing the differences can lead to misunderstanding, unnecessary conflict and counter productive relations.

• **Role Perception**: Understand this - you and every person you meet and interact with cannot not play a role. Role perception may be viewed as the preferred role of each one of the sixteen styles. Put another way, it is living up to a real or imaginative model of the ideal way of being in the respective MBTI styles.

• **Conflict Resolution**: Here we are attempting to provide you with some beginning insights as to how and what is possible to reduce conflict. Each style experiences conflict differently, mainly as a result of differences in expectations and values. Consider each one of the sixteen types as a value programmed differently and appropriately so.

• **Modes of Learning**: We define the concept as how someone of a given type best acquires new knowledge or develops specific skills. You will soon discover that each style has natural tendencies of assimilating and comprehending new data and ways of accomplishing whatever that someone sets out to do.

• **Blind Spots and Pitfalls**: In this last section, we outline what might be labeled the lowest awareness level. Think about the concept this way: styles particularly gifted in one direction cannot always comprehend the "shadow." That is, in moving toward whatever result is desired, it is useful to accept that conflict may be experienced by other types with a different value orientation.

Welcome to the section which we hope will have long-term meaning, significance and value for you.

ESTP

The theme of the ESTP is promoting. Adept at picking up on minimal non-verbal cues, ESTPs are able to anticipate the actions and reactions of others and charm them into having confidence in them. They are highly gifted negotiators, entrepreneurs and salespersons, and they know how to maximize every moment of their waking hours. Indeed, they are the people who love life in the fast lane and they are masterful at inching things in their direction when it comes to interpersonal interactions. They thrive on action and the use of all available resources at hand, sometimes to the point where the goal justifies the means.

CHARACTERISTICS	IMPLICATIONS

MANAGEMENT STYLE

The management style of the ESTP is pragmatic and expedient. With distinct flair, the ESTP does whatever needs to be done to get the job done now, usually with the least possible effort.	The ideal work environment is one providing opportunities, choices and flexibility. The ESTP enjoys a comfortable and physically attractive work space.
ESTPs are at their best when responding to crisis situations and when they know there is an opportunity to impact others via their own hopefully magnificent performance.	It is important to keep ESTPs mobile, moving them into positions that present problems to be solved and crises to handle.
They manage in a highly action-oriented way, focusing on the job to be done, not always taking into account the organization or the people in it.	They are impatient with abstractions unless they can see and experience immediate applications and payoff.

ESTP

CHARACTERISTICS	IMPLICATIONS

ESTPs enjoy variety in what they do.

Routines and day-to-day steady work are not their forte.

Their commitment is to solve concrete problems. They have no need to fight the system, they just go ahead and take the necessary action. Established norms and procedures pique the pride and cleverness of ESTPs. They are likely to ask themselves, "How can I obtain an objective with minimal interference from the system?"

ESTPs ignore authority, hence other types can be annoyed with their focus on expediting the task irrespective of violations of rules. ESTPs can effortlessly ask peers or superiors the question, "What policy are you talking about?"

As leaders ESTPs are often viewed as outstanding troubleshooters since they work to solve problems. They have a keen sense of reality and can spot trouble early. Their capacity to focus 100% on the present situation often leads to effective and beneficial results.

If crises and problems do not abound in the organization, ESTPs may create them in order to derive a continued sense of satisfaction and excitement from their work environment.

They can be counted on to get things going, to get the ball rolling—albeit at times the ball may accelerate faster than anyone anticipated.

ESTPs are always looking for ways to be useful. Wherever there are ESTPs, there is always excitement and involvement. They refuse to be an audience or stand on the sidelines. Not having anything to do is the worst of all situations for an ESTP.

Their keen sense for opportunity may lead ESTPs to start a number of projects only to eventually be criticized for not

Consequently, do not expect them to be the kind of people who will settle in a normal day-to-day "business as usual" type

CHARACTERISTICS

IMPLICATIONS

necessarily following through as boredom may set in before a state of completion has been obtained.

organization. Let the other types follow through. ESTPs need a well-organized support staff to provide reminders of commitments and follow through.

ESTPs may direct an abundance of energy toward a specific project or assignment, especially if it is considered significant and exciting. The reason is obvious: ESTPs derive a great deal of satisfaction from making an impact in problem-solving situations.

Do not always take their willingness to work hard for granted, unless there is an expected return commensurate with their investment of energy.

ESTPs are the greatest "jury-riggers" around—they just make things happen. Addicted to enjoying immediate gratification, their willingness to take a risk and gamble on the outcome may lead to more than they bargained for.

Other types may be uneasy with their willingness to ignore traditions, policies, belief systems, or relationships in order to get the job done. ESTPs may even be dubbed "trouble makers."

ESTPs tend to be easy to get along with and people seem to enjoy cooperating with them. They are comfortable in giving verbal praise. The feedback provided by the ESTP tends to encompass whatever it takes to get people to do the job.

People tend to like to work for ESTPs so long as not too many rules are broken or there is not too much interpersonal chaos.

ESTP

CHARACTERISTICS	IMPLICATIONS
Always with an eye out for new opportunities, ESTPs change their positions quickly as new facts are presented.	They are likely to ask of a planned change: "Will it work?" or "Is it practical?" or "When do I have to come in and salvage or clean up the mess created by individuals not capable of coping with the demands of the moment?"
However, they tend to dislike the unfamiliar and may be uncomfortable with changes they have not instigated or somehow been involved in creating.	
While ESTP managers quickly can adapt to changing circumstances, they tend to apply solutions to problematic situations they know from experience will work. Indeed, they are superb in applying variations on a theme they know works.	

VALUES

ESTPs value action—living on the edge of great challenges or disaster can be very exciting.	They do not care about explaining actions or justifying them. They are more interested in just going on to the next action.
ESTPs need variation, challenges and opportunities to demonstrate their great skills in dealing with the unexpected.	The highest and best use of their time and energy is to allow them to take advantage of adverse circumstances and create success where others have failed. Indeed, their great gift is to make immediate arrangements for immediate effect.

CHARACTERISTICS	IMPLICATIONS

They abhor routine rules and rigid adherence to hierarchy and structure.

They may rebel in large and small ways against too many constraints to their freedom. Therefore, it is best to approach an ESTP with the attitude of guidance instead of control.

ESTPs typically tend to avoid ties, plans, commitments or obligations that get in the way of exercising their freedom to choose the next act. Tradition tends not to be that important to the ESTP.

ESTP managers are not inclined to theorize and contemplate; rather, they put a great deal of value on achievement and power. A specific project can absorb them so totally that they can become driven to maximize the performance potential to the point of believing that the goals may justify the means.

ESTPs don't care much about the rationale behind an event or a policy, or about the authority to implement it. Likewise, they tend not to hold much respect or esteem for those who insist on following the rules for rules' sake.

Fostering, improving and honing skills and behavioral effectiveness can be quite important to them.

Expect ESTPs to exercise their skills of gamesmanship, promotion and negotiation in all manner of environments. They need and very much want to have an impact on those around them.

CHARACTERISTICS	IMPLICATIONS

ATTITUDE

The basic attitude of ESTPs is one of optimism. They expect the lucky break and the windfall to be just around the corner. It should come as no surprise that ESTP managers have a "can do" instinct to them. Nothing is impossible.

Since they expect things to turn out well, they take what may seem to others as inappropriate risks, without any notice or apparent concern for the possibility of failure.

They enjoy a challenge and their attitude when the going gets tough is one of high energy and blind faith that they actually can accomplish the impossible.

They are impatient with predictions of doom and gloom and dire consequences. Such predictions raise the hackles of ESTPs and may be taken as threats to be adamantly countered.

On the other hand, ESTPs tend to be realistic about the motivation and intent of others to the point of being cynical. Expect ESTP managers to be keenly aware that in the real world everyone is out for him or herself— and in the final analysis, it is the fittest who survive.

ESTP managers may at times appear somewhat moody, especially when their expectations are shattered. Their attitudes then can be quite cynical, skeptical and kind of "knowing" that the world has turned against them— which at times, of course, may not be true at all.

ESTPs ignore and avoid ambiguous situations.

They have no intention of making the ambiguous clear. In fact, if they can use an ambiguous situation to their advantage, they will; otherwise, they will just go elsewhere.

SKILLS

ESTPs are skilled at anything tactical, maneuvering to overcome obstacles. They are quite

If you want ESTP employees to give a superior performance, be sure the job provides opportuni-

ESTP

CHARACTERISTICS	IMPLICATIONS
resourceful and able to use whatever is at hand to get the job done.	ties for maneuvering and wheeling and dealing.
Promoting for them is an external process. ESTPs are keen observers of human behavior, even minute variations and alterations of non-verbal clues, and they put this skill to use in promoting and negotiating.	Their hypersensitivity to minimal cues provides an essential ingredient for skillful manipulation of the external environment.
They have a capacity for variations on a theme and for executing minute changes which allows them to adroitly operate/manipulate people as well as machines, materials and objects.	It is often difficult to predict their next move. This factor alone often keeps most opponents off guard.
ESTPs are concrete and specific in their speech. Language is but a tool in their repertoire of things to use to get things done. Their language is likely to be full of realistic and concrete images, but the most gifted among them can use abstract language to meet their ends.	When engaged in conversation, ESTPs mirror the language of the person(s) they are speaking with—again, responding to those minimal cues.
As a result, they are magnificent negotiators. For them, nothing is constant and there are no standards etched in cement. They comfortably function in a state of animated suspension, and where others fail to obtain what they hope to achieve, ESTPs succeed in spades. Beware—no one can charm the socks off of	The reason ESTPs tend to negotiate so well can be found in their understanding of power. They know instinctively that gaining an advantage comes from finessing the power base. For them, the fun is to experience the "play" in getting to where they want and the real glory does not lie in creating a "win-lose" situ-

CHARACTERISTICS   IMPLICATIONS

people much better than the ESTP—the only contest would perhaps come from the ESFP.

ation; rather, it is one of assisting everyone in believing they "won." Behind closed doors, however, you may find ESTP managers grinning, as when everything is said and done, they really won—covertly.

ESTP managers can be exhilarating, exciting, energizing, charming, witty and gregarious beyond anybody's expectations. On the other hand, do not be surprised if the characteristics are reversed and the ESTPs turn all those wonderful traits off only to become everything but charming and understanding. If they decide they want to, no one can play hard ball much better than they can.

However, their ability to display an uncanny, charismatic, magnetic charm melts down barriers faster than ice on a warm summer day. They tend to be disarmingly charming, they rely on their ability to create the situations they want instead of being responsive to the needs of others.

DRIVING FORCE

ESTPs have a very high need for action, spontaneity and variation. They abhor repetition, rules, routines and hierarchies.

When engaged in repetitious actions, they quickly find ways to vary routines in order to test limits and discover breaking points.

ESTPs have a hunger for excitement that may lead them to operate on the brink of disaster. They pride themselves on being able to trust their impulses and rise to any occasion, thus more often than not avoiding impending disasters.

They may be driven to act on their impulses, seemingly caught up in the action itself. This kind of absorption in activity comes naturally to ESTPs; to do things because of duty, responsibility, relationship or insight has no pull. Others rarely experience this kind of immersion.

CHARACTERISTICS

IMPLICATIONS

ENERGY DIRECTION

Given these skills, values and attitudes, ESTPs direct their energy toward exciting and impactful performances.

If ESTPs are not having an impact on their environment, they find ways to create the impact (sometimes troublesome ways) or just drop out.

Within the organization their energy will be directed toward taking expedient action, if necessary taking shortcuts and finding quick fixes.

ESTPs are exceptionally resourceful; the greater the challenge, the higher the odds, the more interest they exhibit in overcoming obstacles.

A great deal of their energy is directed toward optimizing every valuable moment of life.

When the going is good for ESTP managers, nothing could be better. On the other hand, if things turn sour, it is difficult for them to keep the faith. As a result, they can become frustrated and fed up. Know this: when an ESTP has come to the end of the line, there is usually no way back.

Turn ons are practical and expedient ways to get things done.

Without turn ons and stimulation, ESTPs find life's restlessness unbearable.

AUTHORITY ORIENTATION

If ESTPs are in charge, they expect to be obeyed and not questioned, and they often are by virtue of their sure and confident demeanor. Authority is granted not by title and tenure but by commanding behavior.

To challenge their authority is like asking for a reprisal; they may respond either by immediate and direct confrontation or delayed and subtle intervention—depending on which style best fits the situation.

ESTP

CHARACTERISTICS

IMPLICATIONS

ESTPs have little or no patience for those who question their authority. Yet, as followers, they readily challenge authority or ignore it if it does not suit their purposes.

A manager has to earn the right to manage ESTPs by taking action and being straightforward.

ESTPs are autonomous, wanting to call the shots on their own actions. In reporting relationships with their superiors, ESTPs tend to be masterful at getting out of a situation what they want. For example, they may be told to take specific corrective action when circumstances are turning out negatively or adversely. While they typically will agree to do whatever they are asked to, it is quite likely that they will do what they think is appropriate anyway. More often than not, their action tends to be the better choice, particularly if they find themselves in a crisis situation.

A consistent and firm approach leads to the best results when confronting them. Nonetheless, when directly confronted and threatened with the possible consequences of their actions, they may dig in their heels and become even more insistent on doing what they want. Therefore, it is most often appropriate not to threaten ESTPs. The reason is obvious: freedom for them is held in extraordinarily high esteem and anyone attempting to diminish, harm or threaten that freedom is, one way or another, heading for trouble. Keep in mind that under adverse circumstances ESTPs seldom build up antagonism and grudges. Rather, they tend to get even and then go on with the art of living.

ROLE PERCEPTION

ESTPs tend to be proactive in relationships; that is, they take the first step in defining the relationship. They do not hesitate at all to tell another person what is to be done. They are the masters at one-upmanship.

ESTPs hold firmly to the belief that they know what is best for another individual in a relationship. They can be relentless in their adherence to a belief which pertains to another person, and there are times when their focus

CHARACTERISTICS

IMPLICATIONS

should be on themselves, in addition to the prevailing external circumstances.

CONFLICT RESOLUTION

ESTPs do not tend to avoid confrontation. They are not afraid of "calling them like they see them." Hence, they tend to be great tacticians and deal with adverse circumstances with a great deal of flair and energy. The above should not be confused with having analytical skills, however. While an analytical mind may not have the affinity for subtle tactical issues, focus will ultimately be on the source of the conflict—and that is not the natural forte of an ESTP.

ESTPs have little patience with anxiety and interpersonal tensions. They are likely to avoid such situations or even leave when they perceive them to be insurmountable.

MODES OF LEARNING

ESTPs prefer to learn through hands-on methods such as projects. They prefer to be shown how to do something rather than hear about it.

Frequently they do not read directions, so confident are they that they can solve concrete problems. However, refusing to read directions sometimes results in doing things the hard way.

They have an exceptional talent for accurate observation and like to use their skills in learning.

ESTPs enjoy translating their observations and skills into tangible (visible) and immediate results.

CHARACTERISTICS	**IMPLICATIONS**

Since the consciousness of ES-TPs is concrete and specific, they may have difficulty buying into abstract presentations.

Abstraction requires extra energy for them since it is counter to their concrete, "here and now" consciousness. Neither do the hyper awareness and impulsivity of ESTPs lend themselves to the patience required for this process.

Learning is not undertaken for learning's sake, but for the results it can produce, the tools it provides them with or how much fun it is.

ESTPs are not adverse to learning; they place far greater emphasis upon putting what they have learned into immediate action.

BLIND SPOTS AND PITFALLS

ESTPs may focus so much on keeping things moving and fast action that they may ignore the human element, the people needs. Indeed, being so improvisation oriented, they may miss implications of their actions.

It would be helpful for them to see the perspectives of others as "factors" to be considered before acting.

At times ESTPs may be inconsiderate and demanding.

ESTPs may need to be reminded to take time to listen to others, and there are times when the mere discipline of listening for intent rather than the concrete and specific can be a difficult and frustrating challenge for them.

The ESTP tends to look for the quick fix and may be impatient with longer-range solutions.

If the situation is drawn out and time consuming, an ESTP may lose interest.

CHARACTERISTICS	IMPLICATIONS
With their extreme hunger for spontaneity, ESTPs may be seen as too irresponsible for the job.	ESTPs might have to be reminded of the necessity to meet deadlines and finish projects. In such cases, they may best be moved to a situation requiring action.
They are so ready to change course that they may not provide the stabilizing force an organization needs at certain times.	
Since they have a strong distaste for the negative, they may whistle in the dark and not seek to solve major problems, especially interpersonal ones.	
Their focus on concrete data and details may make them "blind" to the more subtle factors in group behavior and meaningful interpersonal relationships.	They may be well-advised to seek out information about the broader perspectives and subtle implications of a proposed action or decision (i.e., consult an NF on the values implications or an NT on the long-range consequences).
They focus so much on facts, data and details and take such an objective stance that they may at times be viewed as cold and inappropriately impersonal.	ESTPs may thus be misperceived as uncaring when in fact they do care. Likewise, others may take their objectivity as criticism and dislike.
Sometimes it may be difficult for ESTPs to listen, especially if they are in pursuit in one specific area of concentration. It is	The outer world is such a great source of energy for ESTP managers that to introspect just does not occur to them; if so, an ESTP

ESTP

ESTP

CHARACTERISTICS	IMPLICATIONS
as if an ESTP has a hunting instinct and tremendously desires to gain the upper hand. Being wise and insightful in those kinds of situations can be very difficult.	type can almost be threatening to individuals who tend to experience their realities in an inner world.

CHARACTERISTICS	IMPLICATIONS

ISTP

The theme of the ISTP is instrumentation. ISTPs are natural masters at using tools and instruments; they take pride in their skill and virtuosity, and they are exceptionally coordinated. They are keen observers of the environment and they tend to pick up signs in the external environment faster than most. They can be a storehouse of data and facts about things and events they find particularly interesting.

CHARACTERISTICS	IMPLICATIONS

MANAGEMENT STYLE

The management style of the ISTP is egalitarian, pragmatic and expedient. As a manager, the ISTP does whatever needs to be done to get the job done with the least possible effort.

The ideal work environment for the ISTP manager is one where there are specific and concrete problems to solve, and where there is an absence of routine and required procedures.

ISTPs tend to do exceptionally well when responding to crisis situations.

Without an occasional crisis, ISTPs may lose interest.

They manage in an action-oriented way, focusing on the job to be done, not necessarily the organization or the people in it. ISTPs need variety in what they do. They are challenged and excited when working on tasks where the outcome is not known.

At times people view ISTPs as uncaring and insensitive. It is important to remember that ISTPs focus more on the task to be completed than the individuals doing the work.

ISTP

CHARACTERISTICS	IMPLICATIONS

They naturally enjoy solving extensive, concrete problems.

They can be quite impatient with abstractions unless these can be shown to have immediate applications and payoff. For ISTP managers, it is the present, the here and now, that counts.

They have no need to fight conventional systems and procedures. If these systems work and facilitate ISTP managers, fine; if not, independent necessary action is called for.

They flow with events as they occur, and the highest and best use of their time, at least in the mind of ISTP managers, is to be useful and make the best possible contribution. NOW!

As managers, ISTPs tend to devote all their attention to the immediate needs of people or the organization. They enjoy crisis situations and troubleshooting because solving immediate, here-and-now problems allows ISTP managers to impact others and enjoy a sense of immediate payoff for the contribution they are able to make.

It is important to keep ISTPs on the move, directing them into situations and positions that present problems to be solved and crises to handle, especially when their current assignment is ready to become routine and stable.

ISTP managers are not particularly enamored with routines and day-to-day procedures. They thrive on challenges and novelties. To master the impossible and deliver a superb, even if impossible, admirable performance is a driving force in their lives.

Expect ISTP managers to be superb hands-on problem-solvers. If and when there is a malfunction or an operational problem, they seem to have a great capacity to mobilize whatever forces and energies are needed.

When engrossed, the element of time means little or nothing to the ISTP, but perfection is im-

In the long haul, it is important for the ISTP manager to reach a performance level as close to

CHARACTERISTICS

IMPLICATIONS

portant. If whatever is produced, delivered or turned out is not perfect, the ISTP manager is not likely to be in great spirits.

perfect as possible; therefore, you can expect the ISTP supervisor to direct a great deal of energy toward optimizing results.

ISTP managers tend not to be concerned about a setback or two. Typically, they trust their ability— circumstances eventually turn out favorably.

Just for effect, however, they may visibly display their displeasure and impatience.

ISTP managers are not particularly conceptual; rather, they are concrete, linear thinkers and doers. For the typical ISTP, theories and philosophies are not valued a great deal.

ISTP managers tend to want to touch, see and feel problems and opportunities. In other words, their style is not to deal with abstractions, at least if they cannot be translated into meaningful, rather immediate action.

It is not easy for most ISTPs to provide subordinates with feedback since they tend not to enjoy verbal communication.

Unless skillful in giving feedback, ISTP managers typically devote time and energy to providing information as to the performance assessment of subordinates. It is unrealistic to expect impromptu, natural feedback from them.

ISTP managers are typically very flexible, therefore it is relatively natural and easy for the ISTP-type manager to change position on an issue.

Unlike other more structured managers, ISTP supervisors have no difficulty in dropping whatever they are doing to assist and help in more pressing matters.

Typically, ISTP managers tend not to be bound by conventions, systems, routines and procedures. If there is a solution to a problem or a complex situation,

It might be tempting to assume that ISTP managers tend to be rebels and more or less fight red tape and bureaucracy. That is not necessarily the case; rather,

CHARACTERISTICS	IMPLICATIONS
they tend to mobilize the forces required to get results, even if it means cutting some red tape here and there, and making up rules as they go along.	they merely have little use for and tend not to accept a situation where restrictions prevent them from reaching desired results. Consequently, do not be surprised if ISTP managers elegantly and effortlessly leap tall buildings and achieve whatever they want without sticking to the conventional fabric, so to speak.
ISTPs not only resist regimentation, they insist upon the freedom to vary each next move.	If and when ISTP managers are required to follow specific procedures and systems to attain desired objectives, they are more likely to attempt to improve on whatever exists. Hence, it can be very tough and difficult for them to adapt to circumstances which seem to function against their better judgment.
To expect ISTP managers to follow rules according to the way things are supposed to be done is not realistic. Often the notion of "not invented here" applies. In other words, ISTP managers may be quite uncomfortable with changes they themselves have not instigated.	ISTPs are most successful when they originate changes; they are least successful in implementing the changes of others, often because these do not measure up to the perfection of the ISTP.

VALUES

ISTP managers appreciate and value variation on just about any theme. They may not be all that strategic, yet they can be highly	It may not be all that realistic to assume that ISTP managers will invent new processes and systems. It is reasonable, however,

CHARACTERISTICS	IMPLICATIONS

tactical using the tools available to them. For them, immediate action should yield immediate results.

to assume that they are masterful in evolving improved and better ways of achieving immediate goals and results. Consider them, if you will, eminently capable of troubleshooting and making things work, even if it requires a jury-rig.

ISTP managers know that nothing will remain constant, and they enjoy the risk that goes with change. Usually the risk tends to be calculated, and at times the ISTP leader has been known to be an excellent hip shooter.

ISTP managers do not derive a great deal of satisfaction from attempting a constant state of "business as usual." Do not be surprised if your ISTP supervisor will walk fairly far out on a limb, willing to risk short-term setbacks in the anticipation of reaching the pot of gold at the end of the rainbow.

ISTP managers particularly appreciate the opportunity to make an important and memorable contribution. Indeed, they value the opportunity to be virtuosos by delivering magnificent, action-filled performances.

It makes a great deal of sense to think of ISTP managers as people who are tremendously motivated to achieving the impossible—preferably now. In other words, the ISTP types tend to direct an amazing amount of energy toward reaching a stage of perfection when involved with specific assignments. Do not be surprised, then, that when their projects end, they feel a certain amount of emptiness. They don't know exactly what to do and where to turn next.

CHARACTERISTICS	IMPLICATIONS

ISTP managers are pleased when they are provided opportunities to autonomously and individually make an important contribution in making something function. Indeed, they are great jury-riggers.

ISTP managers are not natural team players. That is not to suggest that the typical ISTP leaders are loners; they are totally capable of working with the team and making significant contributions. It is realistic to assume, however, that they tend to enjoy personal achievements more than group or team accomplishments.

ISTPs are gifted when it comes to aesthetics. They value just about any art form, relying on the five senses in their appreciation. They quickly see how colors match or blend. They tend to be gastronomic connoisseurs and they can appreciate music like no one else.

In a work situation, ISTPs have a unique gift in determining how things match or mismatch. As managers, they can be masterful in determining exactly what needs to be achieved to have the right kind of impact.

ATTITUDE

The basic attitude of ISTPs is one of optimism. They expect the lucky break, the windfall, to always be just around the corner, and therefore, as we already have mentioned, ISTP managers consider risk-taking to sometimes be the oxygen of life.

Since they expect things to turn out well, they take risks in the eyes of others without much notice of the possibility of failure.

Hand in hand with this attitude of optimism goes cheerfulness, sometimes blind faith, and a great deal of trust that eventually everything will move in the right direction.

They are impatient with predictions of gloom and doom and dire consequences. Such predictions raise the hackles of the ISTP and may be taken as threats to be adamantly countered.

CHARACTERISTICS

IMPLICATIONS

When put down, criticized, ridiculed or treated in a negative fashion, however, an ISTP may exhibit natural cynicism, expecting others to be looking out for themselves in an egotistic, nonconsiderate manner.

If the work environment becomes highly political and the path to success is one of strategically positioning oneself in an organizational hierarchy, do not expect the ISTP manager to excel in that kind of environment. Indeed, with an ISTP manager, what you see is what you get.

Ambiguity holds no fascination for ISTPs. In fact, they will tend to avoid it.

ISTPs can find ambiguous situations quite frustrating, especially if they take up time and impede action.

SKILLS

ISTPs are usually very skilled at the use of tools. They typically have a great deal of mechanical and technical talent and can easily become virtuosos at operating equipment, tools, weapons, and all kinds of instruments. They have a great capacity for variations on a theme and for executing minute changes which allows them to operate/manipulate situations, machine materials and objects with a great deal of skill.

If you want ISTP employees to deliver a superior performance, be sure the job provides opportunities to solve problems, especially of a kind where there is a need for "hands on" contributions. Do not expect ISTP managers to either have the time or the inclination to philosophize. They want action, and the action is now.

They are quite resourceful and are capable of using whatever props or resources are at hand to get the job done.

CHARACTERISTICS	IMPLICATIONS

Due to the fact that ISTPs tend to be unconventional and situationally adept, expect them to demonstrate great creativity and a desire to make things work, especially when the odds suggest otherwise.

Do not expect ISTPs to display new and different modes of creativity, however. Since they have reached a sense of perfection in the execution of just about any task, they would rather add some bells and whistles than come up with a whole new different approach.

ISTPs are concrete and specific in their speech. They are usually individuals of few words, except in regard to their areas of interest; then they are prone to communicate at length, in great detail, and with full use of the lexicon of that area. Having little interest in developing language skills, their general manner of speaking is likely to be terse and sparse with realistic and concrete images, but the most gifted among them can use abstract language to meet their ends.

You would make a fairly serious mistake if you expect ISTP managers to enjoy small talk and/or long-winded conversations. ISTPs are people of few words and when they communicate they tend to use language economically and to the point. They tend to be uncomfortable in situations where there is a need for a great deal of instruction along with having patience.

The ISTP manager has an ever-observant mind—eyeing variations and opportunities. At times, an ISTP is so skillful in knowing what needs to be done that impulse strikes before thought intervenes.

At times trusting the impulse of an ISTP manager can bring about phenomenal results, at other times these impulses are best checked against long-range strategy.

DRIVING FORCE

ISTP managers have a high need for action, spontaneity and variation. Routine instructions

If forced to engage in repetitious actions, they will find ways to vary the action in order to test

CHARACTERISTICS

IMPLICATIONS

and how to deliver day-to-day predictable performance are not their bag.

Their excitement and desire for action is a very natural internal process welling up from inside. ISTPs are more alive when they are engaging in action that is self-directed. They typically are very skillful and coordinated in any movements of their hands; hence, tools can become an extension of their highly creative capabilities, and they become virtuosos in performing both simple and complex tasks such as shaping an artistic object, conducting a symphony or delivering breathtaking results in a crisis work situation.

ISTPs have an insatiable hunger for excitement that at times may lead them to operating on the brink of disaster. The reason is simple: they pride themselves on being able to trust their impulses and rise to the occasion, thus avoiding adversities, malfunctioning and even a disaster.

ENERGY DIRECTION

Given these skills, values and attitudes, ISTPs direct their energy toward exciting action and impactful performance. ISTP managers are people who tend

the limits and explore alternatives.

They may be driven to act on their impulses, seemingly caught up in the action itself. This kind of absorption in the activity comes naturally to them. ISTP managers will seldom initiate any action motivated by a sense of duty, responsibility and great insights. Rather, they tend to do whatever seems to be needed under changing circumstances. This provides ISTP leaders with a type of action-focused energy not readily available to others.

This kind of situation brings out the best abilities of an ISTP.

"Living" for them is a matter of action, involvement and focusing energies toward expedient solutions. It is not atypical for ISTP managers to become cyni-

CHARACTERISTICS	**IMPLICATIONS**

to function in a somewhat detached role. Frequently, they view themselves in more of a consultative than managerial role. Solving here and now operational problems can be counted as one of their primary sources of great strength and energy.

cal and worry a great deal if things are not being resolved expeditiously and as perfectly as possible. Waiting for things to be resolved tomorrow or sometime in the future is not something they particularly endure with a great deal of grace and patience.

ISTPs are usually able to pace themselves quite well and rarely do they experience fatigue.

Their energy does not vanish or go away in non-work situations. To the contrary, ISTPs enjoy all kinds of activities, especially those connected with sports and the out-of-doors. Indeed, for the diehard ISTPs, work is play and play is play, as opposed to the NTs where work is play and play is work.

Within the organization, the energy of ISTPs is directed toward taking expedient action and shortcuts and finding quick fixes.

ISTPs do not waste personal energy on others.

ISTP managers enjoy the opportunity to resolve unusual and difficult problems so they can constantly make full use of their gifts.

Turn ons, above all, tend to be practical in nature, along with finding expedient ways to get things done.

Turn offs are people who tend to be risk avoidant and either philosophize without action or remain loyal and rigid to the tried and true systems and procedures.

CHARACTERISTICS

IMPLICATIONS

AUTHORITY ORIENTATION

ISTP managers tend not to consider hierarchies and pecking orders to be important; rather, they are egalitarian in their approach to others. They expect to be respected and obeyed, especially if they have "grown up through the ranks." For ISTPs, power and authority is seldom a matter of rank; rather it is an issue of competency and ability to think on one's feet.

A manager has to earn the right to manage ISTPs by taking appropriate action and demonstrating superior capabilities. Do not expect ISTPs to be particularly impressed by anyone attempting to exercise any form of hierarchy or power-based authority to get things done. ISTPs respect proven performance beyond anything else.

As followers, ISTPs readily ignore authority if it does not seem to be getting things done or is blocking their own action.

When directly confronted and "threatened" with the possible consequences of their actions, they may dig in their heels and become even more insistent on doing what they think is appropriate and what they want.

ISTPs tend to be autonomous, wanting to call the shots on their own actions.

ROLE PERCEPTION

ISTPs tend to be responsive in relationships, that is, they wait and respond to another's first step in defining the relationship. Once that first step is made, they are more likely to be directive in their relationships.

When they are not proactive, most likely their level of interest is half-hearted.

CHARACTERISTICS	IMPLICATIONS
They are inclined to give orders rather than information. This directive nature may be as much non-verbal as verbal.	Giving information means waiting for others to act. ISTPs want action now. Being one up is part of their nature and they are masters at keeping others guessing about what they, the ISTPs, are up to!

CONFLICT RESOLUTION

If a conflict provides an opportunity for "battle," the battle leader side of the ISTP comes forward and takes charge. Then the ISTP will notice and capitalize on the weaknesses and mistakes of the "opponent."	The ISTP manager is a tactician by nature. That does not mean that your ISTP manager is particularly strategic, i.e., thinking about the long haul consequences and bringing the most favorable conditions to his/her side. Rather, the ISTP type instinctively knows what to do as a battle is raging. Under such circumstances, "winning" is not everything—it is the only thing for the diehard ISTP.
ISTPs have little patience with anxiety and interpersonal tensions.	They are likely to avoid such situations, at times, by physically departing from the whole situation.
ISTPs may be put off by efforts to get to the source of a conflict, believing as they tend to do that analysis is a waste of time.	Interpersonal skills tend not to be an area of strength for ISTPs; therefore, in their mind, why waste time trying to understand interpersonal conflict?

MODES OF LEARNING

ISTPs prefer to learn through hands-on methods, such as	Frequently they do not read directions, so confident are they

CHARACTERISTICS	IMPLICATIONS

projects. They prefer to be shown how to do something rather than hear about it.

They have an ability for accurate observation and like to use their skills in learning. Since the consciousness of ISTPs is concrete and specific, they may have difficulty buying into abstract presentations.

Learning is not undertaken for learning's sake, but for the results it can produce, the tools it can provide, or how much fun it is.

BLIND SPOTS AND PITFALLS

ISTPs may focus so much on keeping things moving and on fast action that they may ignore the human element—people needs.

Being so improvisation oriented, they may miss implications of their actions.

ISTPs tend to look for the quick fix and may be impatient with longer-range solutions.

that they can solve concrete problems even better than the manual and conventional directions.

One reason it is so difficult for ISTPs to indulge in any kind of theory or book learning may be that they do not enjoy preparing for anything. They are on stage, ready to perform with great flair.

ISTPs require immediate results.

It may help them to see the perspectives of others as "factors" to be considered before acting. They may need to be reminded from time to time to really listen to others.

In an orderly, predictable and routine-oriented environment, ISTP managers may find themselves snubbed or punished by policies and procedures imposing a threat to their need for a sense of freedom.

Action is what the ISTPs want and need. As a result, their tendency to not carefully think

CHARACTERISTICS	IMPLICATIONS

ISTP

	through the consequences of their often immediate and impulsive response may cause frustration and misunderstanding on the part of others.
With their extreme hunger for spontaneity, they may be viewed as too irresponsible for the job.	Organizations where the overall driving force is tradition, predictability, and dependence on the tried and true procedures may react negatively to ISTP managers who typically are looking for problems to occur in need of ISTP treatment.
They are so ready to change course that they may not provide the stabilizing force an organization needs at certain points in time.	Yet, in the proper position and situation, the contribution of ISTP managers can be invaluable—they are magnificent troubleshooters and extremely valuable when plans and existing processes are failing.
Since they have a strong distaste for the negative, they may whistle in the dark and not seek to solve major problems, especially interpersonal conflict. Their focus on concrete data and details may make them "blind" to the more subtle factors in group behavior and meaningful interpersonal relationships.	It is difficult for ISTP managers to grasp abstract feelings and thoughts. Typically, they bring everything out in the open and call a spade a spade. They may be well advised to seek out information about the broader perspectives and subtle implications of a proposed action or decision.
They may focus so much on facts, data, and details, and take such an objective stance, that they may be seen as cold, impersonal and purely task-oriented individuals.	ISTPs may thus be misperceived as uncaring when in fact they do care. Likewise, others may take their objectivity as criticism and a personal offense when indeed their intent is to clear the air and get on with the task at hand.

CHARACTERISTICS   IMPLICATIONS

ESFP

The theme of the ESFP is performing. Warm, fast, charming and witty, ESFPs want to impact others, to evoke their enjoyment and to stimulate. Seeking to excite and please their "audience," they are masters at entertaining, showmanship and sales. They thrive on social interaction, pleasure and joyful living. Indeed, for ESFP managers, life is a bowl of cherries just about 24 hours a day.

ESFP

CHARACTERISTICS   IMPLICATIONS

MANAGEMENT STYLE

The management style of the ESFP is easy going, yet pragmatic and expedient. As a manager, the ESFP does whatever needs to be done to get the job done with the least possible effort.

The ideal work environment is one with opportunities, choices, flexibility and people. The ESFP does not enjoy being alone and likes a comfortable and physically attractive work space - a space where one can express oneself.

ESFPs are at their best when responding to crises. They especially work well with people in situations calling for immediate action and finding solutions to exciting problems.

It is important to keep ESFPs mobile, moving them into positions that present problems to be solved and crises to handle. Their capacity to make a positive contribution in reducing the effects of crises for others does not mean they are equally effective in resolving personal crises.

They manage in an action-oriented way, focusing on mobilizing people to get the job done, not on the organization and its cumbersome structure. ESFPs like variety in what they do, easily creating variations on a theme.

ESFP

CHARACTERISTICS

IMPLICATIONS

Their commitment is to solve concrete problems. ESFPs have no desire to fight the system, yet if need be they will eliminate the necessary red tape to get the job done. Having ample courage and creativity propels them to move forward and expedite in the least complicated manner.

ESFPs are impatient with abstractions unless they can be shown to have immediate applications. They are hands-on people; there has to be a payoff and tangible results soon (or even better, immediately) as they direct their energy to accomplish.

As leaders they often find themselves in a position of being troubleshooters since they naturally are inclined to work at solving problems. ESFPs have a keen sense of reality and can spot trouble early. Their capacity to focus with undivided attention on the present situation leads to a quick grasp of solutions for all kinds of dilemmas.

Do not expect their best solution to be permanent; tomorrow they may "invent" something which surpasses yesterday's superb improvisation. ESFPs are energized by movement, a fast pace and ever-renewing challenges.

ESFPs can be counted on to get people working together.

Their keen "nose" for opportunity may lead them to start a number of projects in no particular order of priority. To make things worse, ESFPs are not particularly geared to pursue details and really follow through, unless the project continues to capture their interest.

It is a misuse of ESFPs to insist on such follow through. Let the other types follow through. They need a well-organized support staff to provide reminders of commitments and to follow through. Indeed, the ideal work environment for an ESFP is one where life is exciting and somehow enough people are around to execute and get things done.

CHARACTERISTICS	IMPLICATIONS

Acutely aware of the pain and suffering of others, ESFPs are tireless workers when there is a crisis at hand.

If crises and problems do not abound in the organization, they may create them.

ESFPs are not afraid of failure for they are focused on the odds of success. Thus, they typically take risks where no other type would dare.

Other types may be uneasy with their willingness to ignore traditions, policies and the tried and true routines in getting the job done.

People cooperate with them and find them easy to get along with. ESFPs give verbal praise without hesitation. The feedback most often offered by an ESFP is whatever pressure it takes to get people to do what needs to be done.

Their charm results in others responding to their creative lead. Their approach is with gusto, for tomorrow we die.

They seem to have a relentless eye for new opportunities, and ESFPs change their positions quickly as new facts are presented, opening up untold new approaches to alter the present state of just about anything.

They are likely to ask of a planned change, "Will it work? Is it practical? Have you considered the following viewpoint? When do I have to step in to clean up the mess others created?"

However, they tend to dislike the unfamiliar and may be uncomfortable with changes that they themselves have not instigated.

ESFPs have a unique system for approaching challenging situations. Do not expect them to skillfully implement others' systems of approach. "Not invented here" frequently seems to apply.

ESFP

CHARACTERISTICS	IMPLICATIONS

ESFP

VALUES

ESFPs value excitement, variation and impact.

They typically tend to avoid ties, routines, systems, plans, commitments and obligations that conceivably could get in the way of their freedom to choose the next act.

They trust luck, putting their faith in the odds of winning.

ESFPs don't pay a great deal of attention and don't care much about the rationale behind an event or a policy, or about the authority vested in someone to implement it. Hence, do not be surprised if at times they put themselves in relatively dangerous situations to perfect their performance and prove their worth.

Personal skills, coordination and behavioral effectiveness are valued a great deal by ESFPs. Their performance in whatever form must be mastered superbly to a point of perfection. They cannot abide clumsy performance in themselves or others.

You will find ESFPs exercising their skills of showmanship, influencing and promotion in all manner of environments. They experience a strong sense of reward when impacting others.

ESFPs value action - do not expect them to be enamored with theoretical abstractions and philosophical reasoning. If whatever is on the agenda does not require some kind of action, ESFPs get bored.

They do not care about explaining actions or justifying them. They are more interested in just going on to the next task or project.

CHARACTERISTICS	IMPLICATIONS

They abhor routine and rigid adherence to hierarchy. To "follow the book" is not their strong suit - frequently because they have not read the book anyway.

ESFPs may rebel in more ways than one against too many constraints to their freedom. If their job is too routine, they typically will put their own little twist to it to get the variety and enjoyment they need out of an otherwise boring situation.

ESFPs value pleasure and enjoy life to the hilt. In other words, it is the "here and now" which sparks their energy as if there were no tomorrow.

Do not expect dull moments with them; their zest for life and living provides ESFPs with extraordinary energies to make the most out of any situation. Naturally people are drawn to them as they seek to entertain and contribute to the well being of everyone.

ATTITUDE

Their basic attitude is one of optimism. ESFPs expect the lucky break, the exceptional circumstances, and the windfall to be just around the corner.

Since they expect things to turn out well, they take what seems to others as risks without any notice of possible failure.

Hand in hand with this attitude of optimism goes cheerfulness and an upbeat attitude.

They are impatient with predictions of doom and gloom and dire consequences. Such predictions raise the hackles of ESFPs and may be taken as threats to be adamantly countered.

On the other hand, when things are not working out and not going the way the ESFP would like, expect a cynical attitude that others are looking out for their own good and eventual payoff.

Consequently, limiting oneself to functioning in the mode of implementing shortcuts may translate into meagre payoffs and may produce even further cynicism.

CHARACTERISTICS	IMPLICATIONS
ESFPs are likely to ignore ambiguous situations and proceed to action.	In fact, they will try to avoid them.

SKILLS

ESFPs are skilled at anything tactical and they tend to maneuver quickly and with great accuracy to overcome obstacles. They are unusually resourceful and able to use whatever is at hand to get the job done.	If you want ESFP employees to give a superior performance, be sure the job provides stimulation in a lively and festive atmosphere with only the absolute minimum of rules and directives.
Their performing is an external process. ESFPs are keen observers of human behavior; even minute variations and alterations of non-verbal clues, and they put this skill to use to impact others. Their performance builds on the responses they evoke in others.	Do not be surprised or disappointed if ESFPs turn out to be total clowns. They tend to use their whole being to demonstrate the lighter side of life - indeed, ESFPs can be hilariously funny.
ESFPs have a great capacity for evolving variations on a theme and executing minute changes, allowing them to create situations and behaviors which entertain and impact others with infinite variation.	ESFPs thrive on problems and challenges; without these, they become bored, and they are likely to expend their energies in nonproductive ways.
ESFPs are concrete and specific in their speech. Language is but a tool in their repertoire of things to use to get things done. Their language is likely to be full of realistic and concrete images, but the most gifted among them can use abstract language to meet their ends.	Conversation with ESFPs can go on indefinitely. In addition, the conversation is for the most part quite stimulating - at least for the ESFPs.

CHARACTERISTICS	IMPLICATIONS
The ESFP makes an excellent conversationalist with a witty and seemingly endless banter.	Conversation at length is great as long as the ESFP finds it to be entertaining and stimulating; it is not an effective substitute for doing the tasks at hand, however.
They are usually up on the latest and greatest in dress, food and other physical accoutrements.	
Expect ESFPs to be highly gifted in some artistic direction. In other words, they tend to excel in specific areas of interest, be it the performing arts, whipping up fabulous and creative meals, scuba diving, hang gliding, dancing, sculpturing, sports, and on and on and on.	Anything that captures their interest or is a special strength or capability needs to be exercised and perfected. Therefore, encourage and support ESFPs in their artistic direction; after all, they are performing for you, and if there is no audience and shared excitement, what is the use?

DRIVING FORCE

ESFPs have a high need for immediate action, spontaneity and variation. They abhor rules, routines and hierarchies.	When engaged in repetitious actions, they quickly find ways to vary routines in order to test limits and discover breaking points.
ESFPs have an insatiable hunger for action and excitement which at times may lead them to operate at the brink of disaster. Indeed, they consider themselves able to trust their impulses and rise to any occasion, especially unusual, unanticipated circumstances. They move away from impending dangers and adversities with great flair.	ESFPs may be driven to act on their impulses, seemingly caught up in the action itself. This kind of absorption in the activity comes naturally to them. To perform according to duty, responsibility, relationship or insight is not important for them. Others rarely experience this kind of absorption.

ESFP

CHARACTERISTICS	IMPLICATIONS

ENERGY DIRECTION

Given these skills, values and attitudes, ESFPs direct their energy toward exciting and impactful performance, especially in areas where they can make a contribution to the well being of people.

If ESFPs are not having an impact on their environment, they find ways to create impact. More often than not, they seek to influence their environment humanly and with a constructive impact. If, however, they have decided to dislike someone for whatever reason, expect the human warmth to turn to arctic ice.

Within the organization their energy will be directed toward influencing others, socializing and entertaining. In addition, ESFPs are very project oriented and enjoy a challenge where there will be tangible results.

Turn ons are playful and enjoyable ways to get things done, especially if the ESFP is given the opportunity to be the center of attraction.

Turn offs are tasks for the sake of tasks or in service of a long range goal.

AUTHORITY ORIENTATION

If ESFPs are in charge, they expect to be obeyed and not questioned, and they often are by virtue of their ability to influence. However, they can sometimes come across as very friendly while at other times as less charming and understanding, even abrupt.

When necessary, although not by habit or choice, ESFPs are very capable of asserting themselves masterfully. As they move forward swiftly and with a great deal of gusto, expect them at times not to be the best of listeners, as the importance of their own agenda may overpower their otherwise superb people skills.

CHARACTERISTICS	IMPLICATIONS

ESFPs seek to please and prefer to respond favorably to others. Even so, ESFPs are autonomous, wanting to call the shots on their own actions. Their wanting to please others stems more from the desire to have an impact than an obedient attitude. As followers, they may readily challenge authority or ignore it if it does not seem to be getting things done. For the diehard ESFP, authority is not necessarily granted by title and tenure.

When directly confronted and "threatened" with the possible consequences of their actions, ESFPs may dig in their heels and become even more insistent on doing what they want.

ROLE PERCEPTION

ESFPs tend to be proactive in interpersonal relationships; they take the first step in defining the relationship.

Thus they are seen as quite gregarious and friendly.

An ESFP prefers to give information rather than directives.

It is easy to respond to the implied directive in an ESFP's informative and thus wind up in his/her service.

CONFLICT RESOLUTION

Liking things to be upbeat, ESFPs tend to avoid confrontation. They prefer harmonious and pleasant interactions.

The aversion to confrontation blends well with denial and avoidance. Approach ESFPs gently in a conflict situation and reveal your feelings first to keep them from responding defensively.

CHARACTERISTICS

IMPLICATIONS

ESFPs have little patience with anxiety and interpersonal tensions. They are likely to actively avoid conflict situations.

Under stress, this habit results in denial of worsening personal difficulties. It is also useful to know that ESFPs are not very capable of dealing with a lot of personal conflict. In other words, they appreciate harmony and interpersonal understanding. If conflict prevails over long periods of time, do not be surprised if they just pick up and leave, as loyalty to themselves is higher than to the institution.

They may be put off by efforts to get to the source of a conflict, believing as they tend to do that analysis is a waste of time.

Effective conflict resolution with ESFPs might focus on alleviating the pain and suffering of the difficult situation. Sometimes humor will hook them into dealing with the conflict.

Confrontation is probably not the most efficient approach in resolving conflict, where active listening may be. One can invite ESFPs to act out whatever frustration exists. In that process they tend to burn themselves out and eventually alter their position. They may enter the scene of conflict as a roaring lion and leave as a huggy teddy bear.

LEARNING

ESFPs prefer to learn by active personal involvement and through hands-on methods such as projects. They also like group

Frequently they do not read directions or manuals, so confident are they that they can solve concrete problems.

CHARACTERISTICS IMPLICATIONS

interaction and learn well through that process. They prefer to be shown how to do something rather than hear about it.

They have a talent for accurate, action-oriented observation and enjoy honing their skills in learning. Since the consciousness of ESFPs is concrete and specific, they may have difficulty buying into abstract presentations, especially for any length of time.

ESFPs tend not to be concept-driven; rather, their strength is a linear one. Abstract problem-solving is not so much their forte as juryrigging. Moreover, they typically attack problems (where no one really knows the outcome) with great energy and excitement.

Learning is not undertaken for learning's sake, but for the results it can produce, the tools it provides and the fun experienced in the process.

It does not take long for an ESFP to create excitement where dullness and stagnation are to be found.

BLIND SPOTS AND PITFALLS

ESFPs may at times focus so much on exciting and fun interpersonal action that they may neglect the task and the job to be done.

Do not be surprised or dismayed if ESFPs arrive unprepared as they are masterful in winging just about everything.

Being so improvisation oriented, they may miss counterproductive implications of their actions. The ESFP tends to look for the quick fix and may be impatient with longer-range solutions.

The tendency for a short-term focus is of inestimable value for developing ingenious shortcuts in the physical world; this same bulldog tenacity can be a handicap by refusing abstract data.

CHARACTERISTICS	IMPLICATIONS
With their insatiable hunger for spontaneity, ESFPs may at times be considered rather irresponsible in an otherwise structured work environment.	ESFPs are challenged to become more tolerant of a minimal amount of structure. It is important for them to focus on the positive benefits of planned activities and task completion, and thereby avoid inadvertent negative consequences. Even though foresight seems dull and a waste of energy, it can be quite useful to the effervescent, energizing ESFP. The propensity for spontaneity is most effective in arousing a stagnant organization. Few can surpass an ESFP in overturning applecarts.
They may be so ready to change course and experiment with new ideas that they may not provide the stabilizing force an organization needs at times.	ESFPs might have to be reminded of the necessity to meet deadlines and finish projects.
Since they have a strong distaste for the negative, they may tend to whistle in the dark and not seek to solve major problems - especially the interpersonal ones. Their focus on concrete data and details may make them "blind" to the more subtle factors in group behavior and meaningful interpersonal relationships.	They may be well-advised to seek out information about the broader perspectives and subtle implications of a proposed action or decision.
They tend to be very generous and may give too much of themselves, their time and their possessions. ESFPs enjoy sharing their drink, food, thoughts and	It should come as no surprise, then, that in structured and traditional organizational settings, ESFPs do not typically enjoy the everyday discipline of anything;

ESFP

CHARACTERISTICS	IMPLICATIONS

time. Expect the ESFPs to have a very egalitarian attitude: "Everything which is mine is yours - and vice versa." Indeed, they tend to be terrific impulsive givers.

rather, their enjoyment is derived from the opportunity to make drudgery into unscheduled excitement and merrymaking.

ESFPs tend to be project-driven and they will devote tremendous energy and be practically captivated by the task at hand. When they have achieved or conducted whatever they set out to do, the blues may settle in until the next exciting challenge is on the horizon.

Managing ESFPs, then, requires the ability to tap into their realities in terms of their concentrated project focus. It is to be expected that your ESFP colleagues and subordinates experience moments of interim lows as whatever they do is nearing completion. The explanation is simple: ESFPs tremendously enjoy being on a high, and when there is nothing to do, they no longer can reach for the stars.

ESFPs have a very real need for living life on a continuous all-time high. They find it frustrating and difficult not to have the opportunities to unfold their great capacity for creative happiness and feelings of goodwill.

Do not be dismayed or upset if ESFP managers tend to intensely dislike ambivalence and ambiguity. It is difficult for them to accept a great deal of uncertainty for long periods of time.

CHARACTERISTICS	IMPLICATIONS

ISFP

The theme of the ISFP is composing; ISFPs are the impressionistic creators of the moment and they know how to make the most out of it. They want to please and favor through their compositions, frequently in the visual and performing arts. With their senses keenly tuned in, they become totally absorbed in the action of the moment, and for ISFPs, actions speak louder than words.

CHARACTERISTICS	IMPLICATIONS

MANAGEMENT STYLE

The management style of the ISFP is understanding, human and easy going. Moreover, ISFP managers are pragmatic and expedient. They do whatever needs to be done to get the job done with the least possible effort, and a premium is attached to being efficient.

The ideal work environment is one with opportunities, choices, flexibility and relatively few familiar and friendly people.

ISFPs like a comfortable and physically attractive work space.

They may not always keep things neat and tidy but they usually know where everything is and can find whatever they may be looking for very quickly.

ISFPs are at their best when responding to crises. They especially work well with people in crisis and adapt well to what is needed.

It is important to keep ISFPs challenged, moving them into positions that present problems to be solved and crises to handle when their current assignment is near stabilizing; this is a safe path to keep their energies focused and satisfaction achieved. Indeed, the job should be varied and exciting.

CHARACTERISTICS	**IMPLICATIONS**

They manage in an action-oriented way, gently persuading people to get the job done. ISFPs like variety in what they do. Their expertise is to solve immediate and concrete problems. They have no need to fight systems, policies and procedures; they just ignore them if and when these systems prevent ISFPs from achieving whatever has to be done.

They are not particularly enamored with abstraction unless it can be shown to have immediate applications and payoff. For ISFP managers, emphasis is on concrete, specific and pleasing results. They have a well-developed sense of wanting to contribute to others and if whatever they do can have a profound impact on others, it is worth the effort.

As leaders, ISFP managers tend to be action oriented. Not having anything to do is worse than being on overload. They are at their very best when there is an opportunity to find solutions to specific, concrete problems. Often they have an uncanny capacity to spot malfunctions before others, and then they may be so absorbed in solving the problems of the moment that the future doesn't exist in their realities.

Hence, do not be surprised or disappointed if and when ISFP managers have less of a sense of priority and urgency to pursue an agenda. For them, living the here and now is important—the future can wait.

ISFP managers can be individual virtuosos.

They can be so competent and excellent in what they do that delegating comes as a disappointing burden to them; after all, why should they bother teaching others when they are superb?

ISFPs can be counted on to get people working together, and they enjoy harmony and understanding.

The style of management for an ISFP is non-imposing and non-directional; others are given ample opportunity to demonstrate their skills.

CHARACTERISTICS

IMPLICATIONS

Acutely aware of the pain and suffering of others, ISFPs are tireless workers when there is a crisis at hand. They are unconditionally kind and give freely to those who are suffering.

It is difficult for ISFPs to not notice or to ignore the suffering of an associate or a friend. Moreover, ISFP managers are perhaps the most egalitarian of all the types. For them, hierarchies, regimentations and any kind of pecking order only have meaning if people are facilitated and enabled to do their job.

ISFP managers are willing to venture into the unknown as long as they can be in the middle of it. Problems calling for inspired, fast and efficient solutions hit the bull's eye for ISFP managers.

Other types may be uneasy with their willingness to ignore traditions, policies or belief in systems in order to get the job done. Indeed, individuals and coworkers taking pride in and relying upon normalized operations may at times be threatened by their desire to juryrig and make things work in an order all its own.

ISFP managers are typically easy to get along with and they get people to cooperate with them. The feedback most often offered by them focuses on the positive, as they dislike confrontation and negative attitudes.

It is important to realize that ISFPs are autonomous individuals, yet they have a very genuine desire to cause others to enjoy the work environment. Typically, ISFP managers are rather egalitarian types who tend to give of themselves and of course expect everyone else to have a similarly generous attitude.

Always with an eye out for opportunities, ISFPs change their position easily as new facts are presented. They are masterful in picking up subtle signals in just about any situation.

CHARACTERISTICS	IMPLICATIONS

However, they tend to dislike the unfamiliar and may be uncomfortable with changes that they themselves have not instigated.

Typically, ISFPs learn by doing and rehearsing; as a result, they are not comfortable with any kind of change unless they have an opportunity to be involved "hands on." Moreover, whatever they do needs to be perfect (in their own view)—that is why at times coping with change imposed by others is difficult for them.

VALUES

Above all, ISFPs value freedom and a sense of personal dignity.

Consequently, do not be surprised if they may avoid ties, plans, commitments or obligations that get in the way of exercising their freedom to choose their next act.

ISFPs are not people who particularly enjoy relying on established systems and procedures unless they have invented these themselves.

They don't care much about the rationale behind an event or a policy, or about the authority to implement it. Likewise, they do not hold a great deal of respect or esteem for those who insist on following rules for the rules' sake. They may, from time to time, deviate significantly from the established ways and leap into new situations without really being fully aware of the consequences.

Skill and behavioral effectiveness are important to ISFPs. Their performance, in whatever form,

You will find ISFPs exercising their skills of craftsmanship, art and grace in just about every

CHARACTERISTICS	IMPLICATIONS

must be mastered to perfection. It is painful for them to tolerate clumsy performance by both themselves and others.

situation. When they perform their own compositions, they strive to have an impact on those around them.

ISFPs also value action. It is not pleasant for them to have nothing to do for any length of time.

They do not particularly care about explaining actions or justifying them. They are more inclined to just go on to the next action and enjoy the excitement of the next project.

ISFPs abhor routine and rigid adherence to hierarchy and structure. Indeed, they are not the kind of people who prefer or look for specific instructions and policies; rather, they just dive in to both learn and perfect what they do as they move along.

They may rebel in both large and small ways against too many constraints to their freedom. If their job is based on routine, IS-FPs will put their own twists in it to get the variety they need.

ISFPs also value pleasure and enjoying life. They often have an affinity for nature and like the out of doors. Above all, the ISFP enjoys the aesthetics and artful execution of anything. They see beauty in form, action and colors.

Do not expect them to be as excited about financial results as the surroundings creating them. Financial success for an ISFP is not an end in itself; rather, it is the road travelled to get there.

ATTITUDE

The basic attitude of ISFPs is one of optimism. They expect that the lucky break and the windfall might just be around the next corner.

As a result of their eternal optimism, do not be surprised if from time to time ISFP managers may make judgments of an extraordinary nature. In other words, they may optimize the current situation without necessarily having concern for the long-range consequences.

CHARACTERISTICS	IMPLICATIONS
Hand-in-hand with this attitude of optimism goes cheerfulness and looking for the positive and uplifting in just about any situation.	They are not very tolerant of predictions of doom and gloom and dire consequences. Such predictions raise the hackles of the ISFP and may be taken as threats to be adamantly countered.
ISFPs have no need to unravel ambiguities; rather, they are inclined to ignore them.	If ambiguous situations are forced on them, they are inclined to avoid them rather than attempt to solve them.
ISFPs also exhibit a natural cynicism, expecting others to always be looking out for themselves and for the payoff. Yet, they tend to want to be trusting and receptive.	ISFP managers certainly wish that this world would match their image of perfection and aesthetics. Early in life, ISFPs, with perhaps unrealistic expectations, frequently tend to place too much trust in others. If, over time, they are awakened to the imperfections and failings, they may be disappointed, hurt and sorry.

SKILLS

ISFPs are skilled at anything tactical, maneuvering to overcome obstacles. They are quite resourceful and able to use whatever is at hand to get the job done. Count on them to jury-rig just about anything. To make do with what is there is their inclination as opposed to dreaming up some new intangible idea or concept.	If you want ISFP employees to give a superior performance, be sure the job provides variation in a quietly stimulating atmosphere. Allowing them to practice and fine tune their skills in the direction they want in an organizational setting might sometimes be difficult. The problem you will have as a manager, however, is that ISFPs may consciously or unconsciously ignore directives and commands counter to their own, always "better" judgment.

ISFP

CHARACTERISTICS

IMPLICATIONS

The ISFPs' creativity and unique gift of composing is an internal process. Their senses are keenly tuned in to color, line, texture, shading, touch and motion. They tend to become totally absorbed in what they are doing, and they tremendously enjoy contributing to the well being of others through their compositions in whatever form. Their performance of their own compositions builds on the responses and feedback they evoke in others.

While the appearance and performance of ISFPs may be perceived as rather impromptu, bear in mind that they seek perfection in just about everything. Enhancing skills and improving on what they enjoy doing becomes a natural part of living for them.

ISFPs have an unusual capacity for developing variations on a theme and for executing minute changes which allow them to create situations and behaviors with infinite variation.

Often an area of keen interest for ISFPs is the arts—be it performing, composing, shaping or creating great aesthetics; they are always lending themselves with great finesse and with the fostering of their free spirit.

ISFPs are concrete and specific in their speech, and language is generally not their favorite medium of expression. Fundamentally, they prefer actions to words. Exceptions are the gag writer who composes gags, the song writer who writes lyrics, and the occasional novelist like Hemingway. Their language is likely to be full of realistic and concrete images, and the most gifted ISFPs have the ability to use abstract language to better express their intentions.

For ISFPs, language may be a barrier to interpersonal relations. For them, talk is cheap; they want to express themselves through results—it is the tangible and aesthetically pleasing that counts.

ISFP

CHARACTERISTICS	IMPLICATIONS

ISFP

DRIVING FORCE

ISFPs have a high need for action, spontaneity and variation, and they dislike repetition. They are driven to compose in whatever medium they find the free variable, which they can shape, improve and perfect.

If forced to engage in repetitious actions, almost by instinct they will find ways to vary the action in order to test the limits and search for ways to improve and perfect whatever they are working with.

They may be driven to act on impulse, seemingly caught up in the action itself. This kind of absorption in activity comes naturally to the ISFP; to do things because of duty, responsibility, relationships or insight has no pull.

Individuals who typically fit into organizational settings tend to react differently as value is placed on conformity. Do not be surprised if an ISFP is at odds with regimentation, rules and systems as these will take away and threaten the free spirit embodied in the die-hard ISFP.

The ISFP individual is a person who is energized by opportunities to challenge the tried and true, especially if he/she is asked to perform within parameters designed and determined by others.

Consequently, do not be surprised if the ISFP may seek levels of risk somewhat beyond conventional parameters.

ENERGY DIRECTION

Given these skills, values and attitudes, ISFPs direct their energy toward favoring others with their compositions.

If ISFPs are not able to exercise their natural talent for composing some kind of graceful action or artwork, they become stressed and report feeling empty.

Within the organization their energy will be directed toward quietly engaging in whatever

Variety is the fuel which enables ISFPs to quietly persist and persevere.

CHARACTERISTICS

IMPLICATIONS

actions are involved in the job, especially if variation is involved. ISFPs seek to experience intensely the here and now.

Turn ons include pleasing others with their actions or figuring out tactical ways around the rules.

AUTHORITY ORIENTATION

ISFPs seek to please and prefer to respond favorably to others. Even so, ISFPs are autonomous, wanting to call the shots on their own actions. Their wanting to please others stems more from the desire to have an impact rather than an obedient attitude. As followers they may readily challenge authority or ignore it if it does not seem to be getting things done. Authority is not necessarily granted by title and tenure.

When directly confronted and "threatened" with the possible consequences of their actions, they may dig in their heels and become even more insistent on doing what they want. Indeed, ISFPs are not unknown for shaping their opinions and kind of etching them in cement.

ISFPs admire the creative initiative in others. Their understanding of art recognizes that true creations can never be commanded or systematized. Authority for ISFPs is expressed through superior performance, not in promises of the future.

Therefore, it is reasonable to understand that ISFPs seldom seek or desire to have and display authority in interpersonal relations. ISFPs are content to let their creative action and compassions command a timeless sense of authority all of its own, independent from fluttering moments of wanting to command others to perform.

CHARACTERISTICS	IMPLICATIONS

ISFP

ROLE PERCEPTION

ISFPs tend to be reactive in interpersonal relationships; that is, they rarely take the first step in defining the relationship. They prefer to respond to the initiatives of others and accommodate their needs as these emerge.

ISFPs resist efforts which attempt to cramp their style. Of equal significance, they resist cramping the style of others as they tend to have a great deal of respect for the autonomy of others.

They prefer giving information to giving directives.

This does not mean that ISFPs go around spouting information—just that they prefer to inform, rather than command.

CONFLICT RESOLUTION

Liking things to be upbeat, ISFPs tend to avoid confrontation. They prefer harmonious and pleasant interactions. As a result, it is both difficult and painful for them to like and function in conditions where a great deal of ambiguity and conflict exist. Ambivalent conditions do not inspire ISFPs to deliver great performances.

Confrontation works against their perceptions and prevents what is so highly valued and appreciated in a day-to-day role—that of being and living in a framework of free spirit.

ISFPs may be put off by efforts to get to the source of a conflict, believing as they tend to do that analysis is a waste of time, not really contributing to the immediate needs of the moment.

ISFPs have little patience with anxiety and interpersonal tensions. They are likely to actively avoid conflict situations or even leave. Therefore, they are not likely to freely express their opinions, especially if they are negative. If and when they do, it may not be well controlled and may be fairly moralistic.

CHARACTERISTICS

IMPLICATIONS

ISFPs are tender and sensitive. Conflict, in their view, is disruptive to the flow of tenderness, sensitivity, and productive human relationships.

Effective conflict resolution with ISFPs might focus on alleviating the pain and suffering of the difficult situation. At times it is more efficient to refocus their attention on adjacent issues, allowing them to get some distance on the problem at hand and thereby gain a more productive perspective on the conflict.

MODES OF LEARNING

ISFPs prefer to learn through hands-on methods such as participation projects. They prefer to be shown how to do something rather than hear about it.

Frequently they do not read directions and manuals, so confident are they that they can solve concrete problems, and so averse are they to language.

They have a highly developed ability for accurate observation and enjoy using their sensing skills in learning.

ISFPs are keenly alert to their immediate environment.

Since the consciousness of ISFPs is concrete and specific, they may have difficulty buying into abstract presentations, distant theories and theoretical speculations.

The desire to experience the here and now significantly prevails as opposed to abstract thinking.

Learning is not undertaken for learning's sake, but for the results it can produce, the tools it can provide them with or how much fun it is.

Immediate application and practicality has great appeal to an ISFP.

CHARACTERISTICS	IMPLICATIONS

BLIND SPOTS AND PITFALLS

ISFPs tend to be rather egalitarian in their attitudes toward others. They share freely and sometimes in error, and believe that others have a similar attitude—which frequently tends not to be the case.

They may need to seek objective viewpoints from others.

ISFPs may get so involved and caught up in the action of the moment that they fail to direct their energies toward different, sometimes more important objectives.

To expend energy thinking about goals conflicts with living fully in the present moment.

Being so improvisation oriented, they may miss implications of their action in terms of a negative reaction of others.

This often results in misunderstandings when working with other different types.

The ISFP typically tends to go for the quick fix and be impatient with longer-range, more permanent kinds of solutions.

Longer-range solutions take away from intense involvement with the present, which is enjoyed abundantly by the ISFP.

With their extreme hunger for spontaneity, ISFPs may come across to others as so situational that the future may have to suffer. Indeed, they are so ready to change course that they may challenge the traditional stabilizing force an organization depends upon.

There is a great deal of strength in these characteristics of ISFPs if these are properly understood. Their important contribution is in making things happen—right now—and they need a minimum of applause and grandiose feedback. They know what is right and they have a clear idea of what is wrong—right now—and not in some intangible distant future.

CHARACTERISTICS

IMPLICATIONS

Since they have a strong distaste for the negative, they may choose to whistle in the dark and not attempt to solve major problems, especially interpersonal ones. Their focus on concrete data and details may make them "blind" to the more subtle factors in group behavior and established and tradition-bound interpersonal relationships.

For ISFPs to work with someone they have decided not to like becomes very difficult, sometimes to the point of impossibility.

They tend to be unusually generous and may give more of themselves, their time and their possessions when compared to the rest of the world.

They may be well-advised to seek out information about the broader perspectives and subtle implications of a proposed action or decision. Yet, do not expect them to do that without major effort, as dealing with the future does not come easily to them.

Given their impulsivity, ISFPs value variety and sensual experiences. They seek to accept the world as it is and maximize living life in the present. They could easily say, "Tomorrow may never arrive—live today," or "Eat, drink and be merry because tomorrow may never arrive."

CHARACTERISTICS	IMPLICATIONS

ESTJ

The theme of the ESTJ is supervising, with an eye to the traditions and regulations of the group. ESTJs are interested in ensuring that the standards are met and the consequences for not following those standards are delivered. They want to keep order so that the organization, group, family and culture will be preserved.

CHARACTERISTICS	IMPLICATIONS

MANAGEMENT STYLE

The management style of the ESTJ is results-oriented, cooperative, authoritarian and quite decisive. An ESTJ manager expects everyone to follow the rules and standard operating procedures without question. Title, position, and hierarchies are important and to be respected.

The ideal work environment for an ESTJ is a predictable, stable and orderly one where tasks are defined and everyone knows what is expected, both individually and departmentally.

ESTJs tend to manage themselves and the circumstances provided for them in a task-oriented, no-nonsense fashion. They are not the ones engaging in small talk; for them, efficiency is important and paying attention to anything that doesn't accomplish the task to be done is a waste.

Moreover, the preferred overall work culture is one of valuing efficiency, that is, achieving results according to plans and on time. It is important that everyone be accountable through deed, not verbiage, and that their contribution be significant and of sustainable value. Anyone not adhering to and respecting this culture may fall out of their good graces.

CHARACTERISTICS

IMPLICATIONS

ESTJ

While ESTJ managers may appear formal and at times impersonal, their fundamental motivation is one of achieving superior results with people working together.

ESTJs like to manage according to plan, so that whatever they do shall impact people and the organization in a constructive, results-oriented fashion. They are typically viewed as conservative. They run efficient meetings with an agenda, preferring things to be on time and on schedule. Their commitment is to the establishment of stability and predictability, with no negative surprises in their work environment.

As leaders, ESTJs work to preserve traditions. They instinctively know the value of rituals, ceremonies, and celebrations in providing a sense of belonging and permanence in the organization so that it can perpetuate itself, grow stronger, and become more productive day by day.

ESTJs enjoy a team approach to work where no one individual would attempt to outshine or draw more attention to him or herself than the group as a whole.

They are likely to ask of a planned change, "Is it useful? Practical? Has it worked before?" Moreover, they tend to be wary of any change, both in terms of usefulness and workability. It is not advisable to recommend major changes in systems and procedures for ESTJs with a great deal of enthusiasm and hoopla, without thorough assurance that whatever is suggested has proven reliable, predictable, and worked exceedingly well in similar kinds of situations.

If traditions do not abound in the organization, ESTJ managers will, over time, establish activities and procedures which clearly provide people with a sense of belonging. Pride and recognition for accomplishments are high on the agenda for them to establish; consequently, a manifestation of success anchored in the security of past events is important to them in enforcing the spirit of accomplishment.

CHARACTERISTICS

IMPLICATIONS

ESTJs, above all, are realistic, concrete and specific.

You can rely upon ESTJs for precise instructions.

You can count on ESTJs to follow through. And, very little, if anything, is left to chance. While they tend to comprehend the whole operational picture, they can be sticklers for detail.

Not surprisingly, then, they are likely to be disappointed when others do not follow through. To ESTJs such behavior means not caring enough to be responsible for obtaining the results deemed appropriate. As a result, they may be quite harsh and demanding, demonstrating a lack of any understanding or empathy when performance is declining.

ESTJs want to be accountable and responsible. They are known to be diligent, focused, energetic workers. Indeed, they tend to demand more from themselves than anyone else.

Their strong sense of responsibility may lead them to take on too much work and get overloaded to the point of exhaustion. Therefore, it is important to realize that ESTJs can become stressed because of their never-ending desire to carry out all their often self-assigned burdens and tasks to be accomplished.

ESTJs are steady, dependable and predictable workers.

They may be impatient with the less steady pace of other types.

ESTJs tend to believe that appreciation must be earned and must not be given to those who are not the most worthy. Moreover, it is sometimes difficult for them to provide positive feedback to others simply because they tend to set very high stan-

They sometimes tend to ignore or overlook the small steps toward a specific goal or predetermined improvement. As a result, they may reward only those in first, second and third place. It is useful for them to understand the value of providing positive

CHARACTERISTICS	IMPLICATIONS
dards, first for themselves and then for others. Compromise on these standards is unacceptable.	feedback. Eventually it would be valuable for them to learn that absence of feedback is often perceived by others as criticism, which frequently results in a decline in productivity and reduces motivation to deliver superior performance.
The feedback most often offered by the ESTJ is in directing an individual to get back on course and in correcting deviations from predetermined standards.	This, too, is frequently perceived negatively by others.
ESTJs tend to be exceptionally loyal to any organization they join. Their contribution is one of assuring that the integrity and goodness of the organization is perpetuated and solidified over time.	Organizations and predictable systems are the heart and soul of an ESTJ - they provide an incredible sense of stability.
ESTJs like predictability and consistency in what they are required to do to be most effective.	ESTJs are masters at carrying out tasks and following routines. Changes are disruptive to their speedy style - after all, every change requires adaptation which slows down their pace.

VALUES

ESTJs support the preservation of the time-tested values, beliefs and norms of life which frequently translate into economics as a way of satisfying needs. They need to know that there is a tangible, worthwhile payoff in	It is neither natural nor comfortable for ESTJs to deviate, question or challenge any lifestyle which, through tradition, has proven to provide stability, predictability and results. Therefore, an ESTJ is more likely to

ESTJ

CHARACTERISTICS

IMPLICATIONS

return for the effort they expend toward some achievement. Expect an ESTJ to energetically pursue a task, assignment or goal when there is a common benefit for everyone involved at the end of the line.

join existing and proven systems, organizations and approaches, expecting the results to emerge as they always have.

ESTJs are comfortable with proven authority and are likely to put faith and trust in credentials, hierarchies and systems which have served organizational purposes well.

They tend not to challenge the rationale behind systems, procedures and policies. Theirs is a world of implementation. To achieve and accomplish whatever they think is expected of them provides them with a sense of inner peace and satisfaction. Not surprisingly, they do not hold much respect or esteem for those who attempt to breach the rules, even if in their respective minds the deviations are attempted for all kinds of plausible reasons.

Belonging, camaraderie, and being an integral part of the whole group is important to ESTJs. Hence, you will find them belonging to different kinds of organizations and clubs. Membership constitutes a productive way of gaining a sense of stability and belonging, preserving and enhancing the known and valued styles of living.

ESTJs tend not to be loners and it is important for them to take part in their communities. Hence, you will find that they enjoy the sharing and inclusion in respected and significant societies and social organizations, and they often contribute much value to their respective communities. Don't be surprised to find ESTJs actively involved in service clubs, church work, PTA and other organizations serving the common good.

ESTJ

CHARACTERISTICS	IMPLICATIONS

ESTJs also value ownership. They seek to possess and preserve objects of importance to them.

Typically, ESTJs enjoy the freedom of having no encumbrances; therefore, they will strive to own outright and individually any properties or objects of importance to them.

They abhor dereliction of duty. Anyone not carrying their load and doing their share of expected work is looked down upon.

ESTJs are very attentive to such derelictions and can be very harsh in their treatment of such matters. "Ignorance of the law" is no excuse; one should be responsible.

ATTITUDE

The basic attitude of ESTJs is one of fatalism. They tend to believe that things are what they are and little can be done to change them. One is well advised to accept one's lot in life because that is the way it is.

Thus they are not motivated to promote changes unless they can rest assured that the changes will work. Moreover, they are not likely to be great risk takers.

Because ESTJs are concrete in their attitudes, "to have and to hold" is important to them.

Everything paid for, not financed, gives them a very real sense of peace of mind.

ESTJs rarely see the world in terms of gray. It is either black or white.

Thus they have little tolerance for ambiguity and tend to get angry and bogged down by ambiguous situations.

In a sense, ESTJs seem to know that their role in life is to make the most out of what is there for them to deal with. Their energies are not directed toward questioning, challenging and tam-

It would be paradoxical to assume that ESTJs would accept, much less enjoy, an environment where everyone would be "doing their own thing." To the contrary, their real sense of joy

CHARACTERISTICS

IMPLICATIONS

pering with existing realities; rather, the challenge is one of fitting into and enhancing what is there. They prefer to make the very best out of the given situation without attempting to start a minor revolution when there is a breakdown.

and satisfaction fully comes to the fore when everyone is contributing in a commonly shared, harmonious fashion.

SKILLS

ESTJs are typically both highly gifted and skilled at anything having to do with logistics. They are masterful in getting the right things in the right place in the right quantity and the right quality at the right time and to the right people.

They are at their best when things work the way they are supposed to. To get to such a stage, they will be tough, usually tougher on themselves than their direct reports. Their level of expectation is uncompromising and as high as they can comprehend.

It is useful to realize that ESTJs are doers, movers and shakers. They like to get things done as efficiently and economically as possible within known systems and procedures. Therefore, it is unrealistic and inappropriate to assume that ESTJs derive a great deal of joy from theory and abstract concepts. Their contribution is to make things work and work well. Given the opportunity, they have to be outstanding implementers.

Keep in mind that efficiency (doing things right the first time) is a guiding light for ESTJs. Effectively doing the right things does not always rate as high in their minds. Consequently, ESTJs may perform beautifully in a project or assignment and be task oriented and focused upon getting the job done. They may ignore important aspects of communications with others such as relating to peers and others at work in a personal way.

For ESTJs, supervising is an external process. They are excellent at plan execution, assuring that their subordinates are doing what they are supposed to be doing.

ESTJs obtain results given their ability to be decisive and realistic.

CHARACTERISTICS

IMPLICATIONS

ESTJs have a well-developed capacity for understanding and knowing how an organization is supposed to function, and they make proper decisions and the adjustments necessary to maintain and enhance the overall efficiency of existing policies and procedures.

It is useful to understand that in the shadow of the great strength of ESTJs—that of delivering results and commanding the resources of an organization—is sometimes a lack of awareness of individual needs for personal warmth and more attention to the human side of enterprise. Indeed, ESTJs at times may be falsely judged as callous, cold and not understanding.

ESTJs are concrete and specific in their speech. ESTJs tend to provide specific, detailed, and relevant information, especially about the steps involved in achieving specific results.

Some other types may feel put down by such detailed instructions and get restive.

Their thought process is linear. They tend to be very focused and direct their thoughts toward problem-solving situations in a step-by-step linear fashion. In other words, their thinking process is one of building on cognitions, associations and blocks of sequential, orderly information, as opposed to concepts, in an intuitive, less structured manner.

DRIVING FORCE

ESTJs have a high need for security and stability. In order to establish such a state of affairs,

They have a strong need for control. Any effort which seeks to undermine or diminish their

CHARACTERISTICS

IMPLICATIONS

they will seek out the means to be in charge of their own destiny. Therefore, they are driven by opportunities to be responsible, accountable, and to acquire the necessary authority to enact and implement whatever they think is appropriate and fitting, given specific circumstances.

control is subject to a major reprisal from our administrative ESTJs.

ESTJs have a hunger for responsibility, leading them to take on more and more of it. They pride themselves on being accountable and they are compelled to always do their duty and follow through on their often self-imposed responsibilities.

It is difficult for ESTJs to observe, much less accept, irresponsible actions and attitudes. Theirs is a world of taking on and dutifully carrying out whatever responsibility is assigned to them. They are eager-to-please individuals who are results oriented and respect the goals and objectives to be attained by the organization and its sub-groups.

ENERGY DIRECTION

Given these beliefs, values and attitudes, ESTJs direct their energy toward setting things right and meeting the standards set by those whom they respect and who have the authority and proper experience to determine the correct course of action.

Expect ESTJs to quickly determine what needs to be done and then go do it. They are "take charge" individuals, and if their superiors fail to articulate clearly what is expected of them, ESTJs are not likely to demonstrate a great deal of warmth and understanding.

ESTJ

CHARACTERISTICS

IMPLICATIONS

Within the organization, their energy will be directed toward stability and the reinforcement of time-tested practices and procedures. This further enables the organization and its members to stabilize and derive a sense of belonging and comfort in the entities they rely upon to achieve their goals and aspirations.

ESTJs depend upon the organization to support individuals and groups in achieving their goals and performing their duties. If and when there is a systems failure or malfunction, do not be surprised if ESTJs can become quite disappointed, upset and stressed, even to the point of losing their ability to function properly.

They are cooperators, driven to establish and maintain the necessary regulatory processes to allow everyone to work both toward their own goals and, more importantly, the goals of the organization.

Originality is not important for ESTJs; being a team player, however, is. It is safe to assume that while ESTJs are often quite competitive, they will play by the rules and not attempt to take unfair advantage of anything or anyone by making up their own agenda.

ESTJs direct unlimited amounts of energy toward accomplishment. They have little or no patience with interruptions and interferences preventing the organization from living up to and attaining superior results.

For ESTJs, work is work and play is play. Therefore, do not expect them to take their work situation lightly. They are serious, goal oriented and highly motivated to make a team contribution. Moreover, do not expect them to become particularly enamored with visions and lofty unproven ideas at the price of achieving what is expected in the immediate future. That is not the natural modus operandi of an ESTJ.

ESTJ

CHARACTERISTICS

IMPLICATIONS

AUTHORITY ORIENTATION

ESTJs expect the person in charge to be obeyed and not questioned. Authority is granted often over time and by title and tenure.

ESTJs expect those in management positions to have earned their title over time and hence be qualified and capable of handling themselves in a professional and prudent fashion. Demonstrating the ability to handle the position is quite important for ESTJs. If, for whatever reason, a superior does not live up to their expectations, the work relationship is not likely to be successful over the long haul.

The ESTJ usually has little or no patience for those who question time-tested and proven authority.

In the eyes of an ESTJ, to question that which is established is a waste of time; rather, the challenge is to make use of the establishment.

ROLE PERCEPTION

ESTJs tend to be proactive in relationships, that is, they take the first step in defining the relationship. They do not hesitate at all to tell another person what they should or should not do.

It is expected that ESTJs are anything but passive in any situation. They like to know where they stand at all times, and only under unusual circumstances will they take a back seat in any conversation pertaining to them or in the establishment of role relationships. Moreover, it is quite normal for ESTJs to be assertive. In other words, they have a need to control the behavior of others through their own "take charge" behavior.

CHARACTERISTICS	IMPLICATIONS

CONFLICT RESOLUTION

ESTJs tend to confront those who do not conform to the rules, right or wrong.

ESTJs tend to have a very clear concept of what is right, wrong, proper, improper and appropriate in any given circumstance. Those attempting to deviate from standard operating procedures and high work ethics could find themselves on the wrong side of the ESTJ.

However, ESTJs may be put off by efforts to get to the source of the conflict, believing as they do that one should pull oneself up by one's boot straps and get on with carrying out one's assigned duty.

Do not expect ESTJs to demonstrate a great deal of psychological insight and understanding. Most of the time, for them the world can be only black and white - subtle shadings of gray may indeed be totally lost on them. Consequently, expect ESTJs to, in no uncertain terms, air their opinions if and when people do not conform to their personal sense of what is appropriate.

MODES OF LEARNING

ESTJs prefer to learn through concrete methods such as workbooks requiring memorization, recall and drill. They are linear thinkers. Moreover, they tend to be visual and concrete.

Consequently, a learning environment which best facilitates their acquisition of new knowledge and skills is more practical and applied than theoretical. Specific examples and comparisons make theories work better for them.

ESTJs have an ability to accurately observe quantities and excel at measurement.

Since their consciousness is concrete and specific, they may have difficulty recognizing that there

ESTJ

CHARACTERISTICS   IMPLICATIONS

is more to learning than that which can be quantitatively measured.

Sequencing is their natural organizing style.

Learning experiences which are properly sequenced provide them with the most success.

BLIND SPOTS AND PITFALLS

ESTJs may focus so much of their thought and energies on the task to be accomplished that they may subordinate the human element to attaining their own ambitious goals and objectives. Moreover, they may focus so much on systems, policies and regulations that they lose sight of individuals and their needs.

Individuals who are less concrete and performance oriented may unfairly judge ESTJs to be harsh and difficult to communicate with, or perceive them as insensitive.

It is important to understand that an ESTJ is a person who takes great pride in supporting, nurturing, and developing organizational frameworks with the sole intent of achieving the best possible results. Hence, do not be surprised if procedures and predetermined processes themselves become so important to them that they might lose sight of the fundamental purpose of what these were installed for in the first place.

It is useful to understand that their perspective is not one of being impersonal, cold, callous or lacking in human understanding. To the contrary, ESTJs care very much about people and their well being. Where they differ is in their belief that it is the organization itself which constitutes the vehicle to eternal happiness.

ESTJ

CHARACTERISTICS	IMPLICATIONS
ESTJs tend to work with a steady energy and may not have a great deal of patience with individuals who have a lower energy level or different work ethic.	They would benefit from understanding that others may not possess this ability and actually produce superior results in bursts of energy.
With their inner drive for responsibility and accomplishment, ESTJs may find it difficult to abstain from taking on more work than they should.	Consequently, it is not uncommon that they can become quite stressed—carrying a self-imposed overload.
Blind sided by their never-ending desire to achieve and attain results, preferably now, it is difficult for ESTJs to take time out and really listen to others.	They strive so hard to be efficient and do things right that at times they would benefit from a clearer focus on what is required to be effective (do the right things).
ESTJs enjoy making decisions when they have a good grasp on probabilities and possibilities for obtaining the results they want. Moreover, ESTJs at times make decisions too fast. People not performing, both in form and substance, to the standards or comfort level of an ESTJ are very likely to be criticized or, even worse, subject to ridicule by the offended ESTJ.	Often for them the tendency to expect others to be like themselves is so strongly in place it blinds them to other points of view. Know this: ESTJs could better themselves by slowing down their decision-making process.
ESTJs are so tuned in to what should be done and what the prescribed procedure is that they may not be responsive to the potentially changing needs in a given situation. Therefore, they may experience frustration and have trouble changing course.	Expediting - getting on with it - is important for an ESTJ. Do something - don't just stand there - tends to describe the modus operandi of an ESTJ. Don't be surprised, then, if there are times when the quality of ESTJ decisions suffers in the interest of time and expediency.

ESTJ

CHARACTERISTICS

IMPLICATIONS

ESTJs usually have a strong belief in good and bad. They tend to be blaming and negative when things do not go the way they should. As natural worriers, ESTJs may be overly concerned with the possibility of negatives.

ESTJs are steeped in tradition. They know what is right, wrong, good, bad, appropriate or inappropriate. People living and functioning outside of these norms of reality tend to be viewed anywhere from with utter distaste to a source of great irritation by the ESTJ.

Beauty for an ESTJ occurs when things work and work well.

Consequently, when someone tampers with systems and procedures, expect the ESTJ to be less than enthused and happy.

Their constant focus on concrete, specific data and significant details may "blind" ESTJs to the more subtle and abstract reasons behind why situations emerge, often in conflict with their own views and values.

They may be well advised to seek out information about the broader perspectives and subtle implications of a proposed action or decision, taking advantage of perspectives different from their own such as those of the NT, SP or NF.

They focus so much on facts, data and details and take such an objective stance that they may be experienced by others as hard, cold, calculating, lacking in insight and misunderstanding how others may be perceiving a given situation.

ESTJs may thus be misperceived as uncaring, insensitive, egotistical and driven to achieve only what they want when in fact they do care and they are vulnerable to criticism. Likewise, others may experience their objectivity as criticism and dislike. Frequently ESTJs could benefit from practicing active listening and acquiring a repertoire of "warm fuzzy" words and responses so that they can facilitate others in dealing with their respective realities.

CHARACTERISTICS	IMPLICATIONS

ISTJ

The theme of the ISTJ is inspecting, looking for discrepancies and omissions, and reporting these deviations from the set standards to the appropriate authority. ISTJs want to conserve the resources of the organization, group, family or culture and can be depended upon to persevere toward that goal.

CHARACTERISTICS	IMPLICATIONS

MANAGEMENT STYLE

The management style of the ISTJ is authoritarian and decisive. As a manager, the ISTJ expects others to follow the rules and procedures without question. Hierarchy is respected.

The ideal work environment is a stable and orderly one in which tasks are defined and everyone knows what is to be done, who is to do it and by what completion date.

ISTJs tend to manage in a predictable and formal way, focusing on the organization, because they are unusually loyal to the organization and the tasks to be performed. There are times when people feel subordinated to the ISTJ manager's high task orientation, which more often than not is unintended.

ISTJs focus extensively upon meeting objectives in a no-nonsense fashion; for this reason they may be perceived as uncaring and controlling. Indeed, they care a great deal about people but frequently find it awkward to express appreciation for work well done.

ISTJs run efficient meetings with an agenda, preferring things to be on time and on schedule.

They are annoyed when meetings bog down with too much process and they may tend to bypass some necessary wheel-greasing.

ISTJ

CHARACTERISTICS	IMPLICATIONS

Their commitment is to the establishment of stability. It is very important to ISTJs to have a sense that life will go on as it has and they consider it their duty to make sure the organization is preserved.

Thus they are likely to ask of a planned change, "Is it useful? Is it practical? Has it worked before?" Look for ISTJs to support a change. That change must not be perceived as a threat to the stability and preservation of the organization.

As leaders, they are sometimes called the "traditionalists," since they work to preserve traditions. ISTJs appreciate the value of rituals, ceremonies and celebrations in providing a sense of belonging and permanence in the organization.

If traditions do not abound in the organization, ISTJs will eventually create them. They require and create stability. Those traditions which survive with the passing of time are inherently stable. Tradition and stability go hand in hand.

ISTJs can be counted on to follow through and make sure necessary supplies and other things will be there for the job to be done.

They are likely to be quite disappointed when others do not follow through and may respond harshly.

ISTJs are very hard workers and willingly accept major responsibility. They hold themselves accountable and are quite trustworthy with anything that requires safekeeping.

Their strong sense of responsibility may lead them to take on too much work and get overloaded to the point of exhaustion.

ISTJs are quite dedicated to getting the job done and do so without fanfare.

This dedication may go unnoticed and unappreciated. The tendency for responsibly carrying a large work load combined with a lack of acknowledgment may from time to time lead to depression and excess fatigue.

CHARACTERISTICS	IMPLICATIONS
ISTJs are steady, dependable, loyal and dedicated workers. They keep to routines and schedules and expect others to do so as well.	They may be impatient with the less steady pace of others.
ISTJs tend to believe that appreciation must be earned and must not be given to those who fall short in dedication and efficiency.	They tend to ignore the small steps toward the goal or betterment and reward only those in "first, second and third place." They may need encouragement and coaching to give attention and praise to those who are not as visibly productive as they are.
When ISTJs must give feedback, the focus is on the necessity of getting back on course and how to correct deviations from the standard.	They need to learn that such feedback is most often perceived as criticism, resulting in lower productivity and a decline in the innovation that keeps the organization alive. Therefore, ISTJ managers are well advised to determine expectations prior to any performance - so no one is surprised and disappointed in a feedback session.
ISTJs are very loyal to the organization. Indeed, they will undertake even distasteful tasks for the good of the organization.	ISTJs can be depended upon to complete all assignments, for it is crucial to their sense of stability that their organization survive.
They like predictability and constancy in what they are required to do.	ISTJs are highly organized. Constancy allows them to maximize completing the task at hand. Changes, alterations and deviations interrupt their steady and direct focus.

ISTJ

ISTJ

CHARACTERISTICS

IMPLICATIONS

VALUES

ISTJs value the preservation of life, which almost always translates into economics as a way of satisfying needs. Conservation of the resources of the organization may be foremost in their minds. These values show in their focus on utility, production and not taking chances.

Abhorring poverty as they do, ISTJs are frequently financially successful. They know all too well the many nights when they worked until midnight. Hence, they expect and demand ample reward.

They trust authority, putting their faith in credentials. These credentials are earned by putting in the time to gain the experience or the education that gives a solid foundation.

They don't care as much about the rationale behind an event or a policy as about the authority to implement it. Likewise, they do not hold any respect or esteem for those who breach the rules, even if for good reason.

Belonging is important to ISTJs; thus you will find them as active participants in organizations, membership being one way to gain a sense of stability. If outside organizations are for some reason considered less important for ISTJ managers, expect a great deal of emphasis on membership in terms of family and selected life-long friends.

Do not expect working with ISTJ managers to be a roller coaster experience; to the contrary, expect the opposite - the salt of the earth, predictable, and what might be labeled as a "long-cycle" working relationship.

ISTJs also value ownership. They seek to possess and preserve objects as well as property.

Ownership provides a sense of stability and security, both qualities being of crucial significance for ISTJs.

They abhor dereliction of duty and would not even think of dis-

ISTJs are natural soldiers determined to see the job through to

CHARACTERISTICS	IMPLICATIONS
honoring a contract or not keeping their word.	the end. They can be quite harsh on those who change horses midstream and thus do not do their duty and keep their commitments.

ATTITUDE

The basic attitude of the ISTJ is one of fatalism: things are what they are and little can be done to change them.	Thus, the ISTJ is not easily persuaded to change things.
Hand in hand with this attitude of fatalism is an attitude of concern. ISTJs tend to be quiet, very serious and concerned about procedures and rules, especially when others are not doing their duty.	Sometimes this concern translates into excessive worry or the expectation of negative outcomes.
ISTJs tend to see things in black and white, and rarely in shades of gray.	Thus, the ambiguous and uncertain holds no fascination for them and indeed results in their getting bogged down and frustrated.

SKILLS

ISTJs are skilled at anything having to do with logistics and materiel. Getting things in the right place at the right time and in the right quantity and the right quality is a point of honor to them.	If you want ISTJ employees to give a superior performance, be sure the job provides opportunities for use of these quantitative and standardizing skills.

ISTJ

CHARACTERISTICS	**IMPLICATIONS**

ISTJs have a natural talent for taking nothing for granted and not reading more into a situation than is present; therefore, they are thorough in the inspection of contracts and documents of importance for the well-being of their organization.

Inspecting is an internal process for ISTJs. They are excellent at comparing a performance or product to a standard and do so with a thoroughness rare in the other types.

Their internal images of the standards are so strong that they feel very sure of their "rightness." This facilitates keen surveillance of quality control applying these standards.

ISTJs have a capacity for attention to detail and gathering facts. They are likely to handle complex figures and make sense out of them with ease.

One of the greatest gifts provided for ISTJs is that of measuring variance. Their affinity to register that something is out of place is highly developed.

ISTJs are concrete and specific in their speech. They tend to give sufficient information, especially about the steps involved in doing something.

More interested in the facts, they may ignore important implications of a communication.

Their thought process is linear and step-by-step rather than several things being processed at once and in no particular sequence.

Environments where things happen on many levels at once are stressful to them. ISTJs prefer to spend a little time and thoroughly assess a situation prior to making a decision.

DRIVING FORCE

ISTJs have a very high need for security and stability and the pathway to that stability is responsibility.

ISTJs thrive on responsibility. Rarely do they hesitate to take on more responsibility.

CHARACTERISTICS

IMPLICATIONS

ISTJs have a hunger for responsibility that leads them to take on more and more of it. They pride themselves on being accountable and must do their duty.

They are driven to fulfill their duty even when they must make many sacrifices to carry out responsibilities.

ENERGY DIRECTION

Given these skills, values and attitudes, ISTJs direct their energy toward observing discrepancies, omissions and deviations so as to conserve the resources (often financial) and meet the standards set by those with adequate experience and authority.

ISTJs have a keen sense for noting what others overlook. Even when they are not at work, their minds continue to churn in ways which benefit the organization.

Within the organization, an ISTJ's energy will be directed toward stability and preservation of the organization.

The blood within an ISTJ is opposite the blood of a revolutionary. A revolutionary tears down the old to pave the way for something different and new; an ISTJ places additional reinforcing rods in concrete which was set up years ago.

ISTJs are cooperators, driven to establish and maintain the necessary regulatory processes to allow everyone to work toward the goals of the organization.

They are cooperative as long as the interest and well-being of the organization is at heart. Anyone not playing by the rules may become focal points for their drive to correct deviations.

Turn ons are practical and "realistic" ways to get more production.

If you were to provide an ISTJ with incentives, they would have to be anchored in reality, tangible, tried and proven.

CHARACTERISTICS	**IMPLICATIONS**

Turn offs include having to work with "irresponsible people."

Do not be surprised if the ISTJ manager can be quite harsh and demonstrate disgust for low performance.

AUTHORITY ORIENTATION

The ISTJ expects the person in charge to be obeyed and not questioned. Authority is granted by title and tenure.

To question the authority of an ISTJ is to insult an ISTJ.

ISTJs have little or no patience for those who question authority.

They may need to listen at times to those who do question authority.

ROLE PERCEPTION

ISTJs tend not to take the first step in defining a relationship. Once the relationship is defined, they do not hesitate at all to tell another person what they should or should not do.

Consequently, do not expect the ISTJ to relish cold calling or any unstructured form of contact with people.

Even though quiet, ISTJs are quite comfortable providing structure and direction to others. In turn, they expect to be directed.

They are less likely to provide information without some sort of directive. Indeed, they find it unsettling when someone just gives them information and does not indicate the desired action.

ISTJs prefer relating with others from a position of strength.

They tend to think that those who do not take the initiative come from a position of weakness.

CHARACTERISTICS	**IMPLICATIONS**

CONFLICT RESOLUTION

ISTJs do not see it as their job to confront those who do not conform to the rules and who fail to distinguish between right and wrong. Rather, they report the deviation to the appropriate authority.

They **do** want the "deviants" to be confronted, and they may be forced to do the confronting themselves. If so, they may deal with them quite caustically.

However, they may be put off by efforts to get to the source of conflict, believing as they do that we should pull ourselves up by our bootstraps and carry out our duty.

ISTJs are not known for their patience in dealing with others' problems, especially when a conflict appears to have irresponsibility, impracticality and disloyalty at its base.

MODES OF LEARNING

ISTJs prefer to learn through concrete methods such as workbooks that require memorization, recall and drill where progress can be monitored and registered.

ISTJs shun abstraction. They respond as if the abstract world is untrustworthy and unreliable.

They have an ability to accurately observe quantities and excel at measurement. They learn faster if they are given concrete examples and comparisons.

Since the consciousness of ISTJs is concrete and specific, they may have difficulty recognizing that there are qualitative and abstract dimensions in any learning situation which may be equally important in broadening their awareness.

BLIND SPOTS AND PITFALLS

ISTJs may focus so much on the task of a situation that they may ignore the human element.

It may help them to see the perspectives of others as "facts" to be considered in making decisions.

CHARACTERISTICS	IMPLICATIONS

They may focus so much on rules and regulations that they lose sight of people needs.

From time to time ISTJs may need to be reminded to take time to listen to others without judgment.

Being so stability oriented, they may insist on procedures for procedures' sake and retain the procedures beyond their utility. They may not be responsive to the need for change.

ISTJs derive a sense of security from the tried and tested. Moreover, they would rather not learn new procedures, having mastered the ones they are accustomed to. If a change is deemed important, ISTJs may adjust better if it is presented in terms of the usefulness or practicality of the change.

ISTJs tend to work with a steady energy and may not have patience with those who do not.

ISTJs expect those they manage to exhibit reliable and persevering efforts at all times. They will feel more at ease if they can understand that those who work in bursts of energy are more productive that way.

With their extreme hunger for responsibility, ISTJs may have trouble saying no and may get overloaded. Since they are perfectionists, it may be difficult for them to delegate unless they have a great deal of confidence that their subordinate will follow through.

They may need to remind themselves to delegate and take on less themselves.

Since they have a strong belief in right and wrong, they may tend to be blaming and negative.

Yes, if you step out of line, the austere and serious ISTJs may reprimand on the spot.

CHARACTERISTICS	**IMPLICATIONS**
They may be overly concerned with the possibility of the negative.	There is a tendency to be too cautious, but the positive aspects of this trait frequently help them avoid snares before they happen.
Their focus on concrete data and details may make them "blind" to the more subtle factors in group behavior.	They may be well-advised to seek out information about the broader perspectives and subtle implications of a proposed action or decision (i.e., consult an NF on the implications of the values). They may well use outside facilitators when their group bogs down.
ISTJs focus so much on facts, data and details, and take such an objective stance, that they may be seen as cold.	They may thus be misperceived as uncaring when in fact they do care and they are vulnerable to criticism.
Likewise, others may take their objectivity as criticism and dislike. ISTJs are not noted for effusive interpersonal warmth.	They may benefit from practice in active listening and acquire a repertoire of "warm fuzzy" words and behaviors.
ISTJs tend to relatively quickly form a first impression of anyone they meet or work with. Whatever the impression, it tends to remain for a relatively long time.	Commitment to a self-constructed and imposed impression may be wrong - and to admit that can be quite painful for less enlightened ISTJs.

ISTJ

CHARACTERISTICS	IMPLICATIONS

ESFJ

The theme of the ESFJ is providing, making sure physical needs are met. ESFJs are genuinely concerned about the welfare of others, making sure they are comfortable and involved. They use their sociability to nurture established institutions. They are congenial, helpful, considerate, thoughtful and wish to please.

CHARACTERISTICS	IMPLICATIONS

MANAGEMENT STYLE

The management style of the ESFJ is softly authoritarian and decisive. As a manager, the ESFJ expects others to follow the rules and procedures without question. Hierarchy is respected.

The ideal work environment is a stable and orderly one, yet personal, in which tasks are defined and everyone knows what is to be done, who is to do it and by what completion date.

ESFJs manage in a personal way, focusing on harmony in the organization. They want people to fit in and be comfortable.

In an ideal environment, everyone would get along.

They pay attention to what people want and need. They are conscientious about responsibilities and tend to be orderly.

They may assume they **know** what people want based on what people usually want (the norm) and may need to be reminded to listen to others to find out what they really want.

Their commitment is to the establishment of stability, paying close attention to appearances and the opinions of others regarding acceptable social standards.

They are likely to ask of a planned change, "Is it useful? Is it practical? Has it worked before? Is it socially acceptable?" For them to support a planned change, it must be deemed appropriate.

ESFJ

ESFJ

CHARACTERISTICS	IMPLICATIONS
As leaders, ESFJs are sometimes called the "traditionalists," since they work to preserve traditions. They instinctively know the value of rituals, ceremonies and celebrations in providing a sense of belonging and permanence in the organization.	If traditions do not abound in the organization, ESFJs will create and nurture them with great gusto. Birthdays, company anniversaries and holidays are occasions for ceremony and celebration. Other rituals will be instituted as needed on a regular basis.
ESFJs can be counted on to follow through and will make sure necessary supplies and other things will be there for the job to be done.	They are likely to be quite disappointed and upset when others do not follow through and things do not go well. They may be critical and nagging.
Seeking responsibility, ESFJs are very hard workers. They frequently bring an abundance of energy to getting the job done.	Their strong sense of responsibility may lead them to take on too much work and get overloaded to the point of exhaustion.
ESFJs are steady workers.	They may be impatient with the less steady pace of other types, and may benefit from understanding that others are more productive when they work in bursts of energy.
ESFJs tend to believe that appreciation must be earned and must not be given to those who are not worthy.	They tend to overlook the small steps essential for obtaining a goal and reward only those in "first, second and third place." They may need coaching and official sanction to give attention and praise to the lesser achievers.

CHARACTERISTICS	**IMPLICATIONS**

The feedback most often given by ESFJs is that of getting back on course and how to correct deviations from the standard. They can be very blunt.

They need to learn that such feedback is most often perceived as criticism. This may reduce productivity and stifle innovation, both of which are needed to keep the organization growing.

ESFJs are very loyal to their superiors.

They become uncomfortable when a situation conflicts with their need to be loyal.

They like predictability and constancy in what they are required to do.

Uncertainty and the lack of specific and clear instruction are unsettling for an ESFJ.

VALUES

ESFJs value the preservation of life, which almost always translates into economics as a way of satisfying needs. These values show in their focus on making sure physical needs are met and on making life comfortable.

For them, everyone should have a comfortable home base and be happy.

They trust authority, putting their faith in credentials.

They don't care as much about the rationale behind an event or a policy as about the authority to implement it. Likewise, they do not hold any respect or esteem for those who breach the rules, even if for good reason.

Belonging is very important to ESFJs, and thus you will find them belonging to organizations, membership being one way to gain a sense of stability. Organizations provide a place where they can serve and help others.

They put emphasis on social ties. The joy of life is socializing with many lifelong friends.

ESFJ

CHARACTERISTICS	IMPLICATIONS
ESFJs also value ownership. They seek to possess and preserve objects as well as property.	This fulfills their need for roots, which is evident in their respect for tradition and appreciation of home.
They abhor dereliction of duty.	Thus, they are at the ready with "shoulds" and "should nots" so others also do their duty.

ATTITUDE

The basic attitude of the ESFJ is one of fatalism; things are what they are and little can be done to change them.	Believing this, ESFJs often require extraordinary persuasion to change things. Since they require stability, it takes time before they are supportive of efforts which seek to change the status quo.
For ESFJs, hand in hand with this attitude of fatalism is an attitude of concern. They are very serious and concerned about the future, particularly immorality and the disintegration of society.	Not only do ESFJs seek responsibility, they feel personally liable for whatever goes wrong. Hence, ESFJs view major changes and transitions as threatening—anything could happen. Thinking about the past invites gloom and doom if they take the blame for whatever might be wrong, as they are prone to do.
ESFJs rather like things to be definite and do not tolerate ambiguous situations well.	They are anxious to please and to do the right thing. When things are ambiguous, they do not know what is expected of them and can get quite upset.

ESFJ

CHARACTERISTICS | ## IMPLICATIONS

SKILLS

Like the other SJs, ESFJs are skilled at anything having to do with logistics, especially in the service occupations. They are masters at getting the right things in the right place in the right quantity and the right quality at the right time to the right people.

If you want ESFJ employees to give a superior performance, be sure the job makes adequate use of these quantitative and standardizing skills.

Their emphasis on "providing" is an external process. They are quite intent on knowing another's needs and providing for them. Thus they excel at selling tangibles and property.

They so personalize the sales process that buyers feel as if they are buying from the ESFJ, not from the company.

They are so outgoing and sociable that they can talk with anyone about anything, especially when it pertains to problems and events, rather than abstractions.

ESFJs are superb hosts and hostesses who expend energy to promote harmony.

The ESFJs are concrete and specific in their speech. They tend to give lots of information, especially about the steps involved in doing something.

More interested in facts and details, they may fail to recognize important subtle implications of conversation.

Their thought process is linear and step-by-step rather than with several things being processed simultaneously and in no particular sequence.

Complex and multi-faceted challenges may be stressful to ESFJs.

ESFJ

CHARACTERISTICS	IMPLICATIONS

DRIVING FORCE

ESFJs have a very high need for security and stability; the pathway to stability is responsibility.

The search for and acceptance of responsibility inevitably provides an opportunity for the welcome interaction with people.

ESFJs have a hunger for responsibility and being needed that leads them to take on more and more. They pride themselves on being accountable and must do their duty.

If they are not appreciated for who they are and all they do, they may spend a great deal of energy reassuring themselves or seeking reassurance. Without affirmation from others, ESFJs become despondent.

ENERGY DIRECTION

Given these skills, values and attitudes, ESFJs direct their energy toward the many shoulds and should nots that form their foundation for stability.

Shoulds and should nots provide needed order and structure for ESFJs.

Within the organization, their energy is directed toward stability and preservation of the organization. They do whatever is needed to keep the organization running.

ESFJs derive much satisfaction by serving and preserving the organization.

They are cooperators, driven to serve conscientiously and to promote harmony in the organization.

Perceived lack of cooperation can drive them up the wall.

Turn ons are the opportunities to help others and working with people who want to do likewise.

ESFJs are the happiest when their schedule is full and they are in the company of people.

CHARACTERISTICS	IMPLICATIONS

AUTHORITY ORIENTATION

ESFJs expect the person in charge to be obeyed and not questioned. Authority is granted by title and tenure.

For them, failure to comply with their authority is viewed as a personal assault.

ESFJs have little or no patience for those who question authority. They obey orders fervently.

They may need to listen at times to the objections of those who do question authority.

ROLE PERCEPTION

ESFJs tend to take the first step in defining the relationship. However, they hesitate telling another person what role to play. Rather, they give information.

This preference for giving information rather than defining roles can make them seem less structured than they really are. It can also draw them off task more than they would like.

CONFLICT RESOLUTION

ESFJs tend to avoid confrontation, preferring to ignore problems.

If their work requires too much confrontation, they may become ill.

Wanting a harmonious environment, they see little value in conflict.

They may need help in seeing how confronting conflict can increase harmony in the long run.

MODES OF LEARNING

ESFJs prefer to learn through concrete methods such as workbooks that require memorization, recall and drill. They also like cooperative, group processes with lots of contact with people.

Be clear, specific (show by example) and patient when giving instructions for tasks when they involve a series of sequential steps and conceptualization found in abstraction.

CHARACTERISTICS	IMPLICATIONS
They prefer a sequential, organized presentation with examples and comparisons.	When teaching an ESFJ a complex process, be sure to cover each step in sequence. Moving too quickly and conceptually will confuse them.
ESFJs have an ability to accurately determine quantities and excel at measurement. In fact, they prefer measurement to estimation.	Since their consciousness is concrete and specific, ESFJs may have difficulty recognizing those situations when there is more than can be quantitatively measured.

BLIND SPOTS AND PITFALLS

Their strong desire to please and provide for others may lead ESFJs to ignore their own needs.	If they learn to insist upon attendance to their own needs, they can prevent burnout. They may need official sanction for permission to take care of themselves before everyone else is taken care of.
They may focus so much on shoulds and should nots that they lose sight of what people really want and need.	They may need to be reminded to take time to listen to others.
Being so stability oriented, they may insist on procedures for procedures' sake. They may not be responsive to the need for change.	Change does not come easily for ESFJs. It requires adjustment—adjustment of shoulds and should nots, the adoption of new routines and the element of uncertainty—whether or not they will like the changes.
ESFJs tend to work with a steady energy and may not have patience with those who do not.	It may help if they understand that some other types accomplish more in their bursts of energy than when they are regimented.

CHARACTERISTICS	IMPLICATIONS
ESFJs expect their effervescence and warmth to be contagious.	They may be quite disappointed when it is not, and indeed find that it irritates some.
With their extreme hunger for responsibility and pleasing others, they may have trouble saying no and may get overloaded.	The foremost consideration for ESFJs is to do whatever it takes to maintain harmony. They wish to satisfy everyone's needs and thereby overextend themselves unintentionally.
Liking decisions and disliking delays, they may make decisions too fast without adequate data.	
They may be overly concerned with appearances and aware of status.	The sociability of ESFJs requires an eventful, attractive and upbeat life-style.
ESFJs are so focused on what should be done and what the prescribed procedure is that they may not be responsive to the needs of the situation.	When significant changes are inevitable, give advance notice to prepare them and take the necessary time to explain the pros and cons of upcoming modifications.
Since they have a strong belief in good and bad, they may tend to be blaming and negative.	Expect this most when there are transitions, disarray and uncertainty.
ESFJs may be overly concerned with the possibility of the negative.	It sometimes helps to question them in a Socratic way about the real possibilities of some negative event happening.

ESFJ

CHARACTERISTICS	IMPLICATIONS

ISFJ

The theme of the ISFJ is to protect and make sure that one's charges are safe from harm and any damage. Indeed, ISFJs are the caretakers who serve quietly without much fanfare or pomp and circumstance. They are unassuming, polite and tremendously devoted to doing whatever is necessary to ensure shelter and safety for those they are close to.

CHARACTERISTICS	IMPLICATIONS

MANAGEMENT STYLE

The management style of ISFJs is likely to be caring, rule oriented and quiet. They may tend to not insist that others follow through, however, as any form of discord or confrontation is quite unappealing to the peaceful, co-operative ISFJ manager. They expect others to follow the rules and procedures without unnecessary and uncalled for questions. Systems, procedures and organizational hierarchies are expected, respected and adhered to.

The ideal work environment is a stable, orderly and personal one in which tasks are defined and everyone knows what is to be expected and achieved and delivers specified results at a given point in time.

ISFJs manage in a kind, understanding and personal way, focusing on harmony and mutual support and achieving results through teamwork and a sense of mutual belonging.

An ideal environment is one where everyone gets along and enjoys mutuality, camaraderie and a sense of achieving results in a harmonious, mutually supportive and understanding fashion.

CHARACTERISTICS

IMPLICATIONS

ISFJs pay a great deal of attention to what people want and need. To do this job they are conscientious about their assigned responsibilities and tend to be very orderly, predictable and alert to the needs of their subordinates.

They may, sometimes in error, assume they know what people want based on what is customary. If ISFJ managers from time to time would take some time out and listen to others to find out what they really want, however, they may find that the overall effectiveness of the organization would be enhanced.

Their commitment is to the establishment of stability, paying close attention to the needs and the opinions of others regarding acceptable social standards as well as adhering to the appropriate work ethic.

They are likely to ask of a planned change, "Is it useful? Is it practical? Has it worked before? Is it socially acceptable?" Moreover, do not expect ISFJ managers to become all that excited about a great deal of change, especially if it is unanticipated. In fact, they can become downright stubborn if changes may cause disruption, uncertainty and unpredictability in their otherwise perfected world of work.

As managers, ISFJs are considered the "traditionalists" since they work to preserve traditions. They instinctively know the value of rituals, ceremonies and celebrations in providing a sense of belonging and permanence in the organization.

If traditions do not abound in the organization, ISFJs will create them through their highly developed sensitivity to the needs of people. The elements in the tradition they will seek to establish are always people-focused and executed in a kind, unassuming way. Birthdays will be remembered as will special occasions, such as anniversaries, marriages and new additions to the family.

ISFJ

CHARACTERISTICS

IMPLICATIONS

The management style of an ISFJ tends to be low key, conserving and tradition oriented.

Do not expect ISFJ supervisors to come up with incredible ideas and revolutionary concepts; rather, their style is one of supporting, assisting and enabling people to perform.

Above all, ISFJ managers are responsible and loyal to people they work with.

They are likely, however, to be quite irritated when others do not follow through. This irritation is not likely to be overtly expressed; rather it will take the form of interpersonal tension building into stressful situations.

An ISFJ manager is a person who is as dedicated to people as the organization itself. Once a human bond is in place, for it to deteriorate is not thinkable for the ISFJ.

ISFJs are attentive listeners and if they genuinely like the person they are dealing with, they will go out of their way to support and accommodate that individual. For an ISFJ, the element of time does not deteriorate a fundamentally strong and mutually supportive working relationship—twenty years later all the pieces are still there.

ISFJ managers tend to be highly "people" focused. They are magnificent in caring for others, especially those who harmoniously and without a great deal of fanfare fit into the team.

ISFJs tend to be doers. They like to get things done and enjoy working in an orderly and prioritized fashion. As can be expected, they usually enjoy excellent people skills, yet under pressure do not expect them to necessarily practice the humanitarian side of enterprise. When there is a job to be done

ISFJ

CHARACTERISTICS	IMPLICATIONS

<table>
<tr><td></td><td>and deadlines to be met, ISFJs can be sticklers for details and focus on results to the point of limiting their own people sensitivity.</td></tr>
</table>

They typically will ensure that each employee is provided with the necessary support to function well.

Hence, expect the ISFJ supervisor to secure the necessary supplies and staff to get the job done.

Seeking responsibility and opportunities to contribute, ISFJs are diligent, focused and energetic workers.

Their strong sense of responsibility may lead them to take on too much work and get overloaded to the point of exhaustion. Indeed, ISFJ managers tend to be so accountable and concerned that they can become quite stressed.

Their kind of energy is low key, disciplined and long cycled. In other words, ISFJ managers will not display big bursts of energy. Their strength is in tenacity and consistency.

ISFJs may be impatient with the less steady pace of other types. They prefer consistent and dependable co-workers, subordinates and managers. It behooves all individuals who work with ISFJs to put forth their best effort.

ISFJs tend to believe that appreciation must be earned. Anyone not pulling their weight and contributing their share to the overall good of the organization is not held in high esteem, and chances are ISFJ managers will not allow under performers to tarnish the image of their work unit.

They may tend to ignore the small steps toward the goal of betterment and thus reward only those in "first, second and third place." Hence, it may be appropriate for ISFJ managers to become aware of and give attention and praise to those who are less than the star performers.

ISFJ

CHARACTERISTICS

IMPLICATIONS

The feedback most often given by ISFJs is that of getting back on course and correcting deviations from standards. They can be quite blunt, especially with procrastinators.

Declining performers receiving corrective feedback may perceive it mostly as criticism, which in turn may result in further reduction of productivity and necessary innovation. It is also useful to keep in mind that ISFJs tremendously appreciate receiving positive feedback quietly and without fanfare.

ISFJs are unusually loyal to their superiors, subordinates and the overall organization.

Often they are so caring and responsible in establishing supportive interpersonal relationships that when conflict occurs, even outside of their immediate domain, ISFJs carry a great deal of concern for others on their shoulders.

ISFJs enjoy predictability and constancy in what they are required to do.

Organizations where the rules are constantly changing can be quite stressful for the ISFJ.

VALUES

ISFJs place a great deal of value on the preservation of life, which almost always translates into economics as a way of satisfying needs. In other words, they tend to allocate their resources toward maintaining and conserving whatever life provides.

Expect ISFJs to be very conserving of the time-tested values and traditional approaches to just about everything. It should not come as a surprise, therefore, that they at times are known to be kind of set in their ways to the point of being somewhat single-minded and stubborn.

ISFJ

CHARACTERISTICS	IMPLICATIONS
These values show in their focus on making sure the physical needs of others are met along with conserving resources and saving for the future.	They may expend a great deal of time and energy in saving and recycling physical resources.
ISFJs trust traditional authority, putting their faith in credentials and demonstrated capabilities.	They may not question or care as much about the rationale behind systems, procedures and policies as about the authority to implement them. Likewise, they do not hold much respect or esteem for those who breach the rules, even if the reasons could be well justified.
Membership is very important to them and thus you will typically find them belonging to humanitarian organizations which promote the continuation of the culture, the preservation of life.	ISFJs have a high sense of duty. As members of groups, they are very dedicated to the causes, leaders and purposes of the organization, especially as they contribute to a greater social order.
ISFJs also value ownership. They seek to possess and preserve objects as well as property.	While not particularly materialistic, the territorial imperative is an important dimension in the life of an ISFJ; to be "of a place" as opposed to "from a place" is very significant for the ISFJ.
ISFJs abhor dereliction of duty.	For them, dereliction of duty is tantamount to committing the unpardonable sin and they will remember it a long time.

ISFJ

CHARACTERISTICS	IMPLICATIONS

ATTITUDE

The basic attitude of the ISFJ is one of fatalism: things are what they are and little can be done to change them. Indeed, attempting to alter the state in which ISFJs find themselves may be viewed as tampering with the essence of life itself and probably should be off limits.

Since ISFJs expect things to not be changeable, they put little credence in efforts to change the way things are. It is therefore natural and congruent for the ISFJ to adapt to circumstances as opposed to attempting to change them.

As a natural extension of being fatalistic, ISFJ managers tend to be concerned with just about everything. While not with negative intent, a fairly typical trait of ISFJs is to expect for things not to always work out, so they tend to prepare for something less than the very best.

Hopefully, it should not come as a surprise that ISFJs have a built in proclivity to become stressed. Therefore, it is quite appropriate to assure as much as possible that ISFJs not be put in an overload situation simply because they may literally suffer damage.

When ISFJs believe in something or someone, they may not be all that open for reassessing their situation, for they are certain of their beliefs and do not care to challenge or question their often deep-seated beliefs and attitudes.

ISFJs have been known to be somewhat defensive about these beliefs.

They have little tolerance for ambiguity and want a degree of certainty in their lives.

It helps to let them know exactly what is expected of them.

It is not uncommon for ISFJs to carry the sins of the world on their shoulders; and they easily

Also, realize that ISFJs tend to be rather unassuming people, often working behind the scenes

ISFJ

CHARACTERISTICS	IMPLICATIONS
accept the blame for malfunctions and mistakes, even if they did not play a part in creating adverse conditions.	without a great deal of publicity, announcing their concern and sometimes bothersome state only when things do not work out.

SKILLS

Like the other SJs, ISFJs are skilled at anything having to do with logistics, especially in the service occupations. They are masterful in getting the right things in the right place in the right quantity and the right quality at the right time to the right people.	If you want ISFJ employees to provide a superior performance, arrange for opportunities to use some of these quantitative and standardizing skills.
Protecting for ISFJs is a quiet, internal process. They are quite intent on being needed and taking care of the needs of others. They excel at service occupations, easily executing routines.	ISFJs tend to be highly dependable team players, and they unflinchingly exceed the call of duty. When work is not enjoyable, rarely will an ISFJ complain.
They serve with gentleness and care, relating well to people in need of help.	ISFJs are genuine in their concern and their feelings are readily evident through the action they take.
ISFJs are concrete and specific in their speech. They tend to give lots of information, especially about the steps involved in doing something.	They prefer to be given step-by-step instructions rather than a general direction.
Their thought process is linear and step-by-step rather than with	Understand, therefore, that working in an environment with

CHARACTERISTICS

IMPLICATIONS

several things being processed at once and in no particular sequence.

Perhaps the most significant characteristics brought into any work environment by ISFJs are their commitment and tenacity. It may take some time before they come around to fully joining up and investing their total person, as it were, to an organization. Once that threshold is reached, however, there is no pulling back.

DRIVING FORCE

The ISFJ has a high need for security and stability and the pathway to that state is responsibility. Consequently, an ISFJ manager will tend to seek more responsibility, especially in the area of managing people.

ISFJs have a hunger for responsibility and being needed that leads them to take on more and more. They pride themselves on being accountable and feel obligated to fulfill their assigned duties.

multiple focal points can be disturbing and frustrating for the ISFJ.

Consequently, ISFJs tend to be exceptionally dedicated to making organizations to which they are committed work, and they know practically no limit for the contribution they are willing to make. With dedication tends to come a protestant work ethic attitude.

It follows, then, that the ISFJs are not the greatest risk takers in this world. Proof of anything takes time and an ISFJ is not about to flame up in excitement.

Their efforts are frequently taken for granted. If they are not appreciated for themselves and all they do, they may inwardly feel resentful, leading to much suffering. If too deprived, they can even become depressed or at worst physically ill.

ISFJ

CHARACTERISTICS	IMPLICATIONS

ENERGY DIRECTION

Given these skills, values and attitudes, ISFJs direct their energy towards humble service and being team players.

The conditions under which ISFJs will function at their very best are characterized by a non-threatening environment where no one needs to function in a one-upmanship fashion. The team concept is important and has a very real sense of significance for the ISFJ. Achieving goals and aspirations as a team is far more important to the ISFJ than relying on the brilliance of a few.

Within the organization, their energy will be directed toward stability and preservation of the organization by protecting others.

A very real sense of satisfaction for ISFJs comes from knowing that everything works, there are no surprises, and life at work is predictable and stable. As support staff, they will diligently protect the resources of the company, including the time and energy of their superior.

Expect the ISFJ to direct all available energies in a positive and constructive direction.

Being so absorbed in making a contribution, the ISFJ manager may, from time to time, work too hard and not necessarily all that smart.

ISFJs are cooperators, driven to serve conscientiously and to put in long, hard hours to get the job done.

They execute routines with a great deal of ease and rarely view work as drudgery.

CHARACTERISTICS

IMPLICATIONS

The biggest, most significant turn on for them is the opportunity to help others.

This provides ISFJs with a great deal of satisfaction and a very real sense of being a meaningful contributor.

AUTHORITY ORIENTATION

ISFJs expect the person in charge to be obeyed and not questioned. Authority is granted by title and tenure. They have little or no patience for those who question authority, and they obey orders, usually without question.

The top priority is devotion and loyalty to the boss. Even though ISFJs respect authority, they may overstep any rule which conflicts with their requirement to back up their boss. They may need to listen at times to those who do question authority.

The ISFJ has a great deal of respect for individuals and institutions with a proven track record. People who are recognized for their expertise are frequently admired by the ISFJ.

In the mind of an ISFJ, competency is a matter of past performance and not a future promise. Those having paid their dues from an educational, achievement or organizational point of view are likely to evoke positive sentiments in an ISFJ type.

ROLE PERCEPTION

ISFJs tend to be reactive in interpersonal relationships; they wait and expect someone else to take the first step in defining any kind of relationship. As a result, they hesitate to tell another person what role to play; they are much more comfortable providing information and waiting for the roles to be assigned and then inform of their willingness to play an assigned role.

ISFJs are sympathetic listeners. They are supportive in relationships and make minimal demands on others. They much prefer giving information rather than forceful directives.

ISFJ

CHARACTERISTICS	IMPLICATIONS

CONFLICT RESOLUTION

ISFJs tend to avoid confrontation, preferring to sort of look the other way and ignore problems. However, should anyone strive to undermine their boss, ISFJs will defend their superior to the utmost.

If their work requires a great deal of confrontation, they will make every effort to avoid negative circumstances. If these persist, ISFJs can become physically ill.

Wanting a harmonious environment, ISFJs view conflict as counter productive, and to be avoided at all costs.

They may need help in understanding how confronting conflict can increase harmony in the long run; yet, do not expect an ISFJ to readily accept this premise.

MODES OF LEARNING

ISFJs prefer to learn through concrete methods such as workbooks that require memorization, recall and drill. Indeed, ISFJs are linear learners.

They are specific and looking for concrete payoff in anything they undertake from a learning point of view. Utility in what they learn is quite important to them.

They have an ability to accurately assess quantities and excel at measurement.

Since the consciousness of ISFJs is concrete and specific, they may have difficulty recognizing that there is more than can be quantitatively measured. Moreover, theories and abstract ideas tend not to be all that enjoyable for them.

Even though they focus on the facts, they will learn faster if given examples that allow them to personalize what is presented

CHARACTERISTICS

IMPLICATIONS

and compare it to past experiences.

BLIND SPOTS AND PITFALLS

Their strong desire to serve and protect may lead ISFJs to ignore their own needs. They may have difficulty saying no.

Therefore, encouraging them to attend to their own needs may prevent them from early burnout. It may help for a higher authority to give them permission to say no.

Also, do not be surprised if ISFJs from time to time may turn out to be quite stubborn.

Their loyalty to what works and has been in place for years is higher than the untested, unproven ideas about the future.

They may focus so much on the shoulds and should nots that they lose sight of what people really want and need.

Even though the boss is listened to very carefully, ISFJs may need to be reminded to take time to listen to others as well.

Being stability oriented, ISFJs may insist on procedures for procedures' sake and continue with procedures beyond their utility. Not surprisingly, they may not be all that responsive to the need for change.

ISFJs are particularly gifted in bringing about conditions of mutuality and stability. Since they invest so much of themselves in attaining such an idealistic state, it follows that any kind of change may threaten what exists and therefore produce resentment.

ISFJs tend to work with a steadfast energy; therefore, they may not have patience with those who direct their energies in a more erratic fashion.

It helps them to understand that other types can produce more by following their own rhythm of working in bursts of energy.

CHARACTERISTICS	IMPLICATIONS
They may put too much value on external appearances and be too aware of status.	ISFJs are aware of status, but they do not directly require to be in the limelight. Rather, they often are a bastion of support and untiring encouragement for someone who is in the limelight, and in that process they may be overlooked and taken for granted.
Since they have a strong belief in good and bad, they may tend to be blaming and negative.	ISFJs have definite opinions; they do not vacillate in their beliefs and the intensity of their feelings will invariably increase when unjustifiably accused of any unintentional wrongdoing.
They may be overly concerned with the possibility of the negative.	Consequently, in a threatening and ambiguous situation, an ISFJ may accentuate the negative aspects, anticipating that whatever can go wrong will happen—and when it does, it may just become a self-fulfilling prophecy.
There may be times when ISFJs become so protective and dedicated to people they serve in one capacity or another that they fail to understand and realize broader and more strategic perspectives.	Over time, ISFJs build a great deal of loyalty and superb interpersonal relationships. When these bonds take precedence over developing the potential of the overall organization, ISFJ managers may cause themselves some unintended damage.

ISFJ

CHARACTERISTICS

IMPLICATIONS

ISFJs naturally and instinctively are so considerate of people and their feelings that they fail to confront anyone or anything—even on a friendly, supportive basis.

Finally, it should not be forgotten that ISFJs may at times find it difficult to actually communicate what they would like to, particularly in adverse circumstances. Being polite and considerate may overrule the desire to take action.

ISFJ

CHARACTERISTICS	IMPLICATIONS

ENTJ

The theme of the ENTJ is commanding. ENTJs devise strategy, provide structures, establish plans, sequence events, and direct others in reaching the goals dictated by the vision of the organization. They are the natural organization builders and cannot not lead.

CHARACTERISTICS	IMPLICATIONS

MANAGEMENT STYLE

The management style of ENTJs is likely to be action oriented. They are the visionaries who communicate a vision of how the organization can change, marshalling the human and material forces to achieve future goals and objectives.

The ideal corporate structure is one in which they are provided with opportunities to take command and guide the organization toward solutions to distant significant goals.

ENTJs typically take charge and command with such assurance that others usually follow easily (unless they are so highly conceptual that would-be followers become concerned about a lack of realism). ENTJs expect others to autonomously and independently implement outlined plans.

They may be disappointed and even baffled when others do not act as independently as they themselves do. Moreover, individuals incapable of demonstrating some capacity for contributing toward the future may find themselves left behind in the dust.

Although preferring to be in charge and soaring with the eagles, they can be team players if that is what it takes to get the job done, for the focus is on efficiency, i.e., get the most for the least.

Team playing will not be for its own sake and will be readily abandoned when no longer efficient and effective.

ENTJ

CHARACTERISTICS	IMPLICATIONS

ENTJs like to make decisions and, as managers, their focus is on policy and goals and a vision of where the organization is going. They are keenly aware of the inner workings of the whole organization and its various subsystems.

Consider the typical ENTJ manager a "trail blazer" - even if at times the trail does not lead in the general direction of the rest of the organization.

ENTJs abhor redundancy and hesitate to state the obvious, so their communications are frequently terse, and they assume that they are understood. While they may communicate the essential aspects of their vision, they may leave others in the dark about the details of the vision and, as a result, they are sometimes considered quite arrogant.

They often need to pay special attention to spell out the details of their vision or work with someone who can assist them. Sometimes they are puzzled that others do not pick up as fast as they do; and when they experience resistance, doubt and hesitation, they can become quite frustrated.

Rationalizing that praise may appear redundant and obvious, ENTJs may not give praise and feedback as often as others need it. If the truth were known, it may be that they are embarrassed by praise, both in giving and receiving it.

They may need to be coached on how to show appreciation to others. They can easily see that praise is needed if they know the practical value of it, but they may need reminding.

While empty praise turns them off, ENTJs do value feedback from someone whom they judge to be competent to give it. They want to know when their ideas worked and their efforts yielded results.

The praise givers may not see the impact of their positive comments to the ENTJ. Do not be discouraged. Keep those positive comments coming.

ENTJ

CHARACTERISTICS	IMPLICATIONS

It helps to apologize ahead of time for asking ENTJs to repeat themselves or to explain a phenomenon in a different manner.

ENTJs are frequently impatient with errors, snarled messes, covering ground already covered and other signs of inefficiency.

They tolerate prescribed procedures only when they contribute toward the goals of the organization.

It is an especially attractive and productive environment that allows ENTJs to take charge and devise strategies for whatever arena can be theirs. Don't expect their strategies to be constant for very long since they are always in search of new and better ways to achieve goals.

VALUES

ENTJs value the theoretical, wanting insight, understanding, comprehension, knowledge, genius and precision.

They may ask incessant questions, especially "why" questions, and are not afraid to split hairs. They disagree intellectually and keep debates going not because they necessarily want to "win" - rather, their appetite for knowledge is insatiable.

They seek efficiency, i.e., getting the most for the least effort in all that they are associated with.

They are ready to abandon anyone and anything that is not efficient, and they are known for not having a very long fuse.

ENTJs trust logical reasoning above all.

Be prepared to offer them the rationale behind an event or a policy and understand that they seldom can accept anything merely for what it is.

They abhor a lack of willpower.

ENTJs expend great energy; they expect those in their association to do likewise.

CHARACTERISTICS	IMPLICATIONS

ATTITUDE

The basic attitude of ENTJs is one of, "There's got to be a better mouse trap." While they are always open to new ideas, they tend to be skeptical of their validity until logically proven otherwise.

Expect them to question anything and everything. Yet when in pursuit of a new idea or concept, they can demonstrate a great deal of tenacity in order to learn and find out. While others experience hindrances as stumbling blocks, ENTJs typically view them as stepping stones.

Usually they find the ambiguous fascinating and seek clarity.

However, they may be overly driven to seek clarity in the face of extreme ambiguity or they may block and become paralyzed by their view of the whole and all its parts.

SKILLS

ENTJs are skilled at analysis, recognizing conceptual differences and creating categories. As strategists, they map out all feasible events well in advance, developing an action agenda, a well thought out outline and an overall scheme. They build models, often theoretical ones, to solve complex problems, enigmas and riddles and get people to work toward goals.

If you want ENTJ employees to give a superior performance, just turn them loose to develop a strategy to solve a complex problem or implement a change; provide them with informal assurance and positive feedback, as they usually are ahead of everyone else in attempting to understand causes and reasons.

Not surprisingly, ENTJs enjoy bringing an organization to a point where it delivers superior performance.

Don't expect them, however, to be disciplined day-to-day routine operators. They easily become bored and impatient when their imagination is left in a holding pattern.

ENTJ

CHARACTERISTICS

IMPLICATIONS

ENTJs are adept logicians.

In conversations where reasoning and logic are replaced by emotions, ENTJs typically are at a loss. For them, reasoning is reality and sentiments and feelings are very difficult to deal with.

Commanding for ENTJs is an external process, taking command in response to the needs of the organization and the lack of order they perceive around them.

Some ENTJs tend to manage by being controversial. Other ENTJs strive to manage by listening and making "strategic arrangements."

In their never-ending pursuit to achieve their goals, ENTJs marshal the forces. They have a knack for enlisting the aid of others toward the organization's goals.

When called upon to turn things their way, they can be quite surprised by negative reactions and resistance, because they usually experience themselves as being "right on."

ENTJs are precise in their speech. They are adept and energetic conversationalists and speak with wit and plays on words. Easily tracking the complex verbalizations of others, they quickly notice inconsistencies in language, contradictions and shifts in position.

Their number one focus speechwise is to get to the point, and get to it as efficiently as possible. Wasting words and time to the ENTJ is to demonstrate disrespect for others.

DRIVING FORCE

ENTJs have a high need for achievement. However, achievement is typically measured by standards set by them, not by society or the organiza-

Performance feedback and reprimanding that takes this need into account will be much more effective. ENTJs are their own worst critics and already

ENTJ

CHARACTERISTICS	IMPLICATIONS
tion. Their achievement need is reflected in a constant drive for competency and an ever present, even if hidden, fear of failure.	know their "errors" and short-comings. As a result, they are usually quite open to criticism - as long as it is impersonal and to the point.
Their standards for achievement are constantly escalating for self and for others.	At times they may need to be gently reminded of their overly high expectations.

ENERGY DIRECTION

Given these skills, values and attitudes, ENTJs direct all their energy toward acquisition of knowledge, competencies and implementation of their vision of how things can be.	If not given the opportunity to constantly learn, they are likely to lose interest, look depressed, or eventually create their own learning opportunities.
Energetic and tireless in their work, ENTJs are devoted to ac-curacy and precision, especially in charting the actions needed to reach the goal.	Expect them to reject and chal-lenge that which is inaccurately presented and based on inferior data.
They hunger for problems to solve - the more complex, the better - and when they are in pursuit of achieving great and important goals and objectives, the word "no" loses all signifi-cance.	If ENTJs do not have problems to solve, they will make some or will take on someone else's problems. Uninvited, they may readily offer solutions, for it is painful for them to see problems in the organization and not be permitted to solve them or to contribute to their solution.
Within the organization, their energy will be directed toward change and the development of long-range strategies to effect that change.	ENTJs are organization build-ers, especially when circum-stances are changing and there is a high need for their work envi-ronment to be prepared for fu-ture challenges.

ENTJ

CHARACTERISTICS	IMPLICATIONS
Turn ons are logic, calm atmosphere, justice, coherence, accuracy, and a sense of moving away from what is to what can become.	Turn offs are over-emotionalizing, exaggeration and unbridled imagination - all of which represent inaccuracy and "soft" approaches to problems which can in the mind of the ENTJ be solved by logic.

AUTHORITY ORIENTATION

ENTJs want the person in charge to be knowledgeable and competent. Authority is not granted by position. They will question authority and test it, especially in their own area of expertise. Of all the NTs, the ENTJ is most likely to take charge.	If the person in charge is not seen as knowledgeable and competent, there is little hope of getting ENTJs to accept their performance feedback as something worth paying attention to. They may follow orders and direction if they have something to fear such as loss of their job, but they won't do it nearly as well as what they do naturally, and may even "forget" or "bungle."

ROLE PERCEPTION

ENTJs tend to be proactive in relationships, that is, they take the first step in defining the relationship. Like a commander, they do not hesitate to give directions.	Basically, ENTJs do not have enough patience to wait around until someone else decides what steps to take. Sometimes, however, they would be well-advised to invite the respondents to take the initiative.
ENTJs tend to be competitive, sometimes just for the fun of it, and while others are bent on winning, the ENTJ seems to enjoy the process more than the final outcome.	It is useful to understand that ENTJs tend to be "big picture" people. Details, routines and specifics are left to others - sometimes arrogantly considered to be lesser souls.

ENTJ

CHARACTERISTICS	IMPLICATIONS

CONFLICT RESOLUTION

ENTJs enjoy a lively debate and may be quite outspoken, but overall they prefer an atmosphere of calm and self-control. Conflicts are to be resolved logically and rationally and emotionalism avoided.

They may have to be reminded to take care of their feelings and others' feelings, rather than insisting on cool logic. Failure to allow some expression of feeling may indeed result in exactly what they were trying to avoid - emotional outbursts. Active listening is a skill they would do well to master and use.

MODES OF LEARNING

ENTJs learn by conceptualizing, abstracting common properties and developing categories. They are adept at learning abstract ideas and less adept at learning by association and rote.

Sometimes their fear of failure can be their own worst enemy and may inhibit learning, especially if they have an audience or peer group which could assess them as not being very competent.

BLIND SPOTS AND PITFALLS

The ENTJ may overlook the human element in the drive for action that will achieve the goal.

ENTJs are intolerant of "nonsense." Again, some tolerance could be cultivated and put to good use.

They can be bitingly critical and sarcastic and may be seen as cold and distant.

ENTJs may resist efforts at coercion.

Be sure to "manage" them by using their drive for autonomy rather than resisting it.

ENTJ

CHARACTERISTICS

IMPLICATIONS

If they are overwhelmed by a fear of failure, they may prefer to plan rather than act and may develop detailed plans of what they are going to do. More often, however, they may prefer decisive action to careful consideration of all sides of an issue.

ENTJs may be impatient with others who see a need for further reflection and research. Indeed, once "the jury is in," they are not exactly known for re-surfacing and re-thinking decisions. There is always a sense of urgency and a desire to "get on with it." Anyone or anything disrupting their need and desire to expedite, even though it would improve the situation, may be in for some heavy going as the ENTJs of this world always seem to have a self-imposed sense of urgency, sometimes at the cost of perfection.

Sometimes for the sake of the success of the project, they might tie themselves to a chair in order to allow the reflection necessary for perfection.

They may be intellectual snobs, with little patience for those less endowed with abstract intelligence.

Anytime ENTJs have determined that another person lacks in "smarts" or intelligence, do not expect them to display a great deal of understanding and compassion.

They find bureaucracy frustrating, with protocol and paperwork a waste of time that could best be spent planning.

Again, be prepared to offer them the logic or rationale behind the standard operating procedures. Don't expect them to take anything on faith or on "authority."

ENTJ

CHARACTERISTICS	IMPLICATIONS
They may put more faith in the "model," the probable sequences needed to achieve the goal, than the reality of the situation. Thus they may ignore some of the practical factors involved in implementing their vision.	It is essential for them to have a support staff and team members who have a more concrete, practical orientation unless they want to spend a lot of extra time and energy operating out of their "short suit."

ENTJ

CHARACTERISTICS	IMPLICATIONS

INTJ

The theme of the INTJ is planning. INTJs devise strategy, give structure, establish complex plans and outline sequences of events in reaching distant goals dictated by a strong vision of the organization. They thrive on putting theories to work and are open to any and all ideas that can be put to use.

CHARACTERISTICS	IMPLICATIONS

MANAGEMENT STYLE

The management style of INTJs is likely to be planning oriented. They are the visionaries who find applications for theories and models to achieve long-range goals and outline all of the steps necessary to get there.

The ideal corporate structure is one in which they have opportunities to devise and implement long-range strategies aimed at the efficient and effective use of the resources of the organization.

The fiercely independent INTJ prefers autonomy and expects others to act autonomously and independently to implement the outlined plan. INTJs tend to have a real sense of urgency, especially when learning and implementing new concepts.

They may be disappointed and even baffled when others do not act as independently as they do themselves.

They are ruthlessly single-minded in their work toward achieving the goal and, truth be known, the relation of "boss-subordinate" is not as important to them as is being competent, knowledgeable and insightful.

Due to their seemingly unbending desire to improve, achieve and significantly contribute, they can fall out of touch with reality. Indeed, they may be bent on making things so much better in the future that they fall out of touch with the "here and now."

INTJ

CHARACTERISTICS	IMPLICATIONS
Although preferring privacy and autonomy, INTJs can be team players if that is what it takes to get the job done—for the focus is on efficiency.	They particularly enjoy small teams where each member makes a significant contribution.
INTJs like to make decisions carefully, and as managers their focus is on goals and a vision of where the organization is going. They are keenly aware of the inner workings of the whole organization and its various subsystems. Above all, they trust their ability to rely on logic in any decision making situation.	When it comes to significant decision making, INTJs are able to combine the big picture and applicable particulars perhaps better than any of the sixteen types.
They tend to be quite loyal to the organization and the ideas they are pursuing to improve.	Loyalties are to the efficiencies in the system, not the specific people nor anything which resembles red tape and bureaucracy.
INTJs abhor redundancy and hesitate to state the obvious, so their communications are frequently terse, and they assume they are understood.	Consequently, INTJs at times are experienced as secretive and non-communicative, giving the appearance of being covert in their pursuit of whatever they are attempting to achieve.
While they may communicate the essential aspects of their vision, INTJs may leave "lesser souls" in the dark about the details of the vision.	Sometimes against their natural inclination, they may need to pay special attention to spell out the details of their vision or work with someone who can do that for them. And when they do, they may tend to be so conceptual that the translator may find it difficult to translate ideas into meaningful work.

INTJ

CHARACTERISTICS

IMPLICATIONS

Rationalizing that praise may appear redundant and obvious, INTJs may not give praise and feedback as often as others need it. If the truth were known, it may be that they are embarrassed by giving and receiving praise.

They may need to be coached on how to show appreciation to others. They can understand that praise is needed when they know the practical value of it, but they may need reminding—and if they don't take into account the realities of less conceptual types, they easily come across as quite arrogant.

INTJs are frequently impatient with errors, snarled messes, covering ground already covered and other signs of inefficiency.

It helps to apologize ahead of time when asking INTJs to repeat themselves.

INTJs tolerate prescribed procedures only if they are efficient in contributing toward the goals of the organization; if not, they will pass the bureaucracy in the fast lane—very quickly.

It is an especially productive environment that supports their autonomy with opportunities to devise and implement the strategies they so clearly seem able to articulate, but at times find difficult to implement.

VALUES

INTJs value the theoretical, seeking insight, understanding, comprehension, knowledge, genius and precision.

They may ask incessant questions, especially "Why?," "How come?" and "I know that's the way you have done it for a long time—give me one good reason why it is good for the future?"

They also prefer communication which is precise, to the point and not superfluous.

Individuals not getting quickly to the point and using language as a "packaging device" get tuned out.

INTJ

CHARACTERISTICS	IMPLICATIONS
INTJs seek efficiency, i.e., getting the most for the least effort in all that they are associated with. Once they understand how to improve on anything, they are willing to put forth high energies to make whatever they have designed work. When it becomes routine and systems are established, INTJs prefer to disappear.	They are ready to abandon anyone and anything that is not efficient and feel compelled to implement changes that lead to more efficient practices and procedures.
INTJs trust logical reasoning above all.	Be prepared to offer them the rationale behind an event or a policy and be prepared to split hairs.
They abhor a lack of willpower.	INTJs seem to be able to muster enormous willpower. They experience frustration in observing those who refuse to exercise willpower.

ATTITUDE

Their basic attitude is one of skepticism. While ISTJs are open to new ideas, they may be doubtful of their validity and utility, until proven otherwise.	Expect them to be skeptical of anything and everything and if they can improve on what is, they will.
INTJs find confusion fascinating and insist upon clarity. They may be driven to seek clarity in the face of extreme ambiguity or they may block and become paralyzed by their view of the whole and all its parts.	INTJs are obsessed with having a special kind of power; they want and need power over nature. They cannot accept any phenomenon at face value. They need and want to know why things are. Even then, do not expect them to readily accept anything.

INTJ

CHARACTERISTICS   **IMPLICATIONS**

SKILLS

INTJs are skilled at analysis, seeing differences and creating categories. As strategists, they map out all feasible events well in advance, developing an agenda, a well thought out outline, and an overall scheme. They build models, usually theoretical models, solve complex problems, enigmas and riddles. Their focus is on translating theories into actualities.

If you want INTJ employees to give a superior performance, turn them loose to develop a strategy to solve a complex problem or implement a change. Indeed, they are masterful in turning past failures into formidable success stories. Their ability to foresee is highly developed.

Planning for an INTJ is an internal process in which all of the contingencies are covered and there is a backup for every proposed action.

Since INTJs tend to work internally, so to speak, with concepts, ideas and "what if" scenarios, they may come across as somewhat mystical, unpredictable and non-communicative. The reason is obvious: the mind of an INTJ is one of probing and testing—knowing that nothing is constant. Communicating with INTJs, then, at times can be quite challenging and sometimes frustrating, as they instinctively want to change and improve on anything they are confronted with.

INTJs are precise in their speech. Easily tracking the complex verbalizations of others, they notice inconsistencies in language, contradictions and shifts in position.

Their verbal skill combined with their original thinking contributes to their success. On the other hand, INTJ managers can become so obsessed with a specific issue and how to untie some Gordian knot that they lose a holistic perspective.

INTJ

CHARACTERISTICS	**IMPLICATIONS**

DRIVING FORCE

The INTJ has a very high need for achievement. However, the achievement is most often measured by standards set by the INTJ, not by society or the organization.

Not surprisingly, then, INTJs hunger for constant evaluation and reevaluation. They are always ahead of everyone in thinking about issues of the future and being open to change; they tend to appreciate comments and new ideas, allowing them to continue in their never-ending exploration.

This achievement need is reflected in a constant drive for competency and an ever present, even if hidden, fear of failure.

Performance feedback and reprimanding that takes this need into account will be much more effective. INTJs are their own worst critics and will already know their "errors" and shortcomings.

Frequently, what an INTJ is attempting to achieve may not be commensurate with what is practically obtainable.

Therefore, it can be of great benefit to the INTJ to reality check with the more practical sensing types.

Their standards for achievement are constantly escalating for self and for others.

They may need to be gently reminded of their overly high expectations.

ENERGY DIRECTION

Given these skills, values and attitudes, the INTJs direct their energy toward acquisition of knowledge, competencies and implementation of their vision of how things can be.

If not given the opportunity to constantly learn, they are likely to get off task, look depressed and create their own learning opportunities. Moreover, their loyalties are directed toward

CHARACTERISTICS

IMPLICATIONS

knowledge, understanding and searching for better ways. Consequently, they tend not to be enamored with delivery vehicles such as routines, standard operating procedures and going by the book—for INTJs these tend to be boring, and as long as they function well, that is really all they care about.

Tireless in their work, they drive themselves and others to achieve the organization's goals.

INTJs tend to expect as much from others as from themselves, and if and when others do not meet the standards of the INTJ manager, expect detachment and aloof attitudes to prevail, i.e., The Big Chill . . .

INTJs are devoted to accuracy and precision, especially in charting the actions needed to reach the goal. They are turned off by over-emotionalizing, exaggeration and unbridled imagination, all of which represent inaccuracy.

Expect them to reject and challenge that which is inaccurately presented.

They hunger for problems to solve, especially complicated problems. If reduced to conducting "business as usual," chances are that INTJ managers will become disillusioned and turn their energies elsewhere.

If they do not have problems to solve, INTJs will find some or will take on someone else's problems. They may keep their solutions to themselves until asked, but it is painful for them to see problems in the organization and not be permitted to solve them or to contribute to their solution.

INTJ

CHARACTERISTICS	**IMPLICATIONS**

When they have insights about how to solve a problem, they are frequently very sure of their solution, while others may not see how they got there.

Quite often, when they communicate their insights, INTJs come across to others as being arrogant and somewhat condescending.

Within the organization, their energy will be directed toward change and the development of long-range strategies to effect that change. Turn ons are logic, calm atmosphere, justice, coherence and accuracy.

INTJs focus strongly on consequences and long-term results. They have an uncanny ability to project far into the future.

AUTHORITY ORIENTATION

INTJs want the person in charge to be knowledgeable and competent. Authority is not granted by position. They will question authority and test it, especially in their own area of expertise. Reporting to someone less competent than they are becomes difficult and over time can produce cynicism, sarcasm and disassociation.

If the person in charge is not seen as knowledgeable and competent, there is little hope of getting INTJs to accept their performance feedback as something worth paying attention to. They may follow orders and direction if they have something to fear, such as loss of their job, but they won't do it nearly as well as what they do naturally, and may even "forget" or "bungle."

ROLE PERCEPTION

INTJs tend to be directive in relationships, that is, they are quite comfortable structuring others' time and tasks. They are less comfortable making the first move in relationships.

They have no difficulty giving directives necessary to carry out plans.

CHARACTERISTICS	**IMPLICATIONS**

INTJs have a strong need for autonomy.

In-depth relationships develop slowly, and not very often.

CONFLICT RESOLUTION

INTJs enjoy a penetrating and lively debate. They may be quite outspoken, yet the typical INTJ prefers an atmosphere of calm and self-control. Typically, conflicts are to be resolved logically and rationally and emotionalism avoided.

INTJs may at times need to be reminded to consider their feelings and the feelings of others, rather than insisting on cool logic—and that can be very difficult for the clear-headed, cool INTJs—especially if and when they are boiling behind a facade of calmness.

MODES OF LEARNING

INTJs learn by conceptualizing, abstracting common properties and developing categories. They are adept at learning abstract ideas and less adept at learning by association and rote.

Sometimes, their fear of failure can be their own worst enemy and block learning—and for the INTJ, if the learning experience is not of the highest possible quality, it isn't worth it.

BLIND SPOTS AND PITFALLS

INTJs may overlook the human element in the drive for action that will achieve the goal. They are frequently so task oriented and single-minded that they may not realize the impact of their ideas and plans on others.

INTJs are fiercely devoted to their work as tenacious high achievers and frequently people are of secondary importance by comparison.

They can be bitingly critical and sarcastic and may be seen as cold, distant and unapproachable.

They may need to actively ask for feedback, since others may hesitate to approach them.

CHARACTERISTICS	IMPLICATIONS
If they are overwhelmed by a fear of failure, INTJs may prefer to plan rather than act and may develop detailed plans of what they are going to do. Indeed, INTJs sometimes are more enamored with possibilities and probabilities at the expense of reality.	Moreover, as they prefer to live in the future, people who tend to be present in the here and now frequently will criticize INTJs for being so theoretical that their hopes and aspirations cannot be translated into anything real.
They may be impatient with others who do not see a need for reflection and research.	Not surprisingly, then, in the world of work, the INTJs are well advised to benefit from association with individuals who tend to function more comfortably in the realm of being concrete. The energy between the abstract and the concrete, of course, is a frequent ingredient in success.
INTJs may resist efforts to persuade or coerce them.	Be sure to manage them by using their drive for autonomy rather than resisting it.
They may put more faith in the model and the probable sequences needed to achieve the goal than the reality of the situation. Thus they may ignore some of the practical factors involved in implementing their vision.	INTJs trust models because they are the creators of models. Yet no single model can independently cover an entire area. Inevitably, some practical aspects will escape the powerful, abstract mind of an INTJ.
INTJs may prefer the complex, well-laid plans to the careful consideration of all sides of an issue.	Indeed, INTJs get a real kick out of putting into a workable design complex principles and ideas and then having the prototype actually work.

INTJ

CHARACTERISTICS	IMPLICATIONS
They may be perceived as intellectual snobs, with little patience for those less endowed with abstract intelligence.	While they do not intend and seldom want to be perceived as arrogant, it happens as a result of their uncanny capability to predict.
INTJs find bureaucracy frustrating, with protocol and paperwork a waste of time that could best be spent planning. Moreover, it is not uncommon that the INTJs (in no uncertain terms) will underhandedly and subtly communicate to the administrators and managers that they have very little use for their systems, procedures and politics.	Again, be prepared to offer them the logic or rationale behind the standard operating procedures. Don't expect them to take it on faith or on "authority." Consequently, do not expect typical INTJs to be the organizational types. Indeed, in their mind, they sometimes experience such organization as interfering with the success potential of the overall firm.
Strong in making classifications and logical connections, they may be weak in noticing and remembering random associations and quantifications.	Typically INTJs master their thoughts well and unimportant issues are quickly forgotten and left behind in the dust.

INTJ

CHARACTERISTICS	IMPLICATIONS

ENTP

The theme of the ENTP is invention, not just of concrete objects, but also new ways of doing things as a means to an end. ENTPs are interested in the patterns of nearly everything and frequently go from one thing to the next, inventing prototypes and having faith in their ability to improvise rather than extensively prepare. They are the engineers of human relationships and systems as well as the more scientific domains.

CHARACTERISTICS	IMPLICATIONS

MANAGEMENT STYLE

The management style of the ENTP is likely to be one of a visionary who communicates the general outline of the vision, yet lets everyone do their own thing. Preferring to be allowed to operate autonomously, ENTPs assume that others do, too.

The ideal corporate structure is one in which ENTPs have opportunities to invent and improvise solutions to complex problems. They thrive on challenges and the non-routine. They tend not to have the attitude of, "If not invented here, it would not work." Rather, they are great copycats and adaptors and they enjoy improving on everything.

They can be team players for periods of time if that is what it takes to get the job done, for the focus is on efficiency.

A team can be both acceptable and important for an ENTP, especially when there is a project and a significant task to be performed.

They are usually adept at mobilizing others to get the project under way, and they are not opposed to taking the initiative to getting things done.

Indeed, expect ENTPs to be highly energized and sometimes totally consumed by a project or situation which intellectually is challenging.

ENTP

CHARACTERISTICS	IMPLICATIONS

As managers, their focus is on principles of the project or those on which the organization is built. They are keenly aware of the inner workings of the whole organization.

They may need to make an effort to define the details of their vision and to give more detailed explanations of the tasks to others.

ENTPs abhor redundancy and hesitate to state the obvious, so their communications are frequently terse, and they assume that they are understood. While they may communicate the essential aspects of their vision, they may leave others in the dark about the details of the vision.

The terseness disappears when they are in the process of developing an idea and it is through the process of talking that they develop their visions and theories. They may need to pay special attention to spell out the details of their vision or work with someone who can do that for them.

ENTPs typically are very project oriented and they can become obsessed or totally absorbed by an assignment or activity they tremendously enjoy.

Hence, managing ENTPs frequently calls for identification of projects and activities requiring a great deal of enthusiasm and energy.

Rationalizing that praise may appear redundant and obvious, they may not give praise and feedback as often as others need it. If the truth were known, it may be that they are embarrassed by praise, both giving it and receiving it.

They may need to be coached on how to show appreciation to others. They can easily see that praise is needed if they know the practical value of it, but they may need reminding.

ENTPs are frequently impatient with errors, snarled messes, covering ground already covered and other signs of inefficiency.

It helps to apologize ahead of time when asking ENTPs to repeat themselves.

ENTP

CHARACTERISTICS	IMPLICATIONS
It is also useful to keep in mind that for an ENTP, nothing seems constant.	Therefore it can be quite appropriate to change gears, play "what if" games and argue both sides of an issue at the same time.
ENTPs prefer to be in charge of innovative projects in which they may ignore the standard and traditional approaches.	It is an especially productive environment that allows them to adapt and make do with whatever is at hand rather than insist on a carefully drawn up blueprint in advance. In a typical work environment driven by day-to-day routine, ENTPs can get pretty bored and attempt to beef up the monotony with new ideas and approaches. To just do the job without an opportunity to explore and search for a better way can become quite frustrating.

VALUES

ENTPs value the theoretical, wanting insight, understanding, comprehension and knowledge. They admire genius, precision, efficiency and effectiveness and seek these characteristics in all that they do.	Realize that ENTPs tend to be global; they want to understand and comprehend the total situation before delving into details. Moreover, some quite disciplined ENTPs have often developed excellent capabilities to handle important details.
ENTPs trust logical reasoning above all.	Be prepared to offer them the rationale behind an event or a policy.
They abhor a lack of willpower.	Especially when the payoff is important.

ENTP

CHARACTERISTICS	IMPLICATIONS

ATTITUDE

The basic attitude of ENTPs is one of skepticism. While they are open to new ideas, they are skeptical of their validity, until logically proven otherwise.

Expect them to be skeptical of anything and everything and in order to alleviate or reduce resistance, it can be quite productive to involve ENTPs in a hands-on assessment because as soon as they become involved in a process, they tend to buy into it.

They find the ambiguous fascinating and also seek clarity. They may be driven to seek clarity in the face of extreme ambiguity or they may block and become paralyzed by their view of the whole and all its parts.

If they become overwhelmed, they may need assistance in breaking down the problem into workable parts.

SKILLS

ENTPs are skilled at analysis, seeing differences and creating categories. As engineers, they map out all the feasible events well in advance, developing an action agenda, a well thought out outline, an overall scheme (although ENTPs are more content than the NTJs to have only a rough sketch before proceeding). They adapt and improvise means to an end, the building of models (usually theoretical models) and solving complex problems, enigmas and riddles.

If you want ENTP employees to give a superior performance, just turn them loose to design a solution to a complex problem, but do not demand that they stick around to implement every little detail. Consult them about the accurate implementation of their design, but then turn them loose to design some more.

ENTP

CHARACTERISTICS	IMPLICATIONS

ENTPs can keep several issues in their mind at the same time. What is even more amazing, they also seem to be able to talk about them simultaneously.

Not surprisingly, the ENTPs are often viewed as "riding out in all directions at once." The reason is simple: they have a unique ability for multi-focus.

They are adept at improvising an expedient solution to a problem as a situation develops. Behind this skill is a constant awareness of the structure of the situation, relationship or edifice.

Keep in mind that ENTPs are high energy individuals - when they are on the path in problem-solving and finding solutions to complete problems, get out of the way because they can really be on a roll.

Invention for ENTPs is an external process, responding to the situation. They devise tools and techniques as means to achieve an end.

If something does not work right, the ENTPs are not always the first to notice - but they are among the first to fix it - even if it means a little jury-rigging.

ENTPs are precise in their speech. They are adept conversationalists and speak with wit and plays on words. Easily tracking the complex verbalization of others, they notice inconsistencies in language, contradictions and shifts in position. They use these observations to debate either side of an issue, sometimes even as an "opponent" to their own position.

ENTPs are quite adept at communicating superbly with individuals who speak with contradictions. They can make others feel at a loss and stupid and may benefit from tempering their debating and nitpicking with humor or explanation. Indeed, they have been known to speak out of both corners of their mouth at the same time.

DRIVING FORCE

ENTPs have a very high need for achievement. However, the achievement is most often measured by standards set by the

Performance feedback and reprimanding that takes this need into account will be much more effective. ENTPs are their

CHARACTERISTICS	**IMPLICATIONS**

ENTP, not by society or the organization. This achievement need is reflected in a constant drive for competency and an ever present, even if hidden, fear of failure.

own worst critics and will already know their "errors" and shortcomings. Usually, they view confrontation of less than optimal performances as valuable learning experiences.

Not surprisingly, then, ENTPs are highly energetic in their never-ending quest for new insights and improving on what exists.

Expect them to steadily increase their competence and skill development in all their endeavors.

Their standards for achievement are constantly escalating for self and for others.

Sometimes ENTPs may need to be gently reminded of their overly high expectations and tendency to pass others intellectually in the fast lane.

ENERGY DIRECTION

Given these skills, values and attitudes, ENTPs direct their energy toward acquisition of knowledge and competencies.

If not given the opportunity to constantly learn, they are likely to get off task, look depressed and create their own learning opportunities. Moreover, when they are on a roll and in high pursuit of whatever they want, at times ENTPs can come across as overbearing, condescending and even arrogant. From their point of view, that of course is not the case - they are merely driven to understand and achieve.

They are devoted to accuracy and seek precision, often splitting hairs if need be. They are

Expect ENTPs to reject and challenge that which is inaccurately presented. Moreover, if someone

ENTP

CHARACTERISTICS

IMPLICATIONS

turned off by over emo-tionalizing, exaggeration and unbridled imagination, all of which represent inaccuracy.

is judged incompetent by them, it is probably all over. Their impatience with individuals whom they feel do not know what they are doing just shows.

They hunger for problems to solve, especially complicated ones. The more complex the problem, the more ENTPs seem to be turned on.

If they do not have problems to solve, they will make some or will take on someone else's problems. Although if not asked, they may not readily offer a so-lution. It is painful for them to see problems in the organization and not be permitted to solve them or to contribute to their solution.

More often than not, ENTPs seem to believe that there is nothing they cannot do. They typically will attack any task or problem with more human gusto than most.

If, however, in the process of evolving a superior solution, they get bored or lose enthusi-asm, the task or project can just as quickly be moved from the top to the bottom of their prior-ity list, and whoever is waiting for results might find days stretching into weeks and weeks into months.

Within the organization, their energy will be directed toward change and the development of long-range strategies to effect that change or the constant de-sign of new products and revi-sion of present ones.

ENTPs usually enjoy several trails to blaze—all at the same time. The more balls they have in the air at the same time, the better—even though at times one or two priorities may slip.

ENTP

Turn ons are logic, a calm atmos-phere, justice, coherence and accuracy.

Turn offs are over-emotionalism, exaggeration and bungling.

CHARACTERISTICS	**IMPLICATIONS**

AUTHORITY ORIENTATION

ENTPs want the person in charge to be knowledgeable and competent. Authority is not granted by position. They will question authority and test it, especially in their own area of expertise. Individuals they respect tend to be doers, movers and shakers, and to the ENTP, past recognition is just that. It is what one can do that counts.

If the person in charge is not seen as knowledgeable and competent, there is little hope of getting ENTPs to accept their performance feedback as something worth paying attention to. They may follow orders and direction if they have something to fear, such as loss of their job, but they won't do it nearly as well as what they do naturally, and may even "forget" or "bungle."

ROLE PERCEPTION

ENTPs tend to be assertive in relationships, that is, they readily make the first move in defining the nature of a relationship. Indeed, they relish maintaining the one up position they can gain that way.

ENTPs are usually quite clear about what is important and have definite opinions and they don't hesitate to state them.

They prefer to give information rather than directives.

Their preference is to put the information in front of you and leave it to you to respond to it.

ENTPs tend to be competitive, sometimes just for the fun of it. For them the real fun is in playing the game - and not necessarily always winning it.

Expect ENTP managers to tremendously enjoy "the hunt," and in this context, do not be surprised if they drop certain subtle hints about how great they are. While they will never admit it, a standing ovation would not be inappropriate.

CHARACTERISTICS   ## IMPLICATIONS

CONFLICT RESOLUTION

ENTPs enjoy a lively debate and may be quite outspoken, but overall they prefer an atmosphere of calm.

As a matter of fact, it is the process of debating they seem to enjoy the most, and unlike the other types, ENTPs have a great gift for arguing multiple sides of an argument at the same time. For them that is "shedding light" on a situation, while for others it spells confusion.

Conflicts are to be resolved logically and rationally and emotionalism avoided.

They may from time to time need to be reminded to take care of feelings, their own and others', rather than insisting on cool logic.

MODES OF LEARNING

ENTPs learn by conceptualizing, abstracting common properties and developing categories. They are adept at learning abstract ideas and less adept at learning by association and rote.

Sometimes, their fear of failure can be their own worst enemy and block learning. That is why ENTPs at times will hide behind a smokescreen of "knowing it all" - when in reality they are masterful in covering up and looking as if they know what they are presenting.

BLIND SPOTS AND PITFALLS

ENTPs may overlook the human element in the quest for objective truth and understanding.

Certainly, ENTPs do not take any pride in being inconsiderate and tremendously task focused - it is just that there are times when their own enthusiasm overtakes them.

ENTP

CHARACTERISTICS	IMPLICATIONS
They can be bitingly critical and sarcastic and may be seen as cold and distant.	Do not expect many "warm fuzzies" from them, especially if you land on their wrong side.
Willing to proceed with only a rough plan, ENTPs may neglect some very necessary preparations, and they do not enjoy preparing for most events.	ENTPs have been known to move so fast that they meet themselves in the elevator both coming and going. Consequently, in their furious haste to achieve and accomplish, they may overlook trivial details appearing inconsequential in the heat of the battle, only to turn up as quite significant at a later stage.
They may prefer theory to reality and design to implementation.	ENTPs may want to abandon the project to do more design, yet they need to be reminded to stay around to guide the implementation of it or suffer disappointment that the results do not meet their high standards. As a result, it is sometimes difficult to understand their priorities, and indeed there may be none. Acting on hunches often tends to stimulate their imagination more than going by the book.
ENTPs may become phobic and resist efforts at coercion. Be sure to "manage" them by using their drive for autonomy rather than resisting it.	Perhaps the least productive attitude to display in front of an ENTP is one of, "Do I have a deal for you!" Changes are the "winner" in a deal-making scenario for the ENTP, not the initiator.
ENTPs may be intellectual snobs, with little patience for those less endowed with abstract intelligence.	Consequently, individuals of a different type and temperament at times can feel left out in the cold by the all-consuming and "all-knowing" ENTP.

ENTP

CHARACTERISTICS

IMPLICATIONS

ENTPs find bureaucracy frustrating, with protocol and paperwork a waste of time that could best be spent designing and defining.

Again, be prepared to offer them the logic or rationale behind standard operating procedures. Don't expect them to take it on faith or on "authority" - and don't be surprised if they break a rule or two. ENTPs have no patience with red tape or any organizational procedure which will not enable them to reach the results they want in the shortest time and most effortless manner possible.

ENTPs may be oblivious to conventions and protocol. It does not even occur to them to think of attending to them. Likewise, they may be weak in noticing and remembering random associations and quantifications.

Structure, procedures, and pomp and circumstance are not exactly the strong suit of ENTPs. To the contrary, the opportunity to take advantage of a specific situation and the unique circumstances prevailing, and then turn up with a real winner - that's ENTP living at its very best.

ENTP

CHARACTERISTICS	IMPLICATIONS

INTP

The theme of the INTP is designing, not just in the "artistic sense," but in the sense of the precise arrangement of all the elements necessary for objective understanding of that part of the world that interests them. While many INTPs are drawn to science and math, the designing can be in many other realms, and they usually turn out to be superb strategists in whatever endeavor they take on.

CHARACTERISTICS	IMPLICATIONS

MANAGEMENT STYLE

The management style of the INTP is likely to be one of a visionary who communicates the general outline of the vision, yet lets everyone do their own thing. Preferring to be left alone to operate autonomously, INTPs assume that others do, too. They can be team players if that is what is necessary to get the job done.

The ideal corporate structure is one in which they are allowed to solve problems, conceptualize, and have opportunities to design, define, research and develop—and not be bogged down by systems, procedures and day-to-day routine.

If faced with what they perceive as incompetence, INTPs are likely to take on the task themselves rather than see the project fail.

INTP managers may have difficulty delegating, especially if they mistrust the ability of subordinates, and they may need coaching in that skill.

As managers, their focus is on the principles of the project or those on which the organization is built. They are keenly aware of the inner workings of the whole organization as a system.

They may need to make an effort to outline the details of a project and to give more detailed explanations of the tasks to others.

INTP

CHARACTERISTICS	IMPLICATIONS

INTPs abhor redundancy and hesitate to state the obvious, so their communications are frequently terse, and they assume that they are understood. While they may communicate the essential aspects of their vision, they may unintentionally leave others in the dark about the details of the vision. Moreover, sometimes failing to understand that other less conceptual individuals are not tracking them, INTPs are experienced as trying to complicate an issue when in reality they are merely waiting to account for all of the factors involved.

They may need to pay special attention to spelling out the details of their vision or work with someone who can do that for them. It is important to understand that concrete verbal communication for INTPs can be quite energy usurping, since their vision is often quite abstract. They often resort to diagrams and matrices to communicate their abstractions.

On the other hand, when asked to explain something, INTPs may become quite technical, with many details and much complexity. Moreover, they are masterful in the use of language in the sense that they are extremely precise in the choice of words to communicate.

Consider INTPs the consummate "wordsmiths." Their fascination with words and their meanings serves them well when they want to verbalize precisely what they intend.

Rationalizing that praise may appear redundant and obvious, INTPs may not give praise and feedback as often as others need it. If the truth were known, it may be that they are embarrassed by praise, both in giving it and receiving it.

They may need to be coached on how to show appreciation to others. They can easily see that praise is needed if they know the practical value of it, but they may need reminding.

INTP

CHARACTERISTICS

IMPLICATIONS

INTPs are frequently impatient with errors, snarled messes, covering ground already covered and other signs of inefficiency.

It helps to apologize ahead of time when asking INTPs to repeat themselves. Indeed, they are more likely to respond positively if they are requested to explain their viewpoint from a different perspective. They usually will respond well to a statement like, "In other words, you are suggesting that . . ."

INTPs frequently will eschew management positions, preferring to develop their natural gifts as individual and significant technical contributors.

It is an especially productive environment that allows them to remain on a technical track and still be rewarded as much as a manager. Typically, INTPs tend to be better leaders than managers. In other words, they enjoy being leaders, i.e., paving the way and being more concerned with effectiveness than merely being efficient.

VALUES

INTPs value the theoretical, wanting insight, understanding, comprehension and knowledge. They admire genius, precision, efficiency and effectiveness and seek these characteristics in all that they do. Their love of theory is perhaps greater than all the other types, for theory is the way to achieve objective truth.

Conceptual originality, love of analysis, precision in thought and language, as well as a penchant for self-critiquing, provide INTPs with a great capacity for insight and theory development.

INTP

CHARACTERISTICS	IMPLICATIONS

INTPs trust logical reasoning above all else. Emotional responses to just about anything leaves them somewhere between dumbfounded and cold.

Be prepared to offer INTPs the rationale behind an event or a policy. Also, be prepared for probing, questioning and hairsplitting. INTPs are not particularly well known for accepting anything at face value. For them, nothing is permanent, and what may be obvious today is irrelevant tomorrow. As a matter of fact, while others may be concerned with next year's plans, the INTP is somewhere in the next century.

ATTITUDE

The basic attitude of INTPs is one of skepticism. While they are open to new ideas, they are skeptical of their validity, until logically proven otherwise.

Expect them to be skeptical of anything and everything—and yet always willing to explore and improve on whatever exists.

INTPs find the ambiguous fascinating and embrace the search for clarity.

They may be driven to seek clarity in the face of extreme ambiguity or they may block and become overwhelmed by their view of the whole and all its parts. If they become overwhelmed, they may need assistance in breaking down the problem into workable parts and sequencing them.

SKILLS

INTPs are skilled at analysis, seeing differences and developing categories. As strategists,

If you want INTP employees to give a superior performance, just turn them loose to design a solu-

INTP

CHARACTERISTICS

IMPLICATIONS

they map out all feasible events well in advance, developing an action agenda, a well thought out outline and overall scheme (although INTPs are more content than the NTJs to have only a rough sketch before proceeding). They adapt and improvise as means to an end; they build models (usually theoretical models) and solve complex problems, enigmas and riddles.

tion to a complex problem, but don't demand that they stick around to implement every little detail. It is important to realize that whenever an INTP has a complete and full conceptual understanding of a situation, the implementation phase becomes boring, inconsequential and a nuisance. The opportunity lost in redundancy for INTPs can be downright painful. Consequently, consult them about the accurate implementation of their design, and then turn them loose to design some more.

INTPs are adept at determining the most efficient and effective structure, figuring out the simultaneous placements of parts of a whole, be it a building as in architecture, a schematic, or a theory.

For INTPs, the ability and opportunity to shape something of value and significance out of nothing—a vacuum or incoherent, ambiguous pieces of thoughts and ideas—is probably their very highest calling.

INTPs are "wordsmiths"—more than any other type, they seem able to express with great precision exactly what they want to communicate.

Attempting to impress or influence INTPs with assumed verbal communication "strategies" seldom turns out to be adequate, as their skill in communicating with great precision, especially in small groups, is so highly developed.

Designing for INTPs is an internal process, flowing out of their imagination. They define tools and techniques expressed in precise thought. As such, they

You can expect them to point out inconsistencies and contradictions in language and action if they need to jockey for power. Moreover, they can shred incon-

CHARACTERISTICS	IMPLICATIONS
cannot not see inconsistencies in language and contradictions.	sistent views and arguments into tiny pieces if they are determined to get their point across with some force. However, they can make others feel at a loss and stupid and may benefit from tempering their debating and nit-picking with humor or explanation.

DRIVING FORCE

INTPs have a very high need for achievement. However, achievement is most often measured by standards set by the INTP, not by society or the organization. This achievement need is reflected in a constant drive for competency and an ever present, even if hidden, fear of failure.	Performance feedback and reprimanding that takes this need into account is effective. INTPs are their own worst critics and already know their "errors" and shortcomings. More than any other type, they can be very objective about their own performance, accepting of criticism and suggestions for improvements.
Their standards for achievement are constantly escalating for self and others.	At times INTPs may need to be gently reminded of their exceedingly high expectations.
They are driven to understand the laws of the universe.	It is better to not cut INTPs off by suggesting that they need to accept anything according to some other authority.

ENERGY DIRECTION

Given these skills, values and attitudes, INTPs direct their energy toward acquisition of knowledge and competencies.	If not given the opportunity to constantly learn, they are likely to get off task, look depressed and create their own learning

INTP

CHARACTERISTICS	**IMPLICATIONS**
	opportunities. INTPs respond well to challenge; they are ingenious when it comes to incorporating new pieces into a puzzle.
They are devoted to accuracy and seek it, often splitting hairs if need be. They are turned off by over-emotionalizing, exaggeration and unbridled imagination, all of which represent inaccuracy.	Expect them to reject and challenge that which is inaccurately presented.
INTPs abhor a lack of willpower.	They do not consider a lack of willpower an acceptable excuse for failing to achieve.
They hunger for problems to solve, especially complicated ones.	If they do not have problems to solve, they will make some or will take on someone else's problems. If not asked, however, they may not offer a solution. It is very painful for them to experience problems in an organization and not be permitted to solve them or to contribute to their solution.
Within the organization, their energy is directed toward change and the development of long-range strategies to effect that change or the constant design of new products and revision of present ones. Turn ons are logic, a calm atmosphere, justice, coherence and accuracy.	INTPs are intolerant of stagnation. Their minds are tirelessly scanning while seeking to make improvements.

INTP

CHARACTERISTICS	IMPLICATIONS

AUTHORITY ORIENTATION

INTPs want the person in charge to be knowledgeable and competent. Authority is not granted by position. They will question authority and test it, especially in their own area of expertise.

If the person in charge is not seen as knowledgeable and competent, there is little hope of getting INTPs to accept their performance feedback as something worth paying attention to. They may follow orders and direction if they have something to fear, such as loss of their job, but they won't do it nearly as well as what they do naturally, and may even "forget" or "bungle." The bumper sticker "Question Authority" in all probability was contributed by a die-hard INTP. Disqualified directives work better than "orders." Present them with information and let them decide.

ROLE PERCEPTION

INTPs tend to be reactive in relationships, that is, they wait for the relationship to be defined by the other person and then respond to that definition by either accepting it or rejecting it. They prefer to give information rather than orders.

Don't take this tendency to be a respondent as lack of interest or wishy-washy character. INTPs are usually quite clear about what is important and have definite opinions; they just don't put them out there first.

They can become competitive in their relationships, especially within the domain they've identified as theirs.

INTPs do not surrender their destiny to others. They will do whatever it takes to defend their sense of destiny.

INTP

CHARACTERISTICS	**IMPLICATIONS**

CONFLICT RESOLUTION

Preferring an atmosphere of calm, INTPs may avoid conflict.

Sometimes, they may avoid conflict for too long, hoping it will go away.

When there is conflict, they can be very tenacious and stick to their perceptions of the "right" solution, until logically shown otherwise. They will expect conflict to be resolved logically and rationally.

They tend to have an "elephant memory." Whatever is said or debated tends to linger with them. Via induction and reflections, INTPs will change their perceptions (sometimes after more than just a mere night's sleep, however).

MODES OF LEARNING

INTPs learn by conceptualizing, abstracting common properties and creating categories. They are adept at learning abstract ideas and less adept at learning by association and rote.

Sometimes, their fear of failure can be their own worst enemy and block learning. Learning is a lifelong reality for the INTPs of the world, and if the formal requirements are below their expectations, they will evolve higher standards than the establishment.

BLIND SPOTS AND PITFALLS

INTPs may overlook the human element in the quest for objective truth and understanding. They can be bitingly critical and sarcastic and may be seen as cold and distant.

INTPs are often driven by an insatiable desire to optimize and maximize every situation they find themselves involved in. While they do not intentionally want to overlook or neglect the human element, they sometimes become totally consumed by achieving a specific goal.

INTP

CHARACTERISTICS	IMPLICATIONS
They may want to spend too much time planning and thereby delay the actual doing of the project.	Give them a deadline for projects and an action-oriented SP on the team to spur them into action.
INTPs may prefer theory to reality and design to implementation.	They may want to abandon the project to do more design, yet they need to be reminded to stay around to guide the implementation of it or suffer disappointment when the results don't meet their high standards.
INTPs may be intellectual snobs, with little patience for those less endowed with abstract intelligence.	They may be intellectual snobs, but they do have a soft heart.
They tend not to like small talk necessary for social and semi-social situations.	If "chit-chat" is really important to their job, it may help to provide them with a "coach" or a model to learn from (an ENFJ, for example).
INTPs find bureaucracy frustrating, with protocol and paperwork a waste of time that could best be spent designing and defining.	Again, be prepared to offer them the logic or rationale behind the standard operating procedures. Don't expect them to take it on faith or on "authority." As a matter of fact, the only kind of authority which has long-term meaning for an INTP is evidenced in expertise and the ability to explain complex phenomenon with reasons for why things are the way they are.
Institutions are of value to an INTP only to the degree they permit creativity.	Anyone imagining that an INTP really has a great deal of loyalty to time-honored institutions

INTP

CHARACTERISTICS	**IMPLICATIONS**
	(other than perhaps universities and institutions of higher education) probably could not be further from the mark.
INTPs may be oblivious to conventions and protocol. It does not even occur to them to think of attending to them. Likewise, they may be weak in noticing and remembering random associations and quantifications.	Conventions and protocol are an insult to their respect and requirement of individuality.

CHARACTERISTICS	IMPLICATIONS

ENFJ

The theme of the ENFJ is mentoring, leading people to achieve their potential and become more of who they are. ENFJs lead using their empathy, exceptional communication skills, their enthusiasm and warmth to gain cooperation toward meeting the ideals they hold for the organization. They are the catalysts who tremendously enjoy drawing out the best in others.

CHARACTERISTICS	IMPLICATIONS

MANAGEMENT STYLE

The management style of ENFJs is democratic and participative. The nature of their modus operandi is likely to be people-oriented. Indeed, they lead by coaching, encouraging, applauding and providing a lot of positive feedback.

The ideal work environment for an ENFJ is harmonious, people oriented, and encourages cooperation. The worst working environment is political, where whoever plays politics best receives preferential treatment based upon internal maneuvering as opposed to the ENFJ's preference for integrity in delivering good performance.

ENFJs manage in a very personal way, focusing on the individuals in the organization. In other words, while they accept and know that organizations are necessary vehicles to accomplish goals and objectives, in their minds and hearts it is people who make things happen.

The ENFJ expects that there be adequate systems, policies and procedures allowing people to work well together, avoiding conflict and misunderstanding of tasks, roles and purposes. Yet, there would be minimal insistence on rules and procedures for, in the view of the ENFJ, these deny the climate of freedom and autonomy that promotes growth of individuals.

ENFJ

CHARACTERISTICS	IMPLICATIONS
The commitment of ENFJs is to the progress and growth of those around them. Sometimes, this commitment to the development of staff takes precedence over the development of systems and procedures.	They are likely to ask of a planned change, "Is it good for the people?" - and in the long haul, "Will everyone really benefit from a new approach?"
More than the typically task-oriented manager, they are accurately tuned in to the organizational climate.	ENFJs not only listen, they also hear much that is not said.
In addition to improving technologies and efficiencies, the reason things work according to an ENFJ can be attributed to camaraderie, mutual support and a commitment to overall team effort. Consequently, ENFJs naturally become concerned with the personal problems of their co-workers, subordinates and superiors. Whenever possible, they like to lend a helping hand in improving and enhancing the overall work environment.	This may draw them off task at times and they may become preoccupied by their built-in tendency to be concerned about the welfare of others. Indeed, ENFJs tend to be somewhat critical of systems and procedures, as all too often they have experienced how organizations and their policies and procedures tend to squelch human motivation, ultimately resulting in performance decline.
ENFJs are masterful at showing appreciation, both verbal and non-verbal, giving frequent and abundant praise. They seem to know just what to say and do to make the other person feel appreciated.	Not surprisingly, people not used to the genuine warmth and care of ENFJs can almost be at a loss with superiors who seem to be more interested in their subordinates as real people rather than always pushing for performance and completion of tasks.

ENFJ

CHARACTERISTICS

IMPLICATIONS

ENFJs value approval of others and are motivated by positive feedback.

In the absence of this kind of assurance, they are quite likely to internalize negative feedback and feel miserable.

Management by the book, policies, impersonal objectives, criticism, and use of formal power is not exactly a source of great joy for an ENFJ.

Indeed, this kind of management may lead to recalcitrance and even lower performance. Therefore, attempting to manipulate or sweet talk ENFJs into doing something against their better judgment is likely not possible.

ENFJs are very loyal, but their loyalty is more to the people in the organization, and less to the policies and procedures of the institution.

When there are abrupt and frequent staff changes, ENFJs may become demoralized and lose trust and enthusiasm for the job. Even worse, they can become quite upset with purely task-oriented individuals in the organization and as a result start to "fight the system," often more covertly than overtly. Consequently, any change involving people and their perceptions should be carefully contemplated, communicated and never come as a surprise to ENFJs.

They like variety and fun challenges, both individually and as members of the team, so as to develop all of their talents, skills and opportunities to be even more valuable contributors.

They may become frazzled and fragmented from wanting to do too many different things or from being pulled in too many directions all at once.

ENFJs usually have a great sense of humor.

Do not be surprised if they unexpectedly turn out to be practical jokers of some kind.

ENFJ

CHARACTERISTICS	IMPLICATIONS

VALUES

ENFJs value the ethical and the moral, wanting goodness (the "greater good") for all, and they have a never-ending desire to make work meaningful. For an ENFJ, it is important to know that the organization is a valuable vehicle for its members to feel significant and challenged in a friendly, constructive fashion.

ENFJs place extraordinary emphasis upon the meaning of each moment. The disadvantage of this habit - there are times when the demand for "meaning" on a short-term basis should yield to other pressing practicalities. After all, "meaning" is not always understood and, at times, is difficult to define.

ENFJs seek relationships in which they can promote growth and development.

If a relationship becomes stagnant, do not expect an ENFJ to hang around much longer.

ENFJs value people above all else. They are concerned with fairness from the standpoint that everyone be able to maximize their potential.

If an organization is managed predominantly by impersonal task-oriented individuals, ENFJs may find the work environment to be callous, hard, cold and impersonal. Under such conditions, they will eventually crusade to put things right. If they fail to achieve more of a humanitarian organizational climate, they may become informally sarcastic and cynical and eventually divorce themselves from the organization.

ENFJs trust their intuitions and inferences above all and use these strengths to contribute to the benefit of all.

While they may understand and intellectually accept the rationale behind an event or a policy, ENFJs place more value on knowing that whatever is done, the impact on the people affected

CHARACTERISTICS

IMPLICATIONS

is taken into consideration, and that the human organization stands to gain a great deal over time.

They abhor a lack of caring. For them, an organization exists to enable people to perform - not the other way around.

Anyone attempting to manipulate or inappropriately use the organization to derive personal benefits will more or less be viewed as somewhere between useless and a traitor - eventually to be given the cold shoulder treatment, often for a long, long time by our ENFJ. However, if someone finds it necessary to manipulate or bend the rules, he/she will not be viewed dimly by an ENFJ if those efforts are unselfish and beneficial to others.

ATTITUDE

The basic attitude of ENFJs is one of credulism, enthusiasm and idealism. They tend to see the good and the human potential in everyone and everything. They are not troubled by the paradoxical and they relentlessly pursue their high ideals. Often these ideals are non-economic; rather, they tend to be humanitarian and people focused.

Sometimes ENFJs may gloss over and ignore the "dark side," preferring to anticipate goodness instead of badness. With their focus on ideals, they may be disappointed when "reality" doesn't measure up to their high expectations for the human potential. Understand that the ENFJ is a person who lives for what can be.

The enthusiasm of the ENFJ is from time to time dramatically demonstrated with effusive expressions of intense emotion.

To more calm-oriented types, this can seem overdone and may be a turn off. Sometimes others would do well to realize that the impulsive, dramatic flair of an

ENFJ

CHARACTERISTICS	IMPLICATIONS
	ENFJ is yet another way to heighten the overall awareness of issues the ENFJ considers crucial in evolving the organization and its people in a constructive direction.
Typically, ENFJs have a global attitude toward most situations and they prefer to deal with abstractions.	For them, ideas, dreams and aspirations are as real as reality itself.
They find the ambiguous perfectly acceptable, since they expect things to be paradoxical.	Acceptance of paradox allows ENFJs to remain open to new and unusual ideas.

SKILLS

ENFJs are skilled at mentoring, anything having to do with people - handling them, deploying them, training them, motivating them, recruiting them, counseling them, and demonstrating by what they do that they really care.	If you want the ENFJ employee to give a superior performance, be sure the job provides opportunities for interaction and some higher purpose whereby the ENFJ can become enthused.
Also, when ENFJs direct effort and focus their attention on empathic listening, they usually come out second to none.	
ENFJs are willing to get involved in relationships and they seem to have a built-in sixth sense for how to optimize a conversation or interaction with just about everyone they care about.	The greater the number of types ENFJs are able to understand and mutually appreciate, the happier they are. Even with individuals they have not been able to spend time with and care about, ENFJs nonetheless strive to optimize conversation and interaction.

ENFJ

CHARACTERISTICS

IMPLICATIONS

Do not be surprised, therefore, if ENFJ managers become so involved in coaching and assisting people that the tasks to be performed unintentionally take a back seat.

ENFJs enjoy coaching and facilitating others to achieve higher goals and aspirations. For them, the process of being a mentor is external. They are highly gifted at really connecting with individuals, thereby assisting with their growth and development.

ENFJs are global and metaphoric in their speech. They are adept oral communicators with their sensitivity to nuances and unspoken aspects of communications. They are also very skillful listeners with an unusual capacity to understand others' viewpoints and realities.

They are more interested in the implications of what is being said and indeed they may claim to have heard things others did not say simply because they are masters at listening for intent and not overly attentive to whatever verbiage prevails. As a matter of fact, ENFJs are superior listeners-when they want to be. They become so involved in one-to-one communications that they may help whomever they dialogue with finish their sentences in order for the communication to progress as efficiently as possible.

Over time, ENFJs take for granted that they are understood and, indeed, they usually are.

When they are misunderstood, they are frequently surprised and even hurt, especially if the connotations are negative.

Warmth, graciousness and charm are important aspects of the people/communication skills of ENFJs. They are particularly gifted at integration, i.e., how there is consistency in similarities and differences among people.

People usually enjoy working with or for ENFJs, as they are providers of excellent informal feedback. Their whole being communicates an authentic and genuine interest in individuals they come across or who wander in on the same path. Due to

CHARACTERISTICS	IMPLICATIONS

their abstract orientation with people, individuals who tend to be more concrete and task oriented sometimes experience the ENFJs as "too much of a good thing," i.e., they want tangible, visible results now—the human potential movement can appear later.

DRIVING FORCE

The ENFJ has a high need for developing empathic relationships. These must be deep and meaningful to satisfy the intense hunger the ENFJ feels for rapport.

If not given the opportunity to have meaningful relationships, ENFJs may become stressed and have difficulties on the job. In the absence of a meaningful relationship or at least a modicum of effort to build a meaningful relationship, ENFJs may walk away from situations with much at stake. Sooner or later they must accept the fact that some people are unable, unwilling or incapable of investing the required energy to sustain meaningful, interpersonal relationships.

Camaraderie and being "good friends" is important to the ENFJ.

Indeed, if an ENFJ does not experience a working relationship as being friendly, it becomes quite difficult for the ENFJ to function adequately and up to full power, so to speak.

Integrity is the attitudinal hallmark of ENFJ's relationships. They are driven to be as authen-

Since they want to avoid being phony, they may resist assignments that require some pre-

CHARACTERISTICS

IMPLICATIONS

tic and true to their values as possible.

tense. Indeed, being cast into a role which downplays authenticity will cause ENFJs all kinds of grief, and invariably they will work themselves away from situations where they cannot be themselves. As a matter of fact, ENFJs have been known to even become physically ill when having to function under false pretenses. Hence, do not expect the ENFJ to particularly enjoy playing company politics.

ENERGY DIRECTION

Given these skills, values and attitudes, ENFJs direct their energy toward bringing forth the potential in everyone they contact. They are in a never-ending search for their true identity and facilitate the searches of others. In that pursuit, they seem to possess an endless desire to accomplish miracles.

Hence, when they are given responsibility for tasks and people, they tend to focus on opportunities to improve and enhance any situation they find themselves in. Indeed, they are highly proactive and do not necessarily accept "the way we do things around here."

Within the organization, their energy seems to be directed toward whatever changes will facilitate its people to achieve, accomplish, and realize more of their potential than thought possible.

It is difficult for ENFJs to accept the status quo. They know that changes are an inevitable fact of life; therefore, they tend to anticipate, facilitate and foster constructive development, especially of people.

ENFJs find meaning and significance in even the smallest event, and their ability to see relationships between things that are

They are skilled at observing nuances and similarities of seemingly diverse aspects. Hence, they know what flows together

ENFJ

CHARACTERISTICS	IMPLICATIONS
apparently very different enables inferences not available to the rest of us.	and what does not blend. At times, even ENFJs are at a loss in explaining the specifics of "why" they arrive at certain inferences and how it is that they are able to see a relationship between things which appear unrelated to most people.
These are the cooperators and people of vision; they are driven to seek harmony and goodwill, getting people to work together.	They may be wary of what may seem like callousness and anything that smacks of allowing the end to justify the means. If they are required to work in environments not conducive to their beliefs and values, ENFJs are likely to create confusion and bewilderment. Moreover, they are not shy about airing their opinions. If something or someone is significantly disruptive and in conflict with them, they will vent their feelings freely, even to the point of moralizing.
Turn ons are ideas and programs that help people - philosophical discussions to get at the meaning of life, and opportunities for interaction with others.	The energy ENFJs have available to philosophize and explore in order to better cope and understand is inexhaustible. They tremendously enjoy a good discussion on just about anything, as long as it does not turn sour or unfriendly. Their communication skills are superb and they tend to do well in any debate that convinces people to alter or change their point of view.

ENFJ

CHARACTERISTICS

IMPLICATIONS

AUTHORITY ORIENTATION

ENFJs want the person in charge to be ethical and "good." For them, authority is not granted by position and formal power - although their first inclination is to respect established hierarchies, procedures and formalities. It is important for them to have respect for their leader; and if they do, they tend to seek approval from the person in charge. Of all the NFs, ENFJs are most likely to naturally assume leadership of a group. Their leadership style brings out the very best in people.

If the people in charge are not seen as ethical, authentic and caring, there is little hope of getting the ENFJ to accept their leadership and performance feedback as something worth paying attention to. This does not mean that the ENFJ is immune to criticism and sarcasm. Chances are, however, that the ENFJs in this world do not particularly appreciate critique as a rule. Don't critique - appreciate.

ROLE PERCEPTION

ENFJs tend to be proactive and directive in relationships, that is, they take the first step in defining the relationship. They also tend to be proactive in working situations. In other words, they like to anticipate and bring about the most favorable conditions of which they are capable.

ENFJs will not burden people beyond their capacity. Simultaneously, they cast a dim view upon malingering and dishonesty.

ENFJs strive to inspire others while at the same time seeking inspiration from others. To that end, they give directives easily.

ENFJs typically enjoy being part of a team or something more than just themselves. They enjoy working for a worthy cause, a leader or an organization they can identify with.

ENFJ

CHARACTERISTICS	**IMPLICATIONS**

CONFLICT RESOLUTION

ENFJs prefer harmonious situations and tend to ignore conflicts as long as they possibly can.	They may suppress feelings of ill will to the point of irruptions and explosions. Moreover, it becomes very difficult for ENFJs to work with a person they have decided not to like - if the aversion is strong enough, the ENFJs are the first to refuse such an untenable situation.
ENFJs are not usually put off by intense feelings as long as these are not overly critical. As a matter of fact, they typically encourage the free expression of feelings so that the group can move toward consensus.	It is useful to realize that as ENFJs are highly value driven and oriented toward assisting and helping others, negative and condescending criticism cannot be taken lightly. The paradox seems to be one where ENFJs readily make value judgments, but tend not to be all that enthusiastic about taking their own medicine.
ENFJs very quickly tend to personalize conflicts.	It may be appropriate to suggest that they learn to make conflicts more objective rather than personal. Whether or not they can accept such a well-intended piece of advice may at times turn out to be doubtful.

MODES OF LEARNING

ENFJs learn through interaction, in dialogue with others or with the written word. They are global and abstract learners. The behavioral sciences tend to be a	Sometimes their need for relating to the teacher may be their own worst enemy and block learning if that relationship is disappointing to them.

ENFJ

CHARACTERISTICS	IMPLICATIONS

favorite, as there are found ideas, concepts and theories that help develop potential.

They use their ability to see relationships and synthesize to simplify the learning process. No wonder, then, that ENFJs tend to be excellent teachers. Even though they are high-energy people themselves, they usually have a great deal of patience and tremendously enjoy assisting others in the learning process.

Since the consciousness of ENFJs is global and diffuse, they may need to be reminded to focus on the details of what they are learning, for they may stop at the global impression of having learned something. Indeed, an ENFJ often tends to be satisfied with theoretical explanations. When it comes to learning details, routine and specifics, it is not uncommon that the ENFJ quickly becomes bored and switches into a favorite pastime, daydreaming.

ENFJs enjoy any challenge of learning which consistently yields "meaning." Moreover, once they have decided or come to the conclusion that a particular subject or discipline is boring, learning more about it can be painful and useless for them.

If ENFJs find it difficult to be whole-hearted in learning a subject, they would rather avoid the subject altogether.

They are adept at learning abstract ideas and less adept at learning by association and rote.

Consequently, do not expect ENFJs to always learn by the book.

BLIND SPOTS
AND PITFALLS

ENFJs may focus so much on the human element in a situation that they may get off task too much.

They function poorly in a work environment which does not provide people interaction.

ENFJ

CHARACTERISTICS	IMPLICATIONS
They can be so easily involved in meeting the needs of others that they may lose sight of their own needs and suffer from loss of identity and eventual burnout.	It is important that ENFJs schedule time for themselves so as to rejuvenate their energy by taking the necessary rest and relaxation. Also, ENFJs must learn to recognize, speak out and stop situations which rob their energy.
Being so responsive to others can lead to other people's priorities using up their time.	Consequently, there are times when they need to be reminded of the priorities in order to accomplish first things first, and not get side-tracked by human issues (which always are important to the ENFJ). In managing the time and energies of ENFJs, it would probably be a good idea to keep in mind their natural and strong tendency to be involved in people-oriented situations. There may be times when it is appropriate to subordinate these kinds of issues to the tasks at hand, in other words, help the ENFJ to focus on the job to be done.
ENFJs tend to work in bursts of energy which may not coincide with the needs of the job.	The ideal work environment allows them the flexibility to capitalize on these bursts of energy while not berating them for the lulls in between.
With their ability to be so empathic, ENFJs may be seen as agreeing with each person they relate to and get stuck in the middle between opposing forces.	As much as possible, ENFJs need to be encouraged to stay in touch with their own identity and to not personalize each person's conflicts.

ENFJ

CHARACTERISTICS

IMPLICATIONS

They may feel torn between the needs of their supervisors and their subordinates.

They may internalize the failures of others.

The cost of this can be a heavy toll in loss of needed energy.

ENFJs may tend to rescue victims of the system and then be divided in their loyalty.

They can avoid this by allowing and encouraging others to take responsibility.

ENFJs may get too involved with others' problems and create dependency relationships that are difficult to get out of.

Again, the stronger their own sense of identity, the less inclined they are to succumb to such relationships.

ENFJs tend to find bureaucracy frustrating, with protocol and paperwork a waste of time. In their attempts to create a climate of freedom (so people can grow), some mandated procedures may not get done.

ENFJs excel in work environments which allow them to be creative and free while simultaneously having access to people. ENFJs understand that they in their lifetime will never finish their work - a challenge that has no end. Therefore, ENFJs seek shortcuts. They become weary of the unnecessary, especially in their consideration of observing the human condition for what it is, what it is not and that which it can become.

ENFJ

CHARACTERISTICS	IMPLICATIONS

INFJ

The theme of the INFJ is intuition and foresight. INFJs use their insights to deal with complexity in issues and people, often with a strong sense of "knowing" before others know themselves. They trust their inspirations and visions, using them to help others. INFJs tend to be both private and complex, yet they bring a quiet enthusiasm to projects and assignments that are part of their vision and source of inspiration.

CHARACTERISTICS	IMPLICATIONS

MANAGEMENT STYLE

The management style of INFJs is one of striving for and supporting the highest and best use of the human potential. There is authenticity in caring for people, and they are likely to lead quietly and by example. It is important to understand that an INFJ needs to work for a cause, a leader, and a purpose—if possible, of higher calling than just churning out day-to-day work.

The ideal work environment for an INFJ is one which goes to great length in focusing on people and their needs. Moreover, the organization also needs to have an identity and a purpose beyond everyday routine. Both human and organizational resources need to be harnessed to a higher goal beyond the everyday humdrum of business as usual.

INFJs tend to manage in a predictable, orderly and very personal fashion. They enjoy being responsible both to the organization and people they feel responsible for. It is important for the INFJ that good interpersonal relationships are established and that people are part of a well-functioning, harmonious team.

The INFJ sees the value of rules, procedures and systems that allow effective functioning of people. However, they are unlikely to insist on rules and procedures for, in the view of the INFJ, these sometimes deny the climate of freedom and autonomy that promotes growth of individuals.

INFJ

CHARACTERISTICS	IMPLICATIONS
Their commitment is first and foremost to people, yet they are also concerned about their organization and its overall purpose. It is when both individual and organizational goals are attained that INFJs will feel content and satisfied that the job is being done.	They are likely to ask of any proposed change, "Is it good for the people?" both in the short and the long haul. Moreover, they are also concerned with the rate of change - how is it communicated and accepted or rejected by the people? They are not great fans of edicts and pronouncements. To them, meaningful and lasting change evolves over time.
INFJs typically value human relationships so strongly that they instinctively and naturally become concerned with personal as well as interpersonal problems of their co-workers, subordinates or superiors.	This highly developed capacity to create a harmonious environment for people to work in can, at times, cause the INFJ manager to temporarily suspend organizational purposes in order to accommodate human needs. Under a great deal of pressure, an INFJ becomes more distressed than stressed. Due to the fact that the human dimension takes on such great importance for an INFJ, the conflict between organizational demands and human needs at times can cause the INFJ manager to experience frustration and bewilderment as to what to do.
INFJs tend to be dedicated, serious and hard working. They can be so zealous about being perfect that they may actually do more than is required by the task.	Not surprisingly, INFJs may find themselves overwhelmed and overworked when they feel they are expected to deliver a superhuman performance. They tend to be such loyal team workers that when they are asked to go the extra mile, they will go another two or three.

INFJ

CHARACTERISTICS	IMPLICATIONS
They may find interacting with a great number of people all at once unproductive, threatening and disrupting of their energies.	INFJs seem to function best in carrying out tasks providing a singular focus.
INFJs are masterful in showing appreciation, both verbal and non-verbal, by giving praise whenever they find an appropriate opportunity. The contribution and appreciation of INFJs is clearly demonstrated in the way they actively listen and give their full attention to a person. They always seem to have real intuition as to what to say and do to encourage and create a set of conditions causing people to feel appreciated. They enjoy commending and applauding the performance of others.	It follows then that since INFJs tend to provide others with encouragement and warm, understanding feedback; they, too, appreciate recognition. Allowing INFJs to understand that they are appreciated not just for what they do, but also for who they are, can seldom, if ever, backfire—unless the source lacks their confidence and trust.
They need and value approval of others and are motivated by positive feedback.	For corrective feedback to be heard by an INFJ, it is not advisable to begin with criticism, as even the most constructive form of criticism may be taken as a personal offense. Authentic, real and heartfelt appreciation is essential for the effective functioning of the INFJ. Once they know they are appreciated, they can better hear the critique.
INFJs are exceptionally loyal. Their loyalty is directed toward individuals and the organization. Whenever possible, the INFJ	INFJs tend to be loyal both to the organization and the people they work with. It is important to realize, however, that when in

CHARACTERISTICS	IMPLICATIONS
manager will make every effort to arrange for individuals to fit into the organization harmoniously and purposefully—not the other way around.	doubt, their loyalties first and foremost go out in the direction of fellow human beings. If need be, the organization can wait. "Harmony" is perhaps one of the most important goals in the life of INFJs; you will find them seeking and providing harmony in any situation. When there is high turnover and frequent staff changes, INFJs may become demoralized and lose enthusiasm for the job.
Typically, the INFJ tends to take on the concerns and characteristics of others and thus, through a great deal of empathy, identifies with how the other person feels.	Therefore, it is not unusual for INFJs to take criticism of others as if it were their own and then feel responsible for the acts that produced it. They are also likely to strongly identify with the underdog and find themselves in conflict with formal actions and their potentially negative impact on morale.
They enjoy predictability and a sense of order in what they do, and they tend to enjoy the opportunity to complete whatever they set out to accomplish. Starting too many new projects out of sequence is not their idea of effectiveness.	INFJs easily become quite involved in what they want to accomplish, therefore they are not likely to take kindly to abrupt interruptions—even though they may not express much dissatisfaction or frustration.
Patient with complicated situations, INFJs are capable of concentration and dedication to achieve significant and important results.	It is not uncommon for INFJs to become so dedicated and committed to assisting others that they become single-minded and blind sided by their burning de-

INFJ

CHARACTERISTICS

IMPLICATIONS

sire to make a significant contribution. In other words, they may become so selfless that they will subordinate their own wants and needs for a cause, a leader, and a purpose of great significance to them.

INFJs are skillful in observing and taking in accurate information about the sentiments, beliefs, values and norms of importance to others and then translating these into a work situation where people feel significant.

As a result, INFJs tend to be quite accurate in understanding how and what seems to motivate people.

VALUES

INFJs value the ethical and the moral, wanting goodness—the "greater good" —for all, both people and systems.

These values are so strong that they may become over zealous in their pursuit of the good. In an organization, they may become heartbroken if they perceive it is immoral, impersonal or uncaring.

Whatever an INFJ decides to value or favor tends to be carefully selected and, as a result, often turns out to be both highly personal and very deep. Indeed, the values INFJs select over time tend to become the core of their identity and their whole existence.

When anything happens that violates or jeopardizes these values, the usually kind-hearted, agreeable, and understanding INFJs can stand firm and, with deep intensity and a very real sense of compassion, direct a great deal of personal energy toward putting things right—as they perceive right to be.

INFJ

CHARACTERISTICS	**IMPLICATIONS**

INFJs seek and expect relationships to provide growth and development. They tend to accept and know that the world is less than perfect; therefore, they take it upon themselves to build more harmony and understanding. That task is accepted as a life-long and self-imposed assignment.

Rationales for initiating changes in systems or policies at times are viewed as insufficient and will not persuade them, especially if their intuition tells them otherwise, and not enough consideration has been directed toward the human side of enterprise.

INFJs typically learn to trust their intuitions and value assessments very early in life.

As a result, a manager, friend, peer or subordinate attempting to persuade or influence an INFJ to take action counter to his/her convictions and sense of what is appropriate will meet a silent, determined and unbending wall of resistance.

Integrity is critically important to them and, as a result, INFJs have almost psychic insights. Consequently, do not be surprised if anyone working with an INFJ in a manipulative or insincere way is likely to draw the short end of the straw.

INFJs are capable of subtle retaliatory measures and while they seek not to harm anyone, it is not easy to get off their blacklist. The best possible stance in working with an INFJ, or being in a close relationship with an INFJ, is to be authentic, sincere and honest.

INFJs abhor a lack of caring and anyone approaching any situation without a genuine desire to ultimately support and assist people can cause the INFJ a great deal of concern and agony.

It is important to realize that while an INFJ is loyal and often a hard-working team player wanting to contribute to the overall achievement of the enterprise, if and when people become cold, hard and impersonal, the INFJ is not likely to respond very well. As a result, expect the INFJ manager to

CHARACTERISTICS	IMPLICATIONS

question anyone using formal authority without having earned the respect and affection of superiors, peers and subordinates alike.

ATTITUDE

The basic attitude of INFJs is one of being credulous and idealistic. They tend to see good and potential in everyone and everything.

They usually expect goodness, warmth and deep human understanding from everyone with whom they work and may gloss over and ignore the darker side. With their never-ending focus on ideals and harmony, they may be disappointed when the real world doesn't measure up.

Their enthusiasm is rarely demonstrated with effusive expressions of intense emotions. It is there, nonetheless, and surfaces with emphatic intenseness when their values and sense of ethics are violated. Moreover, understand that INFJs are people who have a highly developed capacity to understand what seems to motivate people—someone being non-authentic and attempting to play a role is probably spotted more quickly by an INFJ than any of the other fifteen types.

To purely task-oriented, more calculating individuals, the enthusiasm of an INFJ at times may appear excessive and counterproductive. Such individuals would be well-advised to understand that unlike themselves, INFJs believe that life itself is a drama and therefore they enjoy playing it to the hilt.

INFJ

CHARACTERISTICS	IMPLICATIONS
Over time, INFJs have come to find the ambiguous reasonably acceptable since they so often experience organizational and human needs to be quite paradoxical.	The ability of an INFJ to observe and not judge unusual and different behaviors is highly developed.

SKILLS

INFJs are skilled at anything having to do with people—handling them, employing them, deploying them, training them, motivating them, recruiting them, counseling them, and supporting them in achieving their goals and aspirations.	If you want INFJ employees to deliver a superior performance, provide them with opportunities for solving problems, especially regarding human systems and organizations.
Moreover, INFJs are terrific listeners; they can get so involved and empathic when understanding people from their perspectives that they will get into a string of thoughts midstream and finish the sentence for the person they are listening to with surprising accuracy.	INFJs frequently burden themselves with other people's problems. For this very reason (over identification), they may seem aloof and distant from time to time.
They prefer one-on-one relationships and they seem to know just what the person needs to do next. Intimacy is far more important to them than publicity.	It is critically important for INFJs to like and be liked by whomever they associate with. As a matter of fact, if INFJs have a feeling of hostility or dislike for someone, they covertly or overtly refuse to perform.
They work well in organizations, dealing with others in a sensitive manner. They use their original-	Expect INFJ managers to be unusually devoted, with a genuine desire to create the best possible

INFJ

CHARACTERISTICS	IMPLICATIONS

ity, insight and interpersonal warmth to organize, counsel, inspire and teach—achieving outstanding results by working exceptionally well with people.

working conditions for everyone for whom they are responsible. They typically will take a personal interest in fostering individual growth and development.

Intuiting for INFJs is an internal process. They have a capacity for deep concentration and seem to be tuned in to knowledge and insights the rest of us are not privy to.

Consequently, do not expect INFJs to be all that comfortable in crowds. Typically, they do not enjoy public appearances and addressing large groups of people.

INFJs are global and metaphoric in their speech. They are adept communicators with sensitivity to the nuances and unspoken aspects of communication. INFJs do not take the spoken word at face value. Their ears and eyes are tuned to what lies behind the spoken word.

More interested in the implications of communication, they may hear things others did not even notice or would not even imagine.

Moreover, INFJs are in constant search for meaning—in words, in people and in situations.

For INFJs there is a reason for everything, and understanding the reason for what people say and do is more important for INFJs than the substance of specific events.

They frequently apply their talent for language to the written word and write in a personal way using rich metaphors.

Typically they strive to communicate meaningfulness in their writings. Indeed, they want to provide the reader with better insights and understanding, especially in the human side of enterprise.

INFJ

CHARACTERISTICS	IMPLICATIONS
When INFJs apply themselves to the technical fields (over the more people-oriented professions), they can bring great ingenuity and problem-solving ability to the tasks.	INFJs need to work for a cause, a leader, a purpose—if it is bigger than life itself, then that is perfect. For INFJs the meaning of life seems to be more important than approaching every day as usual—indeed, the spark, the energizer and the clincher for them is when they can contribute the unusual, the incredibly important and valuable in a compassionate, unassuming fashion. INFJs do, however, tend to fit well into everyday work routines, as long as the environment is supportive and harmonious.
INFJs sometimes have difficulty communicating the intensity of what they feel and perceive, tending to strive for perfection in verbal expression.	Consequently, INFJs frequently find written communication a more rewarding and precise outlet for their skilled use of image and metaphor. They usually write well and can often express themselves superbly with an artistic bent. Do not expect INFJs to join the speaker circuit, for they are most comfortable working with small groups who over time become trusted friends, enjoying mutual trust and confidence. While they can comfortably learn to speak up, one of their greatest gifts tends to be reflected in non-verbal communication skills.

INFJ

CHARACTERISTICS	IMPLICATIONS

Warmth, graciousness and charm are important aspects of their people/communication skills.

People usually enjoy working with or for INFJs, as they are particularly gifted in causing people to want to work together. Moreover, they, unlike most, tend to manage people and situations by empathy and listening. They are masterful at providing meaningful performance feedback—even though at times you may have to ask for it.

DRIVING FORCE

INFJs have a high need for empathic relationships. These relationships must be deep and meaningful for them to satisfy the intense hunger that they feel for rapport.

As a result, INFJs tend to be so alert to and focused on the needs of others that they may jeopardize their own situation. It should not come as a surprise then that INFJs do not tend to be involved a great deal in company politics.

The hallmark of their style in relationships is authenticity. They cannot and will not accept the counterfeit, superficiality and any form of manipulation.

Since INFJs want to avoid being phony, they may resist assignments that require some pretense. Moreover, they are not power oriented. Consequently, you cannot expect them to take charge by commanding; to the contrary, they are likely to go out of their way to accommodate.

Also, be mindful of the fact that an INFJ is a compassionate person. The more meaningfulness in a work situation, the more devoted, dedicated and enthused is our INFJ.

While the INFJ typically will be loyal to company policies and procedures, it is unrealistic to assume that an INFJ will subordinate regulations and procedures to important human needs just to get the job done.

INFJ

CHARACTERISTICS	IMPLICATIONS

ENERGY DIRECTION

Given these skills, values and attitudes, INFJs typically direct their energy toward bringing forth the highest and fullest potential in everyone they contact. They are in constant search for their own identity and naturally enjoy facilitating others in their search for meaning and purpose.

If not given the opportunity to have meaningful relationships, they may become stressed and have difficulties on the job, to the point of becoming physically ill.

They find meaning and significance in the smallest event, and their ability to see relationships between events and circumstances that are apparently very different enables inferences not available to most individuals of a different type.

Expect INFJs to make extraordinarily insightful observations in interpersonal relationships. To many, they may come across as having an ability to soothe and heal wounds and conflict-filled situations.

Within the organization, their energy will be directed toward change which will make a better world—toward helping humankind.

INFJs are quick to respond in a moment of need—especially if it is a human need. It is painful for them to perceive the need for change and not be listened to.

These are the cooperators; they are driven to seek harmony and goodwill, arranging for people to work together.

As a result, understand that the chances of their becoming hurt and not feeling understood and accepted by others can be quite high. Indeed, INFJs give "value" higher priority than logic. It is important for them to place trust in others and be trusted in return.

INFJ

CHARACTERISTICS

IMPLICATIONS

INFJs can quietly become enthused about ideas and programs which assist people to become more of what they are capable of being. Moreover, they tend to derive a great deal of energy from philosophical discussions in order to understand the meaning of life and how people can derive more meaningfulness from their respective work environments.

INFJs are masterful at having impact on people's lives—quietly and frequently from behind the scenes.

AUTHORITY ORIENTATION

INFJs want the person in charge to be ethical, authentic and "good." Authority is not granted by position—it is earned over time through dedication and exemplary behavior. Their first inclination is to respect their superior and to seek approval from the person in charge.

If the person in charge is not seen as ethical and caring, there is little hope of getting INFJs to accept their performance feedback as something worth paying attention to. This does not mean that INFJs are immune to harsh criticism and sarcasm. Even if they do not respect their superior, harsh criticism and sarcasm can cause deep injury.

ROLE PERCEPTION

INFJs tend to wait for others to take the first step in defining how a relationship should be established, its parameters and function. They do not mind giving directives and if no one steps up to take charge, they will in the interest of time and task.

An INFJ is the kind of individual who quietly and unassumingly becomes a friend, a supporter and a confidant. That role may not be defined, yet it is always there.

INFJ

CHARACTERISTICS	IMPLICATIONS
It is important to know that IN-FJs are selective in whom they choose to support.	Do not expect INFJs to demonstrate overt eagerness in establishing healthy, mutually supportive relationships. To the contrary, expect a quiet flame to burn in their hearts and minds, establishing long-term valuable, honorable and meaningful relationships.

CONFLICT RESOLUTION

INFJs prefer harmonious situations and tend to ignore conflicts as long as they possibly can. They put forth great effort to make things run harmoniously, and those attempting to get their point of view across in a non-caring, matter-of-fact fashion are virtually assured that the INFJ will spare no energy resisting whatever is being argued.	INFJs may suppress feelings of ill will to the point of immobilization. It is inconceivable for them to engage in a verbal fist fight. As a matter of fact, if they find themselves in the middle of a hot and heavy argument, they would rather leave than win.
Even a reminder to minimize their tendency to personalize a conflict is difficult for them to accept beyond a reasoning level. It is very difficult for INFJs to separate their personal values from the otherwise impersonal world.	INFJs at times approach high levels of exhaustion in taking conflict personally and carrying it in their bosom for a long time.
However, they are not put off by intense feelings. They may even encourage the free expression of feelings so that the group can move towards consensus.	Indeed, a source of great strength for INFJs is their ability to empathize with people they care about and feel responsible for. They tend to be great supporters of freedom of speech, as long as no one gets hurt.

INFJ

CHARACTERISTICS	IMPLICATIONS

MODES OF LEARNING

INFJs learn through interaction, in dialogue with others or with the written word. They enjoy concepts, theories and ideas a great deal— especially those which explain the scientific and human phenomena.

The learning environment is important for INFJs. The more personal mutual understanding there is, the more the learning process is facilitated. They tend not to enjoy a disciplinarian type of instruction. For INFJs, there is very little in this world which can be considered black or white—the shades are preferably warm and gray.

INFJs use their ability to see relationships and to synthesize in order to simplify the learning process.

Since the consciousness of INFJs is global and diffuse, they may need to be reminded to focus on the details of what they are learning, as they naturally may stop at the global impression of having learned something and thus not adequately master the nitty-gritty, boring, mundane, inconsequential details.

INFJs learn easily from lectures and written work that they consider valuable and important. Moreover, they are abstract learners and enjoy expanding their horizons in grasping new ideas and concepts, especially in the humanities and causes of events both past and present.

As a result, INFJs are skillful in understanding human motivation at work and in family situations.

INFJ

CHARACTERISTICS	IMPLICATIONS
A positive relationship with the teacher is as important as is the integrity of the teacher.	Particularly in their younger years, the need for relating to the teacher may turn out to be their own worst enemy and significantly block learning, especially if that relationship was disappointing or discouraging to them. On the other hand, a teacher who understands and accepts the INFJ student can become a useful and influential mentor.

BLIND SPOTS AND PITFALLS

INFJs may focus so much on the human element in any situation that they may get off task too much and lose a sense of perspective.	INFJs are so dedicated and motivated that they may devote their total being to a cause, a purpose, and sometimes a person. They may tend to idealize to the extent that they leave behind their own needs. The result, over time, can be detrimental, as they may come to resent their own actions.
Responsiveness to others may lead to so much energy being devoted to other people's priorities that INFJs expend more of their time than they initially may have intended. Eventually they may lose sight of their own needs and suffer from loss of personal identity and eventual burnout.	Therefore, at times it may be quite appropriate for INFJs to flag some time out and schedule time for themselves to rejuvenate their batteries and personal energy, which is necessary for them to continue to make a major contribution in the lives of others.
INFJs tend to be loyal to both the organization and the people with whom they work. They are steady, dependable, day-to-day	The ideal work environment for INFJs is one which allows them to make a significant contribution to a leader and a worth-

INFJ

CHARACTERISTICS

IMPLICATIONS

contributors. While they can accept and perform within the parameters of daily routine, it seems to be quite important for them to "like" and "be liked." In other words, do not expect an INFJ to function well for any length of time if and when interpersonal conflict exists.

They may get very involved with others' problems and, as a result, create dependency relationships which may be difficult to get out of.

While INFJs usually adapt to established procedures, they tend to find too much bureaucracy frustrating; protocol, routine, and paperwork can be both meaningless and a waste of time. Consequently, in their attempt to create a working environment of freedom and autonomy (that encourages individual growth and development), organizational mandates, systems, and procedures may, at times, suffer accordingly, especially if those who designed and developed the systems are considered inept.

while cause, and where the sum of all human elements delivers super-human results. For the INFJ, nothing is impossible if a dedicated, sincere team is determined to accomplish great things. The problem or reality, of course, is that those kinds of wonderful situations seldom seem to exist.

If standard operating procedures and regulations seem to be getting in the way of individuals using their talents, they may have difficulty working within these constraints and, as a result, find their energy drained. The ideal work environment for an INFJ is one where human qualities, harmony and understanding prevail. Efficiency in a work situation for an INFJ is one where people are allowed to become whatever they are capable of.

INFJ

CHARACTERISTICS	IMPLICATIONS
INFJs tend to be highly perfectionistic and idealistic. As a result, they may put off tasks rather than accept imperfect products and conditions.	Non-manipulative, participative management is an important dimension in the working life of an INFJ. It is important that changes, systems, and procedures are installed and operated for a purpose—a purpose serving both organizational and human purposes.
Finally, INFJs are so gifted in imagination that they may prefer fantasy to reality and dreams to action.	Indeed, happiness in the final analysis for an INFJ is when wonderful dreams come true. If we were to provide the INFJ with a motto, it would probably sound like this: "If I do not envision something better, I am not doing my job."

INFJ

CHARACTERISTICS	IMPLICATIONS

ENFP

The theme of ENFPs is inspiration, both of themselves and others. They lead through their contagious enthusiasm for "causes" that further good and develop latent potential. They are very perceptive of others' motives and interested in what is going on around them. Their inspiration leads them to disclosing and unveiling the fake, the sham and the evil, and enthusiastically communicating their "message."

CHARACTERISTICS	IMPLICATIONS

MANAGEMENT STYLE

The management style of ENFPs is outgoing, democratic and participative. Their style is likely to be highly people oriented and they lead by their energy and enthusiasm for causes.

The ideal work environment is one that is warm, understanding, and very people oriented. Cooperation, support, and making a dream world of harmony come true is the real theme for the ENFP.

ENFPs manage in a very personal way, getting involved with the individuals in the organization. As they live and breathe for creating a wonderful tomorrow, don't be surprised if they forget to cross some t's and dot some i's.

There would be minimal insistence on rules, systems and procedures for, in the view of the ENFP, these mechanical restrictions deny the climate of freedom and autonomy that allow people to reach their very highest potential.

Their commitment is to the progress and growth of those around them and thus on the development of staff instead of the development of systems, procedures and corporate policies.

ENFPs are likely to ask of any change, "Is it good for the people?" and "Will it take away, undermine, or in any way hurt good, human relationships?"

ENFP

CHARACTERISTICS	IMPLICATIONS
They are tuned in to the motivations of others and can spend untold hours on interpersonal intrigues and problems—and love every minute of it.	It is a challenge for an ENFP to reduce the spending of untold hours on interpersonal intrigues, for the purpose of achieving balance.
Seeking relationships, ENFPs easily become concerned with the personal problems of their co-workers, subordinates or superiors. Not surprisingly, these kinds of problems can absorb their energies, sometimes to the detriment of the business itself.	This may draw them off task at times and they may become overwhelmed with their self-assigned responsibility of harmonizing the lives of others.
They do not hesitate to get involved and want to be a part of all that is going on around them, especially if it calls for innovation, realization of dreams, and a better future for those involved.	They sometimes may be viewed as sticking their nose in where it really does not belong or they get "too" involved. Keep in mind, however, that they really have the good of others at heart and are usually willing to risk the consequences of their unsolicited involvement.
ENFPs are masters at showing appreciation, both verbal and non-verbal, giving frequent and abundant praise. They seem to know just what to say and do to make the other person feel appreciated. In fact, they are a natural inspiration and encourage people to reach out.	Their appreciation and investment in being the carrier of good tidings is directed toward their leaders, peers and subordinates as well.
They value approval of others and are motivated by positive feedback. Conversely, negative feedback may be experienced as	Appreciation is essential for the effective functioning of the ENFP. Management by any kind of criticism, including construc-

ENFP

CHARACTERISTICS	IMPLICATIONS

rejection and a personal vendetta, causing all kinds of misery and misgivings.

tive, turns off ENFPs. Their worst working environment is impersonal, political, and one where nobody likes anybody.

ENFPs are very loyal, but their loyalty goes to the people in the organization, not so much to the systems and procedures.

When there are frequent staff changes, ENFPs may become disconcerted and demoralized, eventually losing a sense of enthusiasm for the job. Indeed, they frequently identify strongly with the underdog and find themselves at odds with the system.

ENFPs like variety in what they do, frequently inventing new ways of doing things, and are masterful at "spur of the moment" activities, especially when they involve interacting with people.

As a result, they may become fragmented from wanting to do too many different things all at once and from being pulled in too many directions, seeking to please everyone.

They tend to start many projects with a great deal of gusto, therefore, don't be surprised if some of them fall by the wayside from time to time.

ENFPs easily become bored with routines and may fail to carry out ongoing projects to completion. The ideal work environment for them calls for variety and allows them to exercise their ingenuity and creativity in initiating and maintaining a meaningful work situation.

VALUES

ENFPs value ethics and morals, striving for the "greater good" for all.

This value is so strong that they may become overzealous in their pursuit of the pure. In an organization they may side with de-

ENFP

CHARACTERISTICS	IMPLICATIONS

tractors if they perceive immorality, non-caring, and efforts which only focus on results.

They seek relationships in which they can promote growth and development; "people" are their center of gravity, so to speak.

If they do not have opportunities to promote the growth and development of others, their work becomes devoid of meaning and apathy sets in.

They trust their intuitions and inferences above all and decisions based solely on logical, objective criteria do not evoke their full energy.

At times, the rationale behind an event or a policy may not persuade them, particularly if their intuition tells them otherwise.

Integrity is very important to ENFPs.

Their sometimes uncompromising values and needs may conflict with systems, policies and procedures, and they may choose to ignore "reality" in order to protect their sense of integrity.

They abhor a lack of caring and appreciate the "human side" of the enterprise.

Without a strong appreciation for the "human side," life becomes bland. ENFPs often have a strongly held belief that everyone is obligated to care for everyone.

ATTITUDE

The basic attitude of ENFPs is one of credulity, enthusiasm and idealism. They tend to see good and potential in everyone and everything. They are not troubled by the paradoxical and

They usually expect goodness. With their focus on ideals they may be disappointed when "reality" doesn't measure up. Sometimes, they may be hypersensitive to the "dark

CHARACTERISTICS

IMPLICATIONS

they relentlessly pursue their high ideals.

side," inaccurately interpreting their astute perceptions of hidden motives as negative. Indeed, when they do not receive feedback, they usually experience it in only one way - negatively.

The enthusiasm of the ENFP is dramatically demonstrated with effusive expressions of intense emotion. On the other hand, when whoever or whatever is not living up to expectations, life for the ENFP can be experienced as a bottomless pit and there seems to be no relief in sight.

Individuals not geared toward the realities of an ENFP often tend to become critical of the dramatic flair, the high-energy people focus, and the never-ending concern for making the most (or the least) of interpersonal relations.

ENFPs find the ambiguous perfectly acceptable since they expect things to be paradoxical. Orderly, predictable and bureaucratic systems are turn offs for ENFPs.

They require ample space for their creativity. A great appreciation for the paradoxical allows ENFPs to experience a wide range of the multitudinous human thoughts, feelings and behaviors.

SKILLS

ENFPs are skilled at anything having to do with people - listening, facilitating, deploying, training, motivating, recruiting, counseling and understanding their perspectives.

If you want ENFPs to deliver superior performance, be sure the job provides opportunities for interaction and some higher purpose they can become enthused about.

Typically, ENFPs enjoy and are willing to get involved in relationships. They identify with others to the point of demonstrating perfect empathy and

The ability to identify may put some strain on their own identity. In other words, ENFPs can become so enamored and dedicated in supporting others, es-

ENFP

CHARACTERISTICS	**IMPLICATIONS**

seem to know just what the person needs in order to function better.

pecially when there is a feeling of mutual dependency, that their own needs and wants are subordinated to the cause of supporting others. Sometimes only later do they regret their impulsive generosity.

Inspiring for ENFPs is an external process, emanating from the continuous scanning of the environment for data to confirm their beliefs and values and support their causes. Their natural enthusiasm can be a great source of inspiration for others.

Just as ENFPs naturally inspire others, they seek and require inspiration from others. Enthusiasm, beliefs, values, inspiration and causes are words which apply to ENFPs.

ENFPs are global and metaphoric in their speech. They are adept communicators in their sensitivity to the nuances and unspoken aspects of communication. Indeed, when they apply themselves to human needs, they are superb listeners.

More interested in implications and hidden agendas, they sometimes "hear" things others do not hear and block out that which doesn't confirm their beliefs. ENFPs can become so bent on pursuing their selective perceptions that only a dramatic jolt or flare can move them off the dime, so to speak.

ENFPs are naturals for thinking with imagery. Their writing style captures one's imagination. With their penchant for unveiling and disclosing, their interest in all that is going on around them, and their talent for communicating, they are particularly gifted in reporting and rephrasing events so they become more illuminating, interesting and valuable.

Small wonder they often take up journalism, especially investigative reporting.

ENFP

CHARACTERISTICS	IMPLICATIONS

Warmth, graciousness and charm are natural and important aspects of their people/ communication skills.

Working for and with ENFPs can be quite enjoyable. One is still advised to keep in mind, however, that their work ethic is quite different. On one hand, bursts of energy and enthusiasm are their great contribution. On the other hand, when boredom takes over, few can be less responsive than the ENFP.

DRIVING FORCE

ENFPs have a high need for empathic relationships. These relationships must be deep and meaningful for them to satisfy the intense hunger that they feel for rapport.

One of the greatest joys for an ENFP is getting lost in conversation with another person. Yet, while not necessarily outspoken, ENFPs have a great capacity to determine whom they like and whom they trust; at times they build so much into a relationship that they can easily be taken advantage of and/or disappointed.

There are times when ENFPs emphatically will put their foot down to clearly demonstrate a point, be it in agreement or in opposition.

Realize, however, that behind such a facade of decisiveness, more often than not there is a willingness to be persuaded to change position, as long as the process is enjoyable and very human.

ENFP

CHARACTERISTICS	IMPLICATIONS

The hallmark of an ENFP's relationships is authenticity.

Since ENFPs abhor being phony, they are not likely to perform well in assignments that require pretense or could be merely considered hard, cold and task oriented. It seems that quality human interaction is more important to them than quantity output.

ENERGY DIRECTION

Given these values, beliefs and attitudes, ENFPs direct most of their energy toward bringing forth the potential in everyone they contact. They are in a constant search for their true identity and will go to great lengths in supporting others in search of their highest and best potential.

If not given the opportunity to have meaningful relationships, they may become distressed and find their external work situation increasingly difficult to cope with. While at least for a time they may put forth their best effort to make things work, behind the facade of willing cooperation, their turbulence may be percolating - only to eventually surface, with a certain amount of drama.

ENFPs find meaning and significance in even the smallest event and their ability to see relationships between people, events and things is powerful and different, enabling identification of inferences not available to the rest of us.

There is a disadvantage, however—ENFPs can sometimes draw faulty conclusions from their inferences.

Within the organization, typically their energy is directed toward changes which ultimately result in increased human satisfaction and performance.

ENFPs insist upon human satisfaction first and performance second. They hold that performance increases as interpersonal conflict decreases.

ENFP

CHARACTERISTICS

IMPLICATIONS

Indeed, these are the cooperators. ENFPs are driven to seek harmony and goodwill, arranging for others to enjoy and share in a common cause, a purpose, and a sense of being significant way beyond the trivia of day-to-day work.

They may be wary of what seems like callousness and anything that smacks of the end justifying the means. Anyone attempting to stand out by breaking the implied rules and norms should not be surprised when encouraged by an ENFP to "knock it off and join the team without attempting to be the center of attention."

Natural turn ons for ENFPs are ideas and programs that have value beyond material well being. People actualizing their fullest potential is a never-ending crusade for ENFPs. To that end, philosophical discussions which get at the meaning of just about everything and are an opportunity for interaction with others are important to unlocking the purpose of life.

It should come as no surprise then that while an ENFP may go about everyday work as a loyal, industrious team member, it would be naive to surmise that work for work's sake constitutes sufficient motivation. For the ENFP, the search for a deeper meaning and motivation will never subside.

AUTHORITY ORIENTATION

Above all, ENFPs want the person in charge to be ethical, caring and a good human being. Authority is not granted by the position itself, although their initial inclination is to respect position power and to seek approval from the person in charge.

If the person in charge is not seen as ethical, moral and caring, there is little hope of getting the ENFP to accept his/her authority and performance feedback as something worth striving for, especially if it is negative.

ENFP

CHARACTERISTICS	IMPLICATIONS

ROLE PERCEPTION

While ENFPs tend to be adaptive in their relationships with others, they easily make the first move in defining a relationship. ENFPs respect a strong and capable leader.

Wanting harmony, they frequently adapt to the role set for them, especially if they view someone as their chosen leader, both on a formal and informal basis.

When ENFPs take the lead, they are quite likely to give information rather than directives. They usually expect others to act on the information.

Since they are so tuned into the needs and aspirations of others, their indirect, informative "directives" are frequently followed. When they are not, an ENFP can be quite disappointed.

CONFLICT RESOLUTION

ENFPs prefer harmonious situations and may ignore conflicts as long as they possibly can. They are distressed by conflict and have a tendency to take things quite personally.

They may expend great efforts in conciliation and pacification to avoid conflict. If, however, they are not able to positively impact situations in a constructive, helpful fashion, their natural tendency is to avoid them and depart from the scene.

ENFPs are not, however, put off by intense feelings. They believe that expressing feelings may even encourage others to do so, and thus the group can move toward consensus and a common understanding of how to find a resolution.

They are often masterful at helping others resolve their conflicts.

Their empathic capabilities are so developed that at times they may even personalize conflicts.

They may have to be reminded to not take conflicts personally. Keep in mind, however, reason-

ENFP

CHARACTERISTICS

IMPLICATIONS

ing logically with them may be counterproductive, especially if their feelings are intense.

MODES OF LEARNING

ENFPs learn through interaction, in dialogue with others or with the written word. They are abstract, not linear or concrete, learners. Theory, ideas and concepts can hold their fascination for long periods of time.

Sometimes, their need for relating to the teacher may be their own worst enemy and block learning, especially if the relationship turns out to be disappointing to them.

They use their ability to see relationships and synthesize to simplify the learning process; hence, they may be viewed as global learners. An eye for great detail tends not to be their strength.

Since the consciousness of EN-FPs is global and diffuse, they may need to be reminded to focus on the details of what they are learning, for they are inclined to choose to remain with the global impression of having learned something. To soar with generalities, concepts and ideas, particularly those deemed of benefit to individuals, groups or mankind, is their great source of energy, enthusiasm and new insight.

They are adept at learning abstract ideas and less adept at learning by association and rote. It is safe to assume that "doing things by the book" won't exactly elicit ENFP enthusiasm.

ENFP

CHARACTERISTICS	IMPLICATIONS

BLIND SPOTS AND PITFALLS

ENFPs may focus so much on the human element in any situation that they may subordinate a task to favoring interpersonal and human needs.	It is useful to understand that if ENFPs, for whatever reason, do not like whomever they are working with, the personal sense of discomfort can be so taxing on them that performance could decline.
ENFPs can be so involved in meeting the needs of others that they may lose sight of their own needs and suffer from loss of personal identity and a sense of their own presence.	To schedule time for themselves, to rejuvenate their energy and, in a sense, to refocus their priorities may turn out to be quite helpful, if suggested in a non-threatening, caring way.
Being so responsive to others can lead to meeting other peoples' priorities while jeopardizing their own needs.	Sometimes the responsiveness of ENFPs can take them off task, since they do not prestructure their time. Insomuch as they can be devoted and committed to assisting other individuals, sometimes a "getting the job done" orientation conflicts with the humanistic proclivities of ENFPs.
They frequently do things at the last minute.	It is important to stress deadlines for ENFPs. The deadlines must be real, for they will not respond to contrived deadlines. Somehow the deadline creates a condition under which they can draw on creative juices not otherwise available.
ENFPs tend to work in bursts of energy which may not coincide with the needs of the job.	The ideal work environment is one which allows them the flexibility to capitalize on these

ENFP

CHARACTERISTICS

IMPLICATIONS

bursts of energy while not berating them for the lulls in between.

With their high degree of empathic ability, ENFPs may be experienced as agreeing with each person they relate to, and subsequently they get stuck in the middle between opposing forces, eventually being torn between their own, their supervisor's and their subordinates' needs.

It is important to realize that the realities, the conscious stream of energy, and the natural desire of ENFPs is centered around people and their ability to become everything they possibly can be. As a result, forces interfering with these noble and very worthwhile proclivities are not readily accepted, much less understood, by the ENFP.

They may get so involved in internalizing the failures of others that they put their own priorities in a holding pattern.

ENFPs are people of passion and compassion. They are typically highly focused on bringing about conditions allowing each person they care for to, in a most favorable way, become everything that person seems cut out to be.

As a result, they may tend to rescue victims of the system, policies and procedures only to find themselves in a conflict situation they actually want to defuse.

Because of their warm, authentic and outgoing attitude toward others, they may get too involved with problematic situations external to them and create dependency relationships which may be difficult to terminate without conflict and hurt feelings.

It is very difficult for ENFPs to wrest themselves free from problematic, dependency relationships. It behooves them to insist upon mutuality in relationships.

ENFPs tend to find bureaucracy frustrating, with protocol and

They may have difficulty working within the constraints of

ENFP

CHARACTERISTICS	IMPLICATIONS

paperwork a waste of time. In their attempts to create a climate of freedom, personal integrity and autonomy (so people can grow), some mandated procedures may be left by the wayside- or even worse, way behind in the dust.

standard operating procedures and regulations. As a result, they may find it necessary to challenge and bend rules, procedures and policies.

CHARACTERISTICS	IMPLICATIONS

INFP

The theme of the INFP is one of supporting. INFPs support anything that allows the unfolding of the person, encouraging growth and development with a quiet enthusiasm. They become the advocates and champions of causes, caring deeply about their goals and aspirations, and they naturally tend to relate to and dedicate themselves to a few special people.

CHARACTERISTICS	IMPLICATIONS

MANAGEMENT STYLE

The management style of INFPs is very caring, democratic and participative. Their style is likely to be people oriented and they lead by quietly championing worthwhile causes and encouraging individuals to achieve whatever they are setting out to do.

The ideal work environment for the INFP is one that is highly people oriented and encourages harmony, mutual support and cooperation.

INFPs manage in a very personal, quiet and unassuming way, getting involved with the individuals in the organization one by one and establishing personal relationships based on quality, not quantity.

Typically, there would be minimal focus and insistence on rules and procedures for, in the view of the INFP, these inhibit a climate of freedom and autonomy which fosters growth opportunities for creative individuals.

Their commitment is to the progress and growth of those around them and thus on the development of staff more so than the development of systems and procedures.

They are likely to ask of any proposed change "Is it good for the people?" both in the short and the long haul. Moreover, they are also concerned with the rate of change—how it is communicated and accepted or re-

CHARACTERISTICS	IMPLICATIONS
	jected by the people. They are not great fans of edicts and pronouncements. To them, meaningful and lasting change evolves over time as a result of human qualities.
"Realities" for an INFP are anchored in process. An INFP derives a great deal of satisfaction from the fact that nothing is constant and from the opportunity to quietly and unassumingly influence a cause in a positive and constructive fashion.	
INFPs are naturally tuned in to the emotions and motivations of others, and they are unusually gifted at understanding individual differences.	They have a far greater awareness of the emotions of others than they are able to verbalize.
Seeking relationships, they naturally become concerned with the personal problems of their co-workers, subordinates or superiors and feel a sense of obligation in resolving grievances, conflicts and disagreements, however small.	This may draw them off task at times and they may become more concerned with how an organization and its systems, rules and procedures actually prevent productive change from taking place as opposed to supporting it.
INFPs are usually content to work alone, savoring solitude for contemplation and making a significant contribution.	They may find interacting with a great number of people all at once unproductive, threatening and disrupting of their energies.
They are masterful in showing appreciation, both verbal and non-verbal, by giving praise	Their appreciation is directed at human accomplishment. They are loyal, industrious, and al-

CHARACTERISTICS

whenever they find an appropriate opportunity. INFPs clearly demonstrate their appreciation by the way they actively listen and give their full attention to a person. They always seem to be keenly aware, knowing what to say and do to encourage and create a set of conditions causing people to feel appreciated.

It should come as no surprise, then, that INFPs value the approval of others and are encouraged themselves by positive feedback.

Typically, INFPs tend to take on characteristics of others and thus, through a great deal of empathy, identify with how the other person feels.

INFPs are loyal; their loyalties, however, seem more directed toward the people in the organization, not the systems, procedures and mechanics of keeping an organization going.

IMPLICATIONS

ways alert to the human potential. For the INFP this potential is crucial to work and provides meaning for a cause, a purpose and people. Indeed, it is the being, the quality and the authenticity which matters—from that, superior results will emerge.

Authentic, real and heartfelt appreciation is essential for the effective functioning of the INFP. Managing by objectives, by criticism, by systems, by the book, or by some kind of edict is inconsequential or, even worse, detrimental to the cause of optimizing human potential.

Therefore, it is not unusual for them to take criticism of others as if it were their own and then feel responsible for the acts that produced it.

When there is high turnover and frequent staff changes, INFPs may become demoralized and lose enthusiasm for the job. Unless there is a plausible reason, they are likely to identify strongly with the underdog and find themselves in conflict with the formal actions and their potentially negative impact on morale.

CHARACTERISTICS	IMPLICATIONS
INFPs are loyal, industrious team players who want to please anyone they work for or with. They view any organization as a vehicle for achieving desired results by people working meaningfully and harmoniously together. Basing decisions on hard, cold facts without taking the human element into consideration is out of the question for an INFP.	INFPs have a great enough challenge to temper and balance their own quiet stubbornness, strictness with themselves, making great sacrifices and idealism. Understandably, the work environment must, at a minimum, be meaningful and harmonious.
They enjoy variety in what they do and are frequently drawn to many new projects, ideas and changing activities.	At times, they may become fragmented from wanting to do too many different things or from being pulled in too many directions. It follows, then, that INFPs tend not to be all that enamored with regimented and unimaginative routines.
Patient with complicated situations, INFPs are capable of intense concentration and dedication to achieving significant and important results.	
INFPs are particularly skillful in observing and taking in accurate information about the sentiments, beliefs, values and norms of importance to others.	Thus, they may be aware of issues, concerns and problems that others are not ready to confront.

VALUES

INFPs value the ethical and the moral, wanting goodness—the "greater good"—for all.	These values are so strong that INFPs may become over zealous in their pursuit of the pure. They

CHARACTERISTICS	IMPLICATIONS
	may become apathetic if they perceive the organization as immoral, impersonal and not caring.
Whatever INFPs decide to value or favor tends to be very carefully selected and, as a result, often turns out to be both highly personal and very deep. Indeed, the values they select over time tend to become the core of their identity and existence.	When anything happens that violates or jeopardizes their values, the usually kind-hearted, agreeable and flexible INFPs can stand firm and, with deep intensity and a very real sense of compassion, direct a great deal of personal energy toward putting things right (as they perceive right to be).
INFPs seek and expect relationships to provide growth and development. They accept that nothing is constant; and for them to build more harmony, understanding and a common acceptance is a life-long, self-imposed assignment.	
Intuition speaks loudly to INFPs. They trust both their intuition and their value assessments. Ignoring their own impressions and putting a great deal of faith in objective reasoning can sometimes backfire on them.	Rationales for initiating changes in systems or policies are at times viewed as insufficient and will not persuade them, especially if their intuition tells them otherwise. Experience has taught INFPs that the information derived through their intuition and filtered through their values is more valuable to them than decisions arrived at through reasoning.

CHARACTERISTICS	IMPLICATIONS

Integrity is very important to the INFP.

Anyone working with an INFP in a manipulative or insincere way is likely to draw the short end of the straw. In other words, a manager, friend, peer or subordinate attempting to persuade or influence an INFP to take action counter to his or her convictions and sense of what is appropriate is likely to meet a silent, determined and unbending wall of resistance.

INFPs abhor a lack of caring, and anyone approaching any situation without a genuine desire to ultimately support and assist people can cause the INFP a great deal of concern and agony.

INFPs are extremely intolerant of fraud and dishonesty. It is best for the sensitive and deeply caring INFP to only work in the company of genuine and trustworthy individuals.

ATTITUDE

The basic attitude of INFPs is one of credulity and idealism. They tend to see good and potential in everyone and everything. They are not troubled by the paradoxical and their calling is to relentlessly pursue their high ideals.

They usually expect goodness, warmth and deep human understanding from everyone they work with. With their never-ending focus on ideals and harmony, they may be disappointed when the real world doesn't measure up. Sometimes they may be hypersensitive to the "dark side," expecting it to surface anytime, especially if prior experiences have taught them to be measured, cautious and careful.

CHARACTERISTICS	IMPLICATIONS

The enthusiasm of INFPs is rarely demonstrated with effusive expressions of intense emotion. However, often below the surface they are boiling with conviction and commitment which surfaces in their devotion to their chosen cause. Their deep feelings are hidden by quiet reserve; when their values are stretched or violated beyond an acceptable level, INFPs may intensely and repeatedly vocalize their disenchantment.

More often than not, the intensity of the feeling INFPs experience is far in excess of what they are capable of verbalizing.

Over time, they have come to find the ambiguous perfectly acceptable, since they so often experience organizational and human needs to be quite paradoxical.

Eliminate paradoxes and you destroy all of the fun for INFPs.

SKILLS

INFPs are skilled at anything having to do with people—listening to them, facilitating them, deploying them, training them, motivating them, recruiting them, and counseling them— even though they seem to keep a certain psychological distance.

If you want INFP employees to deliver a superior performance, be sure the job provides opportunities for fostering wholeness, harmony and mental health in others. They will work intently and diligently on or for something they care about, even at tasks which do not utilize their strong diplomatic skills.

INFP

CHARACTERISTICS	IMPLICATIONS
INFPs prefer one-on-one or small group relationships; they are able to identify strongly with others, appearing to know just what the person needs to function better.	The ability to identify may put some strain on their own identity. In other words, INFPs can become so involved and dedicated in supporting others, especially when there is a feeling of mutual dependency, that their own needs and wants are subordinated to the cause, sometimes only to regret their impulsive generosity.
The INFPs' mode of supporting is an internal process, emanating from their strong desire to develop the full potential of the individual. To become an advocate, or a champion, they keenly observe the behavior of individuals they want to be dedicated to, including the hidden agendas, overtones and inferences. Then they submerge themselves in their rich inner world of intuition and feelings, tuning out additional data and insights to better focus on the object (person) of their support.	Do not expect INFPs to join the speaker circuit, for they are most comfortable working with small groups who, over time, become trusted friends enjoying mutual trust and confidence. While INFPs can comfortably learn to speak up, one of their greatest gifts tends to be reflected in nonverbal communication skills.
The INFPs are global and metaphoric in their speech. They write well and can often express themselves superbly with an artistic bent.	
They sometimes have difficulty communicating the intensity of what they feel, tending to strive for perfection in verbal expression.	Consequently, INFPs frequently find written communication a more rewarding and precise outlet for their skilled use of image and metaphor.

CHARACTERISTICS	IMPLICATIONS

With their penchant for crusading for their cause, they make good investigative journalists, understanding why people function and pursue activities and careers the way they do.

INFPs need to work for a cause, a leader, a purpose—if it is bigger than life itself, then that is perfect. For them, the meaning of life seems to be more important than approaching every day "as usual"—indeed, the spark, the energizer and the clincher for INFPs is when they can contribute the unusual, the incredibly important and valuable in a compassionate, unassuming fashion.

DRIVING FORCE

INFPs have a high need for empathic relationships. These relationships must be deep and meaningful for them to satisfy the intense hunger that they feel for rapport and quality in interpersonal communication.

Keep in mind that behind the warm, kind and understanding expressions of an INFP is always the search for meaning and enrichment of any relationship. Consequently, INFPs can get hurt, discouraged and disappointed, especially when their expectations are based upon dreams and hopes beyond reality.

The hallmark of their relationships is authenticity. INFPs cannot abide the counterfeit and superficial.

Since they want to avoid being phony, they may resist assignments that require some pretense.

ENERGY DIRECTION

Given these skills, values and attitudes, INFPs direct a great deal of their energy toward

If not given the opportunity to have meaningful relationships, they may become distressed and

CHARACTERISTICS	IMPLICATIONS

bringing forth the potential in everyone they interact with on a day-to-day basis. They are always in search of their own unique identity and facilitate the same kind of search by others through encouraging and allowing individual potential to further emerge. Their highest goal is optimizing personal insights and self-knowledge for everyone.

have difficulties on the job, even to the point of becoming physically ill.

Their ability to perceive nuances in relationships is highly developed, enabling them to register significant variations both in terms of deterioration and improvements. These kinds of insights are unique and not readily available to other types.

For an INFP, the work situation is merely incidental in the process of living. What counts and has real significance is the quality of human relationships; when people at work have a real and lasting sense of self-fulfillment, the INFP can relax.

Within the organization, the energy of INFPs will typically be directed toward change which results in a better place for individuals to work.

It is not uncommon for INFPs to become so dedicated and committed to assisting others that they become consumed and blind sided by their burning desire to make a significant difference. In other words, they may become so selfless that they will subordinate their own wants and needs for "the cause."

These are the cooperators. They are driven to seek harmony and goodwill, always focused on creating conditions for comfortable people environments.

They are wary of what seems like callousness and manipulation through hidden agendas.

CHARACTERISTICS

IMPLICATIONS

Turn ons are ideas and programs that help people, opportunities for meaningful interaction with others, and philosophical conversations in small, intimate groups to better comprehend and understand the meaning of life.

Turn offs are meaningless routine, policies and procedures; dealing only with data or things; and a lack of harmony in the workplace.

AUTHORITY ORIENTATION

INFPs want the person in charge to be ethical, authentic and "good." Authority is not granted by position; it is earned over time through dedication and exemplary behavior. Their first inclination is to respect their superior and to seek approval from the person in charge.

If the people in charge are not seen as ethical and caring, there is little hope of getting INFPs to accept their performance feedback as something worth paying attention to. However, this does not mean that INFPs are immune to harsh criticism. Indeed, they find it devastating. They will especially take criticism to heart when they respect the person providing it and believe that the intent is honorable and constructive.

ROLE PERCEPTION

INFPs tend to be reactive and adaptive in relationships, i.e., they wait for the relationship to emerge and be defined by the other person. They usually adapt

Do not expect INFPs to take charge in assertive, visible, power-focused situations. Their ways are rather mild and unassuming. Do not be misled, how-

INFP

CHARACTERISTICS	IMPLICATIONS

to the role set for them, especially if they experience their superior as a chosen leader, unless it violates a strongly held value.

ever, for behind the often polite and empathic face of an INFP can be the tenacity and unbendable will of steel which comes forth when their values are violated. Then they actively resist the role defined for them.

The INFP's value on individual freedom requires less structure and rules. They are most comfortable giving information rather than directing others.

Therefore, it stands to reason that their preference would be to not impose structure and rules on others.

Generally, INFPs have a great deal of respect for any human being, and they want to be responsive to others.

This natural responsiveness can cause them to be so focused on the apparent needs of others that whatever task is to be performed, at least for awhile, becomes subordinated to personal agendas.

CONFLICT RESOLUTION

INFPs prefer harmonious situations and may ignore conflicts as long as humanly possible. They typically are very distressed by conflict and find confrontations to be a last resort in resolving differences.

Practically without exception, they will go to great lengths in conciliation and pacification to avoid conflict and disagreements. Loud arguments and visible signs of uncontrolled emotions are painful, disgraceful and very bothersome to INFPs. However, do not confuse avoidance behavior with lack of personal strength. When push comes to shove, INFPs can be a tower of strength in forcing and causing others to resolve their differences.

INFP

CHARACTERISTICS

IMPLICATIONS

They are not, however, put off by intense feelings as long as these are expressed in a non-derogatory and genuine fashion.

INFPs are very familiar with their own history of deep and intense feelings; therefore, they can understand and accept the same in others.

They may personalize conflicts, blaming themselves for difficulties and negative situations, especially the ones their friends and loved ones may find themselves in.

Keep in mind that INFPs, with their great compassion, may internalize the darker side of life being experienced by others. If at all possible, INFPs would be well-advised not to take such experiences personally.

MODES OF LEARNING

INFPs learn easily from lectures and written work they consider valuable and important. Moreover, they are abstract learners and enjoy expanding their horizons in grasping new ideas and concepts, especially in the humanities. Causes of events, both past and present, are sought.

A positive relationship with the teacher is as important as is the integrity of the teacher.

Particularly in their younger years, the need for relating to the teacher may turn out to have been INFPs' own worst enemy and significantly block learning, especially if that relationship was disappointing or discouraging to them.

INFP

CHARACTERISTICS	**IMPLICATIONS**

INFPs use their ability to see relationships and synthesize to simplify the learning process. Learning anything that does not call for the use of their imagination can very quickly become boring and uninteresting for INFPs unless it is related to their cause. Consequently, INFPs are adept at learning from abstract ideas and less adept at learning by association and rote.

The consciousness and the realities of INFPs tend to be global and diffuse; thus, they are well-advised to consciously focus on the details of what they are learning, as they may stop at the global impression of having learned something and not adequately penetrate the nitty-gritty, boring, mundane, inconsequential details.

BLIND SPOTS AND PITFALLS

INFPs become totally absorbed in projects—to such a degree that they can lose sight of what is taking place around them. INFPs are so motivated to devote their total being to a cause, a purpose and sometimes a person whom they may tend to idealize, that they may wash out and leave behind their own needs. The result, over time, can be detrimental in that they may come to resent their own actions.

Therefore, at times it may be quite appropriate for INFPs to flag some time out and rejuvenate their batteries. Personal energy is necessary for them to continue to make a major contribution in the lives of others.

INFPs may focus so much on the human element in any situation that they may get off task too much and lose a sense of perspective. Even more detrimental, they can be so easily involved in meeting the needs of others that eventually they may lose sight of their own needs and suffer from loss of personal identity and burnout.

INFPs are challenged to reduce the extent of their caring for others, whereas most of the rest of humanity could increase their willingness to care about others.

INFP

CHARACTERISTICS

IMPLICATIONS

Being so responsive to others may lead to devoting so much energy to other people's priorities that INFPs use up more of their time than they would want to use.

Small wonder, then, that INFPs find themselves struggling with self-deprecation and martyrdom.

It is not uncommon for INFPs to shun significant and large responsibilities.

If and when an INFP manager appears reluctant to take on a new and large responsibility, understand that the reason more often than not is one of not wanting to make a further commitment where there is a potential for failing—not in accomplishing a task, but in commitment and caring for people.

INFPs tend to work in bursts of energy which may not coincide with the needs of the job. In other words, they tend to be more project-driven than time/priority-driven.

The ideal work environment for INFPs allows them the flexibility to capitalize on these bursts of energy while not berating them for the lulls in between. As a matter of fact, INFPs are the kind of people who thrive on the accomplishment of projects. They have a unique gift for relentlessly devoting themselves to significant tasks. Therefore, a wise manner in which to manage an INFP is to reasonably assure that enough personally meaningful projects are in the pipeline.

CHARACTERISTICS	IMPLICATIONS

With their highly developed empathic skills, INFPs may be experienced as supporting and agreeing with each person they relate to. Not surprisingly, they may get stuck in the middle between opposing forces and feel torn between their own, their supervisor's, and their subordinates' needs.

In an organizational setting, it is reasonable to assume and understand that for an INFP, harmony and a sense of togetherness is important. Consequently, to "like" the place and the people at work is important for the INFP to be fully functioning. Do not expect an INFP to be oblivious to any form of human conflict—that is just not possible.

As a result of their proclivity to be so tuned in, concerned and responsive, INFPs may internalize the failures of others.

Consequently, they may blame themselves for anything and everything that is complained about (even if they were not around at the time of the negative event).

An INFP's compassion for people's needs may interfere with the success of the organization, inadvertently resulting in a loyalty crisis.

Keep in mind that INFPs are particularly sensitive to changes in the environment. Even at the expense of organizational efficiency, INFPs want to create harmony first.

They may get so involved with others' problems that, as a result, they create dependency relationships which may be difficult to get out of.

It might help for them to remind themselves of the importance of independence for full growth.

INFPs tend to find bureaucracy frustrating, where protocol, routine and paperwork can be both meaningless and a waste of time. Consequently, in their attempt to create a working environment of freedom and auton-

They may have difficulty working within the constraints of standard operating procedures and regulations and, as a result, find their energy drained by them.

CHARACTERISTICS	IMPLICATIONS

omy (which encourages individual growth and development), organizational mandates, systems, and procedures may suffer accordingly.

INFPs tend to be highly perfectionistic and idealistic. As a result, they may put off tasks rather than accept imperfect products and conditions.

Finally, INFPs are so gifted in imagination that they may prefer the fantasy to reality and the dream to the action.

If they combine this preference for imagination with their skill for writing lyrically, they may become great novelists. Indeed, happiness for the diehard INFP is when dreams actually come true.

ABOUT THE AUTHORS

ABOUT THE AUTHORS

Olaf Isachsen, Ph.D.

Olaf Isachsen was born in 1933 and grew up in his native country of Norway. He received his M.B.A. from Harvard and his Ph.D. from Michigan State, concentrating on organizational development and communication. In academic life, he has been Associate Professor and Director of the MBA program at California Polytechnic Institute, Visiting Professor at the Stanford Graduate School of Business Administration and guest lecturer at several universities including Brigham Young University and Notre Dame.

Dr. Isachsen has been a consultant to numerous corporations-Bechtel, The Kaiser Companies, Weyerhauser, Olin-American, Hewlett-Packard, Korn/Ferry International and Wells Fargo Bank. He has also worked for the U.S. and Australian Departments of Defense, assisting in developing major defense contracts. A recognized expert in communications, his work centers around integrating the visions and goals of senior managers with the human resources and organizational structure available to them.

As a lecturer and teacher, he addresses organizations and conducts seminars throughout the United States and Europe including the Young Presidents' Organization, the American Bankers Association and the American Society for Training and Development.

A prolific writer, Dr. Isachsen has written case studies on management for Harvard University, and published numerous articles in the *Journal of Applied Management, Training Magazine, The Journal of Thought,* and *Personnel Administrator.* Other recent publications have focused on leadership styles within corporations, corporate life-cycles, innovation, motivation, and strategic planning. He has just completed his third book, *Joining the Entrepreneurial Elite,* and is working on his fourth text, *Get A Life.*

During the past thirteen years, Dr. Isachsen has served as Chairman of the Board and Senior Consultant for the Institute for Management Development where he has devoted a great deal of time and energy to the study of human typology and how the insights of Jung, Myers and Keirsey can be applied in organizations to significantly improve overall performance.

Additionally, he is a regular contributor at conferences hosted by INC. Magazine where he recently was given the highest rating of all participating speakers.

Finally, he is a frequent participant in the Jungian Winter Seminar in Switzerland, and as such has gained invaluable and unconventional insights into how to develop a manager to his or her fullest potential.

Olaf is an INTJ.

Linda V. Berens, Ph.D.

Linda Berens's professional (and private) life has revolved around the study and appreciation of personality differences. She received her Masters Degree in Counseling at California State University, Fullerton in the innovative Counseling/School Psychology Program established by Dr. David Keirsey, who is the developer of the temperament theory of behavior and co-author of the million copy seller *Please Understand Me*. Dr. Berens went on to receive her Doctorate in Psychology at United States International University, San Diego, with Dr. Keirsey as the major advisor on her dissertation, which was a seminal work on temperament theory.

Dr. Berens is a California licensed psychotherapist and Educational Psychologist. She also taught at California State University, Fullerton and Cerritos College. She has served as a change agent, facilitating change in individuals and organizations since 1976.

Beginning in 1980, Dr. Berens participated in the establishment of the Western Region of the Association for Psychological Type. As a board member, she helped that organization grow and spread the word about personality type. From 1986 to 1988, she served as President of the Western Region of the Association for Psychological Type.

In order to continue to "spread the word" and enhance the quality of people's lives, Dr. Berens founded the Temperament Research Institute. As Director, she continues to work closely with David Keirsey to stay abreast of the latest developments in temperament theory and its applications. She sees TRI as the vehicle for dissemination of accurate and effective temperament information and materials to professionals, as well as the general public.

As a nationally recognized expert in personality styles, Dr. Berens presents seminars on applications of Keirseyan Temperament Theory to organizations. She is the co-author of *Introduction to Temperament*, a widely-used booklet outlining the four temperaments and numerous other interpretations.

As a trainer of professionals who use the MBTI and temperament theory, Dr. Berens applies an understanding of temperament theory in team building, problem solving, task and role assignment, career development, motivation and conflict management.

Linda is an INTP.

SUGGESTED READINGS

Berens, Linda V. *A Comparison of Jungian Function Theory and Keirseyan Temperament Theory in the Use of the Myers-Briggs Type Indicator* (Doctoral Dissertation, United States International University, 1985). *Dissertation Abstracts International,* 1985.

Giovannoni, Louise; Berens, Linda V.; and Cooper, Sue A. *Introduction to Temperament.* Huntington Beach, California: Telos Publications, 1987.

Jung, C.G., Psychological Types: *The Collected Works of C.G. Jung, Volume 6.* Princeton University Press, 1971.

Keirsey, David. *Portraits of Temperament.* Del Mar, California: Prometheus Nemesis Books, 1987.

Keirsey, David and Bates, Marilyn. *Please Understand Me,* Third Edition. Del Mar, California: Prometheus Nemesis Books, 1978.

Kretschmer, Ernst. *Physique and Character.* London: Harcourt Brace, 1925.

Myers, Isabel Briggs. *Gifts Differing.* Palo Alto, California: Consulting Psychologists Press, 1980.

Myers, Isabel Briggs and McCaulley, Mary H. *Manual: A Guide to the Development and Use of the Myers-Briggs Type Indicator.* Palo Alto, California: Consulting Psychologists Press, 1985.

Spränger, Eduard. *Types of Men.* New York: Johnson Reprint Company, [1928] 1966.